THE CONSTITUTION OF ATHENS

AND RELATED TEXTS

The Hafner Library of Classics

[Number Thirteen]

ARISTOTLE'S
Constitution of Athens
and Related Texts

Translated with an Introduction and Notes by

KURT VON FRITZ

Professor of Greek and Latin, Columbia University

and

ERNST KAPP

Professor of Greek and Latin, Columbia University

1950

HAFNER PUBLISHING COMPANY · NEW YORK

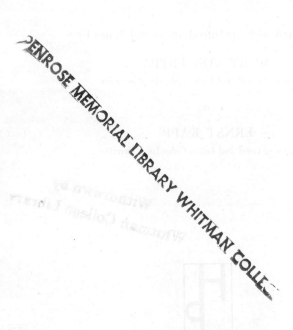

Published at 31 East Tenth Street, New York 3, N. Y.

Printed in the United States of America

THE MURRAY PRINTING COMPANY
WAKEFIELD, MASSACHUSETTS

CONTENTS

v

PREFACE

Aristotle's work on the *Constitution of Athens* is not a work of pure theory, which may be self-explanatory, but deals with a historical subject. It was written at the time to stimulate general theoretical speculations and is now published again in translation for students of political philosophy. Since the majority of readers will undoubtedly not be professional historians, nor will have the time to engage in minute historical research, we have been especially careful to supply these readers with sufficient information.

There is, however, another reason for an extensive commentary. Although most modern scholars still believe that Aristotle's treatise was written for the general public, we have come to the conclusion that, in its present form, it cannot have been intended for publication but was designed primarily to serve the needs of Aristotle himself and of his disciples in the discussions carried on in his school. Whether this assumption is correct or not, no reader who is able to read the Greek text will contest the fact that, in contrast to other works of Aristotle published in his lifetime, this work is written in a very slovenly style and that Aristotle very often did not take the trouble to explain terms and facts which he could assume were familiar to his contemporaries in Athens. As a consequence, many passages in the Greek text and, therefore, by necessity also in a faithful translation, are extremely difficult to understand, not only for the average modern reader but even for the specialist.

Because of the difficulty of the text, there are quite a number of passages which have been understood differently by different modern translators and commentators. In all instances where the difference between our version and other accepted translations touches a point of importance, we have, in a footnote or in the Appendix, given the reasons for our deviation from the *communis opinio*. In a few cases of minor importance, we have

vii

given a literal translation of the Greek words, adding in brackets a few supplementary words to clarify what in our opinion must be the meaning of the passage. Contrary to the method followed by most modern translators, we have given a prose translation of Solon's poems, since, for the purpose of the present edition, accuracy and conciseness in rendering the content of these fragments seemed more important than merely acquainting the reader with their poetic qualities.

To the translation of Aristotle's *Constitution of Athens*, we have added annotated translations of a number of other documents. These documents may be divided into three groups. The first group consists of fragments of the lost parts of Aristotle's treatise which have been preserved by other ancient writers, and of the so-called "Epitome of Heracleides," part of which can also serve to give us some idea of those portions of Aristotle's work that are still lost. The second group consists of the extant fragments of other works of Aristotle, earlier than his *Politics*, which may serve to illustrate the development of his political thought. The third group consists of only one piece — namely, the beginning of Plato's *Seventh Epistle* — in which Plato gives an account of personal political experiences which helped to shape his political philosophy. Since Plato lived through some of the political changes which Aristotle describes in his treatise and reacted passionately to them, inclusion of this document, which is not easily accessible in current translations of Plato's works, seemed appropriate. In the third chapter of our introduction to Aristotle's treatise, we have used these documents of the second and third groups, together with evidence taken from Aristotle's *Ethics* and *Politics*, in order to trace the development of Aristotle as a political thinker, to elucidate his relation to Plato in the political field, and to show the importance of Aristotle's studies in constitutional history for the last phase of his political theory.

In elaborating on the commentaries to the various documents included in this edition, it was of course necessary to make extensive use of the works of other scholars. To trace to its original author every contribution to the interpretation of Aristotle's treatise would, however, have increased the number and extent of the notes beyond all reasonable measure. We have therefore adopted the following principles: With the exception of some works of fundamental importance, we have not quoted any contribution earlier than Sandys' excellent and most extensive commentary, published together with his edition of the Greek text.[1] Since Sandys has given a most conscientious account of the work of his predecessors, anyone who is interested in the history of the interpretation of Aristotle's work may be referred to his edition. We have quoted the authors of those interpretations published later than Sandys' commentary which we have accepted. Of the many more recent suggestions with which, after careful consideration, we were compelled to disagree, we have mentioned only those that seemed to us of the greatest importance. Where a long scholarly controversy developed in regard to such recent suggestions, we have mentioned only what seemed to us the most noteworthy contributions. Since the literature on Aristotle's treatise is widely scattered and not always easy to find, it is quite possible that we have overlooked some interpretations that should have been considered. Where this should be found to be the case, we shall be grateful to reviewers to point out the deficiency.

Since the completion of the manuscript of this present volume, two works relevant to the discussion have been published: one by F. Jacoby, on the local historians of Attica;[2] the other by James H. Oliver, on the Athenian expounders of the sacred law.[3] Jacoby makes four points that deserve mention. First of all, he tries to prove that the reconstruction of the earliest phase of the development of the Athenian constitution — roughly down to the period immediately preceding the Solonian reforms — is essentially the work of Hellanicus of Lesbos, a "historian" of the late fifth century, who tried to fill in, by all sorts of construc-

[1] Sir John Edwin Sandys, *Aristotle's Constitution of Athens*, second edition (London, 1912). A revised and enlarged text, with introduction, critical and explanatory notes, *testimonia*, and indices.

[2] F. Jacoby, *Atthis. The Local Chronicles of Ancient Athens* (Oxford, Clarendon Press, 1949).

[3] James H. Oliver, *The Athenian Expounders of the Sacred and Ancestral Law* (Baltimore, The Johns Hopkins Press, 1950).

tions, the gap between what one may call the mythical or legendary part of Greek tradition concerning a remoter past and the historically more or less reliable tradition concerning the more recent past. In this contention, Jacoby is probably right, although it is not likely that Aristotle used Hellanicus exclusively. At any rate, there can hardly be any doubt that part of that section of Aristotle's work, especially his history of the early development of the archonship, is largely a historical construction based on very scanty evidence (cf. Introduction, pp. 16f.). Also, Jacoby adduces new arguments to show that the "Cylonian affair" and the first trial of the Alcmeonidae actually took place at the times indicated by Aristotle. These arguments may serve to allay to some extent, though perhaps not altogether, the doubts expressed in our Appendix, note 1. Jacoby further tries to show that there was no close relation between the local historians of Attica and the exegetes, or expounders of the sacred law (cf. Introduction, p. 15); that exegetes and soothsayers had nothing to do with each other; and that the exegetes had no special knowledge of ancient institutions and historical events connected with them. On this point Jacoby's theory is partly canceled out by that of Oliver, who tries to prove that the office of exegetes was created only in the early fourth century; that, before that time, exegetes and soothsayers were very closely connected with each other, and that both of them had special knowledge of certain traditions partly related to historical events of religious importance. There now appears, however, to be general agreement that whatever special knowledge the exegetes may have had, if any, is of little consequence for the more important aspects of the history of the Athenian constitution. Finally, Jacoby tries to vindicate Aristotle's account of the chronology of Pisistratus' periods of rule and exile (cf. Introduction, p. 22 and Appendix, note 36) by the assumption that all the confusion in Aristotle's account is due to copyists who failed to copy the figures correctly, and not to Aristotle himself. The fact, however, that Jacoby, after having changed five of the seven figures in the papyrus as copyists' errors, still does not succeed in making all the passages in which Aristotle refers to these events consistent with one another seems conclusive proof that part of the confusion at least must go back to Aristotle, even if one is ready to concede that one or another of the figures in the papyrus may be corrupt. (Cf. also the review of Jacoby's work in *Gnomon*, Vol. XXII.)

In addition to the points already mentioned, James H. Oliver — especially in Chapters IV and V of his book — has made a very interesting attempt to reconstruct certain phases of the history of the Athenian constitution beyond what is found in Aristotle's treatise. The merits of this reconstruction, however, cannot be set forth here; indeed, we have generally refrained in our commentary from discussing any modern attempts to replace Aristotle's account by a better reconstruction of the historical development, except in a few cases where questions of interpretation were involved. A systematic undertaking of this kind would have required a book of its own and is clearly outside the scope of the present edition. Where we have come to the conclusion that Aristotle's account of the historical events is subject to doubt or factually incorrect, we have merely given the reasons for our belief but have not tried to reconstruct the event in question.

Short annotations to the text have been given in footnotes; longer explanations have been placed after the text of the translation as an Appendix. Since the Introduction is in a way also a part of the commentary, one may say that the commentary is given in three different parts: footnotes, Appendix, and Introduction. This arrangement is doubtless unorthodox and may be criticized. Yet, after careful consideration of the special problems presented by Aristotle's treatise, this arrangement appeared most convenient for the reader.

We may be permitted to add that one who reads Aristotle's treatise for the first time will probably profit most if he reads first the translation with the footnotes, then the Introduction, and then again the translation, this time together with the more extensive notes contained in the Appendix.

In conclusion, we wish to thank our colleague, Professor Herbert W. Schneider, for his valuable suggestions in rendering certain passages into English. The responsibility for the translation, however, is entirely ours.

KURT VON FRITZ
ERNST KAPP

SELECTED BIBLIOGRAPHY

Since an excellent account of the history of the interpretation of the *Constitution of Athens* and a full bibliography up to and including 1912 can be found in Sir John E. Sandys, *Aristotle's Constitution of Athens*, 2d ed. (London, Macmillan and Co., Ltd. 1912), only the most important works published after that date are given below.

GENERAL

Jaeger, W., *Aristoteles*. Berlin, 1923. Translated by R. Robinson. Oxford, 1934.

Ross, W. D., *Aristotle*, 3d ed. London, 1937.

EDITIONS AND TRANSLATIONS

Oppermann, H. (ed.), *Aristoteles: Ἀθηναίων Πολιτεία*. Leipzig, 1929. This edition replaces the previous editions of Blass and Thalheim.

Rackham, H. (tr.), *Aristotle: The Athenian Constitution, The Eudemian Ethics, On Virtues, and Vices*. Cambridge, Mass., 1935.

Ross, W. D. (ed.), *The Works of Aristotle* ("Oxford Translation"). Oxford, 1908–1931. See especially Vol. X (1921), containing Sir Frederick G. Kenyon's translation of *Atheniensium Respublica*.

SPECIAL ASPECTS

Bloch, H., "Studies in the Historical Literature of the Fourth Century," *Harvard Studies in Classical Philology*, Special Volume (1940), pp. 303–376.

Bonner, R. J., and G. Smith, *The Administration of Justice from Homer to Aristotle*, Vols. I–II. Chicago, 1930–1938.

Dow, S., "Aristotle, the Kleroterion, and the Courts" *Harvard Studies in Classical Philology*, Vol. 50 (1939), pp. 1–34.

Ferguson, W. S., in the *Cambridge Ancient History (CAH)*, Vol. V, Chs. XI and XII. Cambridge, 1927.

Pritchett, W. K., and O. Neugebauer, *The Athenian Calendars*. Cambridge, Mass., 1947.

The Constitution of Athens

INTRODUCTION

I. Authorship, Text, Style

Aristotle's *Constitution of Athens* formed part of an extensive collection of histories of the constitutions of one hundred and fifty-eight cities and tribes, most of them Greek. More than two hundred fragments from this collection have been preserved in quotations by later Greek authors, eighty-six of which are taken from the *Constitution of Athens*. But, since the majority of these quotations are found in the works of ancient lexicographers, grammarians, and scholiasts, who were interested mainly in anecdotes, mythological details, strange customs, proverbs, and the like, they contain very little that is of interest to the student of politics.

Some of the quotations from the *Constitution of Athens* are, indeed, more informative; but even so, it was quite impossible to form, on this basis, an adequate idea of the contents and the nature of this work. In 1880, there were found two small leaves from a papyrus codex containing passages on the Athenian constitution which, by some scholars, were identified as belonging to the lost work of Aristotle. These leaves, which were acquired by the Egyptian Museum at Berlin, contain passages from what is now counted as Chapters 12–13 and Chapters 21–22 of the present treatise.

In 1890, the British Museum acquired from an unknown source four papyrus rolls containing a continuous text on the history of the Athenian constitution, which were first edited by F. C. Kenyon in January, 1891. Though the text is mutilated at the beginning and the end, and, therefore, the name of the author and the title of the work are missing in the papyrus, Kenyon was convinced from the beginning that the papyrus treatise was identical with Aristotle's famous work. Nevertheless, in the years immediately following its first publication, many scholars tried to prove either that the treatise must be the work of a later

3

author or that the papyrus itself was a modern falsification. Since then, however, the view of the first editor has been confirmed in every possible fashion.

All papyrus experts who have examined the papyrus agree that the assumption that it could be a modern falsification is utterly fantastic; and the historian and philologist, after a careful scrutiny of the contents and form of the treatise, will fully agree with their judgment. The question of Aristotle's authorship, however, must be discussed somewhat more fully, since the purpose of the present edition makes it necessary to determine the relation of the treatise to Aristotle's political theory.

On the front or *recto* side of the papyrus, one finds accounts of receipts and expenditures dated in the year 78/79 A.D. The *Constitution of Athens* is written on the back or *verso* side of the papyrus. As the handwriting shows, this copy was made not later than the earlier part of the second century A.D. Of the eighty-six fragments quoted by ancient authors and either expressly attributed to Aristotle's *Constitution of Athens* or attributed to Aristotle without indication of the work to which they belonged (but of such a nature that their being from this treatise may be assumed), seventy-eight are actually found in the papyrus. Of the remaining eight, four probably belong to the beginning of the treatise, which is not preserved in the papyrus, two must have belonged to the mutilated end, and one comes close enough to a passage in Chapter 54 to be considered as an inaccurate quotation from it. The papyrus contains also the passages previously found in the two leaves of the Berlin papyrus. There cannot be the slightest doubt, therefore, that in the London papyrus we have the work which was considered in late antiquity as Aristotle's treatise on the *Constitution of Athens*.

In view of the fact that the earliest extant ancient quotations from the treatise belong in the second century A.D., it has been argued that the treatise may have been current under the name of Aristotle, although actually the work of some other author, possibly one of Aristotle's disciples. This opinion is supported by the following observations: (1) the style of the treatise differs from that of Aristotle's theoretical works, especially in its showing traces of an avoidance of a clash of vowels, a practice that, although quite common in fourth-century literature, is not observed in Aristotle's theoretical works; (2) the treatise contains a number of terms that are not found elsewhere in Aristotle's writings; (3) neither the *Constitution of Athens*, nor any other part of the collection of histories of constitutions of which it formed a part, is mentioned in Aristotle's *Politics;* (4) the author of the treatise seems to have a somewhat more favorable opinion of democracy than Aristotle reveals in his other political writings. Finally, the defects of the author as a historian have appeared so great to some scholars that they considered it impossible to identify the author with the great philosopher.

In fact, the enormous collection of histories of constitutions to which the *Constitution of Athens* belonged can hardly have been made by Aristotle alone, and the possibility of some collaboration of his friends and disciples in the preparation of the material for the present treatise cannot be denied. But it is noteworthy that the latest date mentioned in the papyrus is the archonship of Cephisophon, that is 329–328 B.C., and that the island of Samos is described as being still under the control of Athens, which was no longer the case after the autumn of the year 322. There can be no doubt, therefore, that the treatise was written before Aristotle's death, but not very long before his death. This also accounts for the fact that the treatise is not quoted in any of Aristotle's other works. Furthermore, since Aristotle's special interest in the constitutional history of Athens can be taken for granted, the fact that this treatise, as far as we know, was always, at least in later antiquity, attributed to Aristotle cannot be disregarded.

The question of the style of the treatise is somewhat more difficult. During the last three decades, Aristotle's authorship has been almost universally accepted, and the difference in style between the treatise and Aristotle's theoretical works has been explained by the assumption that the treatise, in contrast to the extant philosophical works, was written for publication and published to be read by a large audience. This assumption, however, is hardly correct, or must at least be modified, if the nature of the work is to be correctly understood. In actual fact, the extremely slovenly style and sometimes even slovenly syntax[1] of the present treatise is a far cry from the beautiful and elaborate language of most of those fragments of Aristotle's published works that have come down to us in their original wording.

On the other hand, the so-called theoretical works of Aristotle are by no means uniform in style. Probably none of them was destined to be published for a large public. All of them were to be read and discussed in his philosophical school. But, while some of these works seem to represent an unelaborated and immediate reproduction of Aristotle's struggle with his problems and of the often painful and laborious process of his thinking, there are passages in some of these works, especially in the *Nicomachean Ethics*, which come much nearer to the elaborate style of Aristotle's published works than anything that can be found in the *Constitution of Athens*. Nor is it correct to explain these passages as pieces taken over into this work from his published dialogues. There is, after all, nothing strange in the fact that, in those comprehensive manuscripts in which Aristotle put down his thoughts in the various fields of philosophy and science for his own use and for the use of his disciples (both in the narrower and in the broader sense), he should sometimes express his ideas and meditations without paying any attention to style, and sometimes pay close attention to his mode of expression.

Within the body of Aristotle's work, the *Constitution of Athens* occupies a peculiar position, inasmuch as it is not philosophical or scientific, but historical and descriptive. If one takes this fact into consideration, there is nothing in the treatise that does not easily fall within the limits of what, from his other works, is known as the range of Aristotle's style. It is quite natural that, even in a sketch written mainly for private use, the sections consisting of historical narrative should, to some extent, follow the

---

[1] For a particularly striking example, cf. Chapter 4, 2, and Appendix, note 11, where grammatically three entirely different interpretations of the same sentence are equally possible; cf. also, for instance, Appendix, notes 3 and 5; Chapter 7, 3 and Appendix, note 19; Appendix, notes 51, 79, 99, etc.

stylistic rules observed by all historical writers of the time of Aristotle, while in the purely technical and descriptive sections, these stylistic rules might be ignored.

In conclusion, one may say that both the external and the stylistic evidence are entirely in favor of the assumption that the treatise was written by Aristotle himself. But it seems quite impossible that Aristotle intended to publish it, in the form in which we have it, for the general public. This judgment will be confirmed by an analysis of the composition of the work and by a discussion of its historical shortcomings, which will be found in the following chapters.

II. Composition, Sources, Historical Reliability

1

As mentioned before,[1] the beginning of the treatise is missing in the papyrus. But the summary given by Aristotle in Chapter 41 and the "Epitome of Heracleides"[2] show that the lost chapters contained the history of the period of the monarchy.

What is extant clearly falls into two parts. The first of these contains the history of the Athenian constitution from the end of the monarchy to the overthrow of the regime of the so-called "Thirty Tyrants" in 404 B.C. This part extends from Chapter 1 to Chapter 41 of the extant treatise and concludes with a brief survey of the main phases or turning points in the history of the Athenian constitution as described in the preceding chapters. The second part, extending from Chapter 42 to the mutilated end of the papyrus, contains a much more detailed account of the constitutional set-up and of the governmental machinery as it was in the time of Aristotle himself, and as (disregarding some minor later changes) it had evolved in the decade or so following the restoration of democracy, after the overthrow of the "Thirty." It is, however, noteworthy that in this section, which gives such a detailed and technical description of the rules governing the franchise, and of the Council, the magistracies, and the law

[1] See *supra*, p. 3.
[2] See *infra*, pp. 203–207.

courts, we do not find any information concerning the complicated procedure of lawmaking which the Athenian constitution
of the fourth century prescribed; so that whatever knowledge
we are able to acquire concerning this most important constitutional factor has to be obtained from other sources, notably from
some of the speeches of Demosthenes.

The first part presents some very puzzling problems of composition, the most important of which is connected with the constitutional history of Athens before the reforms of Solon. In the
beginning of Chapter 41, Aristotle states that the restoration of
the democracy in the archonship of Pythodorus (404/403) was
the eleventh "change," and then proceeds to enumerate the
various changes.[3] He begins with the statement that the first
change from the original state of things was that effected by Ion
in the division of the people into four tribes. Then, he says, there
was the change introduced by Theseus, which was the first deviation from absolute monarchy and the first change resulting in
something that might justly be called a constitutional order.
This, he continues, was followed by the constitution which existed
under Draco, and then the third which existed under Solon.
Having counted the Solonian constitution as number three, he
goes on counting until, with the restoration of the democracy
in 404, he arrives at number eleven. But it is clear that this
figure, with which his summary started, is obtained only if one
begins to count with the constitution of Theseus; although the
first change in a general sense (and Aristotle had announced that
he was going to count the changes) occurred under Ion, and
although the constitution of Theseus is the first real constitution
and not the first change in the constitution.

To point this out might appear to be sheer quibbling about
words in a case where Aristotle was merely careless in his formulation, were it not for the fact that the problem reappears in a
much more serious form when one analyzes the first extant chapters of the treatise in connection with the summary given in
Chapter 41, a problem that has given rise to endless discussions
among modern scholars. Following a sentence which obviously

[3] Cf. Appendix, notes 138 and 140.

concluded the story of the so-called Cylonian affair,[4] the papyrus begins with a description of the economic conditions and the struggle between the rich and the poor that characterized the period immediately preceding the Solonian reforms (Chapter 2). But the chapter is not, as one is led to expect by its last sentence, followed by an account of these reforms but by a section (Chapter 3) which in its opening sentence *promises* to give a description of the political or constitutional structure of the state *before* Draco; in actual fact, however, it contains a history of the institution of the archonship from the abolition of the monarchy to the introduction of a college of nine Archons and concludes with some remarks concerning the functions of the Areopagus in that period. Finally, the next chapter (Chapter 4) begins with the words: "Such then, was, in outline, the first political order. Not much later, however, in the archonship of Aristaechmus, Draco enacted his laws. His (or 'this')[5] constitution was the following."

On the face of it, then, it would appear that, even if the various stages in the development of the archonship (that is, the archonship for life, the ten-year archonship, the one-year archonship, etc.) are considered as phases of essentially the same constitutional period, as indeed they must be regarded if the chapter is to be understood at all, two different constitutions are described in Chapters 3 and 4, one before Draco and one that lasted from Draco to Solon, but both of them later than, and different from, the restricted monarchy of Theseus and his successors. In fact, this is the way in which the two chapters seem to have been interpreted by all modern commentators, and it is undoubtedly the most natural interpretation of the text as we have it.

Nevertheless, this interpretation is in flagrant conflict with the enumeration of constitutions in Chapter 41, which mentions only one constitution between Theseus and Solon: the constitution of the time of Draco. How is this discrepancy to be explained? In his *Politics*, Aristotle says expressly that Draco made laws, but that he made them "for an already existing constitution,"[6] which

---

[4] Cf. *infra*, p. 69, and Appendix, note 1.
[5] Cf. Appendix, note 9.
[6] Aristotle, *Politics*, 1274b, 15/16.

patently means that he did not introduce or even inaugurate a new constitution; and, in fact, the little we know about Draco from other ancient sources seems to indicate that his law code dealt mostly with what we should call criminal law, and that, though both the creation of an official law code as such and the character of the laws incorporated in it had probably important political implications, the code did not contain any purely political regulations at all. The enumeration of constitutions or changes of the constitutional order in Chapter 41, in which the constitution "under Draco" or "at the time of Draco" is listed as the only constitution between the restricted monarchy of Theseus and the Solonian constitution, is in no way at variance with the statement made by Aristotle in his *Politics*. It merely designates by the name of Draco, the most representative figure of the period, the strictly oligarchic or aristocratic regime which developed after the abolition of the monarchy and continued until the archonship of Solon.

Chapters 3 and 4, on the other hand, as pointed out above, seem to split this period of the constitutional development into two "constitutional orders," one "before" and one "of" Draco. But a somewhat more careful reading of the two chapters reveals that Chapter 4 contains absolutely nothing that represents a definite innovation in comparison with the latest stage of the development described in the preceding chapter. It simply repeats in slightly different words what had been said about the functions and powers of the Areopagus, and gives additional information concerning the mode of election of the leading magistrates of the city, a question that had not been discussed in detail in the preceding chapter. If it were not for the introductory sentences of the two chapters, notably the words "before Draco" in Chapter 3, and the words "not much later" and "this" or "his constitution" in Chapter 4, the two chapters might very well represent parts of a continuous description of the phases of essentially one and only one constitutional period.

Since the introductory sentences mentioned make it impossible to interpret the chapters in exactly this way, these chapters appear rather as two different sketches of the same constitution, one from a more evolutionary, the other from a more stationary, point of view. That this is actually the correct explanation of the relation of the two chapters to each other is confirmed by the fact that the words "not much later" in the second sentence of Chapter 4 have no ascertainable point of reference in the preceding Chapter 3. If still further proof of this seems necessary, it may be pointed out that Chapter 4 begins with the words: "This, then, was the first political order." But, according to the summary given in Chapter 41, the first political order was the restricted monarchy of Theseus, and not what Aristotle describes in Chapter 3.

Two conclusions may be drawn from these observations. In the first place, it now becomes clear that Aristotle at no time, even when he wrote Chapter 4 of the present treatise, meant to correct the statement which he had made in his *Politics* — that Draco gave his laws "for an already existing constitution." The much discussed question, therefore, of whether Aristotle correctly assumed the existence of a specific Dracontian constitution simply does not arise. The "Dracontian constitution" meant to Aristotle at all times a constitution under which Draco lived and of which he was the most characteristic representative at a time when the aristocratic features of this political order had most fully developed; but it never meant to him a constitution created or inaugurated by Draco.

Secondly, it is equally clear that the treatise either was never meant to be published at all, or, at least, was never revised for publication. This conclusion also can be confirmed by many additional observations. Chapters 3 and 4 not only cannot have been written to follow each other; they are also both awkwardly inserted in the place in which we find them. For, as pointed out before, Chapter 2 leads right up to Chapter 5, so that the description of the conditions that led to the Solonian reforms is very inconveniently interrupted by Chapters 3 and 4. This lack of continuity is also illustrated by the repetitions at the end of Chapter 4 and in the beginning of Chapter 5. There are a great many other passages that show that the treatise can never have been revised by its author for publication: for example, the misinterpretation of an inscription in Chapter 7, 4,[7] the inconsistency in the figures given for Pisistratus' periods of rule and of exile in Chapters 14–17,[8] the vagueness of the description of the transition from the oligarchic regime of 411 to the democracy of the last years of the Peloponnesian War in Chapter 33,[9] a description which has given rise to so many different conjectures by modern scholars as to what actually happened — to mention only a few of the most striking instances. Since the same conclusion can be reached by an observation of the stylistic deficiencies and the syntactical obscurity of many parts of the treatise,[10] there can be little doubt as to its correctness.

This does not mean, however, that the treatise as we have it is not of the greatest historical value, much less that it is not of very great importance for a full understanding of the development of Aristotle's political thought. On the contrary, the very fact that the author did not take the time or trouble to revise his treatise for publication and to eliminate the discrepancies resulting from the use of different sources of information makes it possible to gain a much better insight into the nature of the material that he had to use and into the method that he employed in collecting and arranging this material. At the same time, if one wishes to arrive at a just evaluation of what Aristotle actually did achieve and desires to make the best use of it for a full understanding of Aristotle's attitude in regard to the concrete facts of Athenian political life and of the influence of these facts on his political ideas, it is essential to be aware of the fact that the treatise is merely a sketch which was never fully elaborated.

2

A comparison between the various parts of Aristotle's treatise and the relevant sections of the extant works of ancient Greek historians of the period with which he deals, notably Herodotus, Thucydides, and Xenophon, leaves no doubt that Aristotle has made ample use of this source of historical information. But he

[7] Cf. Appendix, note 20.
[8] Cf. Appendix, note 36.
[9] Cf. Appendix, note 117.
[10] See *supra*, p. 6.

not infrequently disagrees with them, and, above all, he tries to give a great deal of additional information, not only concerning his own time, but also in regard to the earlier history of the Athenian constitution. It is generally agreed that, in some cases, Aristotle has made use of documents which he found in the archives of the Athenian state, but that the bulk of the information that cannot be found in the extant works of the great historians mentioned is derived partly from the works of the local historians of Attica who lived in the fourth century B.C., the so-called Atthidographers, and, to a somewhat lesser extent, from party pamphlets which were published in the course of the political struggle of the latter part of the fifth century and which were still extant in the time of Aristotle. However, there is infinite disagreement among modern scholars concerning the question of which specific passages of the present treatise are derived from which specific authors or even from what specific type of sources.

It is patently impossible, within the framework of this introduction, to enter upon such questions of detail; and one may even doubt whether such an investigation would be very profitable, since, with the exception of a few special cases, all conjectures of this kind must, of necessity, remain very uncertain.[11] More-

[11] Herbert Bloch, in an excellent article on the "Historical Literature of the Fourth Century," published in *Harvard Studies in Classical Philology*, special volume (1940), pp. 341ff., has proved, on the basis of incontestable evidence, that Aristotle made use of the Atthis of Androtion in his treatise on the Athenian Constitution. But there is also incontestable evidence to show that occasionally Aristotle differed from Androtion in regard to questions which had been dealt with extensively in Androtion's work, and that, in doing so, he was occasionally right (cf. Appendix, note 25). This alone shows that Aristotle did not follow Androtion, or any other Atthis, slavishly. On the other hand, the fragments of the work of Androtion that have come down to us are still rather scanty, in spite of some recent additions, and it is impossible to determine accurately how far Aristotle's dependence on this kind of sources goes. But, even if it were possible to do this, it would not solve the main problem. For the Atthis of Androtion was probably written only a few years before Aristotle's own work; the other Atthides proper, which were very incomplete, are not earlier than the first half of the fourth century, and even the so-called Atthis of Hellanicus of Lesbus which hardly contained much relevant material except possibly for the chronology, was not much earlier than that.

over, even if we could prove, and not merely conjecture, that
certain sections of the work of Aristotle are derived from the
work of the Atthidographer Androtion, others from the *Atthis*,
that is, local history of Athens, of Cleidemus, and still others from
an oligarchic party pamphlet of the fifth century, this would still
not be very helpful unless we knew also what actual historical
evidence was available to the authors of these works and what
use they made of it.   It is, therefore, much more important to
acquire some insight into the nature of the primary historical
material which Aristotle, or his predecessors, had to use in dealing
with different periods of the history of the Athenian constitution;
and this is quite possible.

Nobody who reads Aristotle's treatise with attention and
understanding can fail to notice the enormous difference between
his description of the Solonian reforms and his account of the
preceding and succeeding periods.   The reason is obvious.   For
the history of the Solonian reforms, Aristotle could use Solon's
own poems; and in this case he has shown that, when he did have
first-rate material, he was quite able to make excellent use of it.
But it must also be observed that Aristotle, while giving the most
vivid and penetrating account of the economic, social, political,
and, to some extent, psychological factors which led to the Solonian reforms, and of Solon's valiant and desperate struggle with
the extreme parties on both sides, offers only a bare outline (one
is tempted to say the mere skeleton) of the new constitutional
order which Solon introduced.   To some extent, the same may
be said of his description of the constitution of Cleisthenes, which
was introduced toward the end of the sixth century.   Certainly
there is a marked difference between his account of this most
important constitutional innovation and the very detailed technical documents which he presents in connection with the much
less important oligarchic constitution of 411, which, after all,
lasted for only a few months.

Again the reason is not difficult to find.   The Solonian law
code was inscribed on the so-called *kyrbeis*, wooden pillars set
up in the portico of the Archon King, where, until the end of
the fifth century at least, everybody could inspect it at any time.

But, toward the end of the fifth century, a commission was appointed to undertake the official task of finding out in detail what the "ancestral" constitutions of Solon and Cleisthenes had been, and this commission, after years of labor, never came to a quite conclusive result. Obviously, this could not have happened if the details of Solon's constitutional regulations had been included in his law code, which was accessible to everybody. The main features of his constitutional order were remembered. Some additional information may have been found in the state archives, but, in regard to the technical details, even the archives obviously had not very much to offer. In fact, everything seems to indicate that not until about the beginning of the fifth century, especially after the Persian Wars, were systematic records made and carefully preserved, first of the most important, then also of less important political regulations and decisions. Solon himself, on the other hand, in his poems, naturally dealt with the causes of the political unrest and disorder which he strove to remedy, with the character of his opponents, and with the general tendency of his innovations, but not with their more technical aspect.

Now, if truly documentary material was so scanty in regard to the constitutional history of the sixth century and was, in all likelihood, practically non-existent concerning any earlier period, what was the source of Aristotle's information concerning the constitutional development before Solon and concerning the period between Solon and the reforms of Cleisthenes? There can be hardly any doubt that Aristotle made extensive use of the works of the local historians of Attica who lived in the fourth century. These historians form a group apart, inasmuch as all of them seem to have had some priestly functions, and most, if not all, of them during part of their lives held the office of interpreter of the sacred law. Though some of the Atthidographers published books on the sacred law, this law was essentially handed down through oral tradition within certain ancient families, and, therefore, the interpreters of the sacred law had to be chosen from those families.

Since, in early times, the sacred law was naturally very closely connected with the political institutions, it is very likely that a good deal of valuable information came down through this channel to the fourth century. The fact, for instance, mentioned by Aristotle in Chapter 3, that the Archon King and, to a lesser extent, the Archon Polemarchus were in charge of the older religious functions, whereas the chief Archon, or Archon Eponymus, had only the more recent of those religious functions that had to be performed by members of the government, is confirmed by incontestable independent evidence. It is, therefore, quite possible that traces of even very early political and social institutions were preserved by the works of those local historians of Attica, who were at the same time interpreters of the sacred law. But it is also obvious that there were natural causes of distortion and error which cannot be neglected in an attempt to determine the historical value of this kind of tradition. On the one hand, there is a natural tendency to preserve most scrupulously the traditional rules governing the correct conduct of the community toward the gods; on the other hand, religion is the field in which legends, especially of aetiological character, most naturally crop up.

Another cause of error, as Aristotle's own treatise shows,[12] may be found in a change, and a consequent uncertainty, of the political nomenclature. When the monarchy was abolished, there, nevertheless, continued to be a "king" who, however, seems to have been restricted to religious and, to some extent, judicial functions. This member of the government was later officially called Archon King, but, in the early period, he seems to have been called simply King. In the case of a specific "king" of the transitional period whose name was known, it may sometimes have been difficult to determine whether he was a real king or a magistrate of that title. Finally, for historians like the Atthidographers who were in possession of very valuable, but at the same time one-sided, specific information and who tried to write a history of Athens from a more general point of view, the temptation must have been very great to engage in historical reconstructions for which their actual material was not quite sufficient. Aristotle's report on the constitutional development

[12] *Cf.* Aristotle, *Constitution of Athens*, Chapters 3 and 4, and Appendix, notes 4 and 10.

from the abolition of the monarchy to Draco in Chapter 3, which is in many respects very vague and which, even where it is less vague, can hardly be quite correct, seems to represent a reconstruction of this kind.[13] A clear indication that, to some extent, this is also true of Chapter 4 can be found in the fact that in this chapter the property qualifications of the different classes of citizens are given in money, although at that time coined money hardly existed and even uncoined precious metal cannot possibly have played the role which a citizen classification on this basis would presuppose. This is also confirmed by the fact that Solon, in the succeeding period, still determined the first class of citizens by their income in natural products rather than in money.

There is still another cause of possible error and distortion which is most important and must be discussed more fully. In the period immediately following the Persian War, the ancient council of the Areopagus acquired a great political ascendancy because of the leading part which it had taken in the direction of this life and death struggle of the Athenian people against the foreign invader. How much of this ascendancy had a foundation in the official constitutional set-up of the Athenian state and how much was due merely to the political situation can no longer be exactly determined. At any rate, when the Areopagus continued to exert its influence on the conservative side, the leaders of the progressive party finally succeeded in depriving it of most of its political powers and influence. But when, after the death of Pericles, the democracy seemed to fail in the conduct of the Peloponnesian War, there was a group of citizens who began to argue that the Athenian state had started on the wrong road when the Areopagus was deprived of its privileges and its power. This point of view was still held by certain groups in the fourth century, and we have an example of their ideas and arguments in one of the extant pamphlets of Isocrates, the *Areopagiticus*. It is only natural that these men should have had a tendency to project into an early period of the constitutional history of Attica those functions, privileges, and powers which, in their opinion, the Areopagus ought to have had at all times; or, in other words,

[13] Cf. Appendix, notes 5 and 7.

that their idea of the history of the Areopagus was colored by their political views. A comparison between Isocrates' pamphlet and those sections in Aristotle's work in which he deals with the earlier history of the Areopagus shows that Aristotle did not entirely escape the influence of these representatives of a movement in favor of greater powers for the Areopagus.

All this does not mean, of course, that the Areopagus was not a pre-Solonian institution, which undoubtedly it was. There are strong indications that the main function of this council in the early period was a judicial one. This does not exclude the possibility that it had other functions also, and that, at times, it may have had considerable political importance. But we must be aware of the fact that most of the material concerning the early history of the institution was so colored by the political discussion of the fifth and fourth centuries that, even if Aristotle had been objectivity itself,[14] he would not have been able to arrive at an accurate knowledge of the nature and extent of its functions in an early period; and, in this respect, we are, of course, in no better position than he was.

The situation in regard to the constitutions of Solon and of Cleisthenes is somewhat different. When in 411 a commission was appointed with the task of finding out what, in detail, the "ancestral" constitutions of Solon and Cleisthenes had been, this appointment was the result of a general tendency prevailing at that time to consider those constitutions as models to which the Athenian state, as far as possible, should return. For some time, indeed, all parties seem to have contended that their aims coincided with the true spirit of these constitutions. But when in 405/4 the radical oligarchs gradually began to pursue political aims and to use methods which, by no stretch of the imagination, could be reconciled with what was known of Solon's principles, they did not shrink from attacking, not only Solon's political and social reforms, but even his personal character. All this goes to show that toward the end of the fifth century the tradition about Solon and also Cleisthenes became strongly colored by the

---

[14] Concerning possible political prejudices of Aristotle himself, cf. the following chapter of the Introduction.

political passions of the day. Some of the main features of these constitutions, however, had been of such decisive and lasting influence on the structure of the Athenian state that their origin and nature could not be forgotten; and in Solon's case, moreover, Aristotle was able to exploit the invaluable documentation which could be found in Solon's own poems. Some points, such as the exact nature of the so-called *seisachtheia*, or abolition of debts, remained somewhat uncertain, nevertheless.[15] Still, Aristotle was able to relate some of the arguments used in the political discussion of the late fifth century concerning these events,[16] without permitting these arguments to influence his own interpretation and political judgment. It is quite possible that his account of this discussion is directly derived from party pamphlets of the late fifth century. But it is an error to believe that everything that looks more or less "objective" is derived from the Atthidographers, and everything that seems somewhat biased in one way or another is derived from "party pamphlets," and it is a mistake to use this assumption as an axiom from which all "source investigations" have to start. This rather primitive method does not lead anywhere, since some of the Atthidographers themselves and especially Androtion, whose Atthis was certainly consulted and used by Aristotle, took a very active part in Athenian party politics.

In regard to the period from Solon to the end of the sixth century, there existed two types of what may be called primary historical material which were available only to a very slight degree, if at all, for the earlier period. Many of the political leaders of the fifth century were descendants of the leading political figures of the sixth century. It is natural that within the families that had remained politically prominent for such a long period the memory of what their "ancestors" had done should have been kept very much alive. Undoubtedly this memory was somewhat colored. But the very fact that Aristotle is able to give an account of changing political alliances among these families seems to indicate that a good deal of very valuable and

[15] *Cf.* Aristotle, Chapter 6 and Appendix, note 15.
[16] *Cf.* Aristotle, Chapters 6 and 9.

probably rather accurate information was preserved in this way.[17]

What is least accurately remembered in this fashion is, of course, the chronology. Here, however, the other type of what may be called primary historical material comes in. There can be hardly any doubt that from the first decade of the sixth century regular records had been kept of the names of the chief archons of every year, and by the end of the fifth century "the

---

[17] In other cases, and especially where the more specific details of an event were concerned, the information derived from this type of source was, of course, somewhat less accurate. An interesting case of this kind is the story of the assassination of the "tyrant" Hipparchus (cf. Aristotle, Chapter 18 and Appendix, note 38). Since the slayers of Hipparchus were later celebrated as tyrannicides, it was quite natural that several generations later, when the particular circumstances had been forgotten, most people believed that Hipparchus had been the ruling tyrant. Thucydides (VI, 54ff.) corrects this version of the story, pointing out that not Hipparchus, but his elder brother, Hippias, was the actual ruler, and then goes on to tell why, according to the information that he had been able to collect, Harmodius and Aristogeiton assassinated Hipparchus instead of Hippias. Aristotle agrees with Thucydides in so far as Hippias's rulership is concerned, but disagrees with him in regard to the rest of the story.

This disagreement is interesting because it illustrates the nature of the primary material which both Thucydides and Aristotle had to use. Before the discovery of Aristotle's treatise, many modern admirers of Thucydides contended that his whole story must be based on "documentary material" because it would have been unworthy of so great an historian to base it on anything less reliable. In actual fact, Thucydides' own argumentation shows clearly that he had documentary evidence only for his contention that Hippias and not Hipparchus was the ruling tyrant. This fact having been established through incontestable evidence, it seemed clear that the overthrow of the tyrants could not have been the main motive of the "tyrannicides." Thucydides, therefore, tried to find out what the real story had been, and since documentary evidence concerning this part of the event was obviously lacking, the only source of information to which he could turn was probably the oral tradition surviving in those families whose ancestors had been involved in one way or another in the overthrow of the tyrants. It is hard to see why he should be blamed for having availed himself of this source of information where no other information was available, though Aristotle later was able to pick up still another version of the story which he probably found in an earlier author but which ultimately must have gone back to the same type of primary information as that from which Thucydides' version had been derived.

list of the archons from Solon downward"[18] had apparently become a well-known and generally accepted means of dating the events of Athenian, and, to a large extent, even of non-Athenian history. Probably, at the same time, attempts were also made to reconstruct for chronological purposes the archonlists farther back, even into the seventh century.

Later, there existed a complete list of all archons, not only from the beginning of the one-year archonship which was dated in the year 683/2 B.C., but even from the abolition of the monarchy which was supposed to have taken place in 1091 B.C., or, according to another version, in 1068, and further on from the introduction of the ten-year archonship, which was supposed to have occurred in 752 B.C. There can be not the slightest doubt that the earliest part of these lists is fictitious, as can be seen from this fact alone: that, according to this list, all the seven ten-year archons actually ruled exactly ten years, which would presuppose that none of them died before he had completed his ten-year term of office. In fact, it is rather doubtful whether there ever was a ten-year archonship. On the other hand, it is quite possible, and it is assumed by many scholars, that the list of annual archons from 683/2 downward is substantially correct. But we cannot be certain about it since there is too little external evidence available to check the later tradition. A great many attempts have been made by modern scholars[19] to reconstruct the history of the Athenian constitution, from the end of the monarchic period to the time of Solon, in greater detail. It is possible that some of these reconstructions come somewhat nearer to the truth than the corresponding chapters in Aristotle's treatise. But, since these reconstructions are based on very scanty evidence, they are not in an essentially different category from Aristotle's own attempt. In regard to the chronology also, it seems preferable not to place too much confidence in any chronological data earlier than the beginning of the sixth century.

[18] Cf. (Pseudo) Plato, *Hippias Major*, p. 285e, where the suggestion is made that Hippias could have recited from memory the names of the Athenian Archons (*eponymoi*, of course) from Solon down to the present.

[19] A. Ledl, *Studien zur älteren athenischen Verfassungsgeschichte*, Heidelberg, 1914.

Beginning with Solon's period, on the other hand, there seem to have been actual records, which, in spite of some minor discrepancies, appear rather reliable; so that, from then on, it becomes possible to establish, to some extent, a regular year-to-year chronology. There is, however, no conclusive evidence to show that in this period the records of the names of the chief Archons in Athens were directly connected with records of other political events. Hence, generally speaking, only those events of that period can be directly dated by means of the archon lists in which an Archon took a leading part or which, for some other reason, became connected with the name of an Archon. Indirectly, however, the events dated in this way could be used to date other events which were in a more or less definite chronological relation to the events so dated. This dependence of the chronology of the period under discussion partly on the Athenian archon lists, and partly on the memory of the important actions, the accomplishments, and the alliances of the great political leaders as it was preserved mainly through oral tradition in the leading families, explains the unevenness of the chronological data supplied by Aristotle for this epoch. It explains also why Aristotle, while sometimes giving an exact date for an event of comparatively minor importance, is vague and inconsistent in regard to the most important question of Pisistratus' period of rule and exile.[20]

There was one more instrument for the fixation of chronological dates which must be mentioned briefly in this connection.[21] These are the lists of the victors in the so-called Olympic games. It was only a short time after the death of Aristotle that the "Olympiades," which could be simply numbered and did not, like the Archon lists, require the constant counting of innumerable names in order to determine the chronological distance of

[20] *Cf.* Aristotle, Chapters 15–17 and Appendix, note 36; cf. also Preface, p. x.

[21] There were also other instruments for chronological dating which had been used before Aristotle; for instance, the list of the Spartan kings, the list of the priestesses of Hera at Argos, etc., but there is no evidence to show that these were used by Aristotle, or by his authorities, in regard to the matters with which he deals in his treatise.

one historical event from another, began to be used as a general chronological framework for Greek history dating from 776, the supposed date of the first Olympic contest. But the list of the victors in the Olympic games back to the beginning of this institution had already been collected, reconstructed, and published by the sophist Hippias toward the end of the fifth century. This list, therefore, at the time of Aristotle, was easily accessible to anyone who wished to make use of it for purposes of historical chronology. Again, as in the case of the Athenian archon lists, we are unable to determine exactly how far back Hippias' list was historically reliable. But, whether the list itself was reliable or not, it could in either case become the source of egregious chronological errors. For the dearth of the chronological data available to Greek historians dealing with the first two centuries after the introduction of the Olympic games resulted in the great temptation to identify, without careful scrutiny, important historical figures with men of the same name who happened to appear in the Olympic victor lists. Erroneous identifications of this kind by ancient authors have wrought havoc with the history of Pythagoras and the Pythagorean order; and it is quite possible that the historical difficulties or improbabilities inherent in Aristotle's account of the so-called Cylonian affair[22] and of its later consequences have a similar cause, since these difficulties disappear if one assumes that Aristotle gives a much too early date for this event, and that he, or the authority which he follows, was deceived by the appearance of a man by the name of Cylon in the Olympic victor list for the second half of the seventh century. In conclusion, therefore, one may say that there existed for the sixth century certain chronological measuring sticks which made exact dating in some cases possible, but this does not mean that all traditional data based on archon lists or Olympiades are correct.

In regard to the fifth century, especially the period after the Persian Wars, the nature of the primary historical material changes again. Generally speaking, the chronology for that period cannot have presented very great difficulties to a careful

[22] *Cf.* Aristotle, Chapter 1 and Appendix, note 1.

investigator, though occasional errors might have crept in and though, in one case,[23] Aristotle, if he is the author of the particular passage, seems to have accepted a political legend which he would probably have rejected if he had paid closer attention to its chronological implications. In fact, even disregarding the chronological difficulties connected with it, this legend is rather incredible; and it is significant, perhaps, that the only story of this kind that has found a place in Aristotle's treatise has to do with the restriction on the privileges and functions of the Areopagus, which played such an important role in the political discussion of the late fifth and of the fourth century. For it indicates clearly that, where the Areopagus was involved, even the tradition concerning this comparatively recent period in the constitutional development was by no means free from political coloring.

Another instance of such coloring is the widespread belief that Aristeides, who had become famous for his disinterestedness, his integrity, and his justice, and who was known to have been a political rival of Themistocles, must have been a leader of the conservative party while Themistocles was the leader of the progressives. In this case, however, Aristotle was able to show convincingly[24] that this tradition which seems to have been widely believed as early as the end of the fifth century can hardly have been quite correct, since in many respects Aristeides was the initiator of the policy which was later carried out by Pericles.

The most important new factor initiated in this period as far as the primary historical material is concerned is, of course, the official record of all the more important public decisions and transactions which began to be kept since about the time of the Persian Wars and which rapidly became more and more complete until it seems to have extended to almost all fields of the public administration. A not inconsiderable part of this record was published on stone and so has been partly preserved in its original form until the present day. But much more than was published must have been preserved in the archives and have been accessible there at the time of Aristotle.

[23] *Ibid.*, Chapter 25 and Appendix, note 74.
[24] *Ibid.*, Chapters 23–24 and Appendix, note 67.

It is in this way that Aristotle was able, not only to give a rather detailed account of the oligarchic government which came to power for a short time in 411, but also to include in his treatise the draft of a constitution which in that year had been drawn up and accepted for the future but which, in actual fact, seems never to have been applied in practice,[25] for the oligarchic government was overthrown while still governing according to a provisional constitution.

These two constitutions, the provisional one which, to some extent at least, seems to have been actually applied for some period of time, and the "final" one which seems to have remained a mere plan for the future, present a number of historical problems. Though no other ancient author, apart from Aristotle, mentions the draft of the "final" constitution at all, there can be hardly any doubt as to its authenticity in the sense that this draft was actually drawn up by the commission appointed for that purpose. This judgment applies also to the temporary regulations of the provisional constitution. But, in regard to the events that led to the adoption of these plans and even in regard to the extent to which these regulations of the provisional constitution were actually carried out in practice, there are a number of discrepancies between the account given by Thucydides and the account given by Aristotle. In addition, there are several points that remain rather obscure in both accounts.

In a way, therefore, one may say that the situation in regard to the constitutional changes of the late fifth century is the reverse of the situation in regard to the tradition concerning the constitutions of the sixth century. As pointed out above,[26] Aristotle knew only the main features of the constitutional innovations of Solon and Cleisthenes, while the more detailed provisions of these constitutions were forgotten beyond recovery as early as the last decades of the fifth century. Such was not the case with the constitutions of the late fifth century. For, by that time, all the drafts of constitutional regulations which were drawn up by the appointed committees, both those which were to be applied

[25] *Ibid.*, Chapter 34 and Appendix, note 117.
[26] Cf. *supra*, pp. 18ff.

immediately and those which were to replace them at some later time, were preserved in the archives of the Athenian state and could be recovered by Aristotle. But the knowledge of the political events that were connected with the adoption of these constitutional regulations had not increased in the same proportion. One cannot say that Thucydides and Aristotle knew less about these events than they knew about the political constellations which led to the reforms of Solon and Cleisthenes. But it is clear from the accounts of both Thucydides and Aristotle that the oligarchic regime of 411 came to power in a rather tumultuous fashion, and that the initiators of the new constitution or constitutions tried to deceive the people in various ways in order to give a cloak of legality to the procedure that they had followed. It is, therefore, not surprising that Thucydides, who was not in Athens at that time and who returned only after other and even more exciting events had obscured the memory of those days, was not able to reconstruct every detail of the events accurately. The same, of course, is true to an even higher degree of Aristotle, who wrote some fourscore years later.

It is, perhaps, not unimportant to have in mind as accurate as possible a picture of the conditions under which Thucydides and Aristotle wrote about this period of Athenian history. If one does, it is impossible to accept the assumption, made by a great many of the most outstanding modern scholars,[27] that the draft of a constitution "for the future," which Aristotle describes in Chapter 30 of this treatise, represents the constitution that was actually in force after the overthrow of the regime of the Four Hundred toward the end of the year 411. If this had been the case, Thucydides could hardly have failed both to know and to mention the fact, even if, in agreement with the nature of his work, he would not have mentioned all the details of the constitutional regulations. Likewise, from the nature of the official records kept at that time, Aristotle could not have failed to notice that this constitution was actually in force for some time. Yet, it is perfectly clear from his account that, in his opinion, it was not.

What has been said about the tradition concerning the events

[27] *Cf.* Aristotle, Chapter 34 and Appendix, note 117.

of 411 is also true, to some extent, concerning the history of the so-called Thirty Tyrants, though Xenophon was present in Athens during that whole period and later wrote about it in the still extant *Hellenica*, which, as mentioned before, were used by Aristotle. The history of this regime, however, was still more tumultuous than that of the oligarchy of 411. Even a person present in Athens at that time, therefore, was not able to observe or to find out accurately everything that happened on the political scene, much less to remember it later; and Xenophon probably wrote this part of his work several decades after the events. Perhaps nothing is more characteristic of the way in which the general public remembered the details of the political events of that period than the fact that, in 398, Lysias, in a speech before an Athenian law court, gave an account of the peace negotiations of 405 which, in regard to some of the most important facts, disagrees completely with the account that Xenophon gives of the same negotiations.[28] For reasons that cannot be explained here, it seems certain that, where the two authors disagree, Xenophon is correct. But if, in 398, Lysias, in a law court consisting of several hundred jurors, could dare to give a very distorted account of matters which, at least partly, had been transacted only seven years earlier in the public assembly of the people, it is not surprising that both Xenophon and Aristotle are occasionally somewhat vague in regard to questions or events of minor importance. In regard to any points of major importance, however, there is no reason to doubt the accuracy of the accounts of either author concerning this period.

Not very much need be said in this connection about the last section of Aristotle's treatise, in which he deals with the political and administrative machinery of the Athenian state as it existed in his own time. For, in contrast to the Solonian laws,[29] the law code which was elaborated after 410 B.C. and completed and adopted shortly after the restoration of the democracy in 404/3 seems to have contained also the constitutional regulations, and

[28] Lysias, *contra Eratosth.* 64ff., and Xenophon, *Hellen.* II, 2,10ff: cf. also Lysias, *c. Agor.*, 5ff.

[29] Cf. *supra*, pp. 18ff. and p. 25.

this code was publicly displayed.   In addition, since everything
in Athens was public, Aristotle or his disciples had merely to go
to the law courts, the administration offices, etc., in order to
observe the machinery of the state in action.   Here, then, we
seem to have an account that is absolutely firsthand;[30] so that
the question of "sources" does not seem to arise.   Nevertheless,
some observations have to be made about this part of the work.
In the first place, Aristotle says nothing about the way in which
the new law code came into being after the democracy had been
restored following the overthrow of the regime of the so-called
Thirty Tyrants, and hardly anything about the minor changes in
the political regulations that were made in the period between
the adoption of this law code and Aristotle's own time.   In the
second place, we find, as pointed out on an earlier occasion,[31]
that in the treatise as we have it no reference is made to the
procedure of lawmaking that was followed in this period, though
the elaborate rules governing this procedure, of which we learn
something, but not enough, through some of Demosthenes'
speeches, seem to have been one of the most important innovations of the new constitution as compared with the democracy
of the second half of the fifth century.

This, however, is by no means the only omission.   For instance,
it was observed long ago that the enumeration in Chapter 59 of
the cases brought before the Thesmothetae is far from complete;
and, generally speaking, one may say that the treatment of the
subject is very uneven, sketchy in some parts but rather full and
detailed in others.   Three different explanations of this unevenness have been offered by modern scholars, namely: (1) that
Aristotle's whole treatise, including the second part, is an extract
from an Atthis, or local history of Attica,[32] (2) that the second
part is essentially an extract from the published law code, and

---

[30] Concerning the suggestion that this section of Aristotle's treatise might
be based on an Atthis or on material collected by his disciple Theophrastus
cf. *infra*.

[31] Cf. *supra*, p. 8.

[32] *Cf*. U. von Wilamowitz-Moellendorf, *Aristoteles und Athen*, Vol. I, pp.
214ff. and 256ff.

(3) that the second part is an extract from a larger collection of similar material which served as basis both for Aristotle's treatise and for the extensive work on laws which was elaborated after Aristotle's death by his disciple Theophrastus. The first of these explanations must be rejected on the ground that it was hardly necessary to consult an Atthis, since the material was directly accessible in the published law code and through observation of the actual procedure followed by administrative offices and law courts in Aristotle's own time. Apart from this, there was scarcely need of an *excerpt* from an Atthis as far as secular matters were concerned, since an Atthis, by its very nature, can itself not have contained more than an extract of all the available material and, in all probability, the Atthides which existed in Aristotle's time gave a *much* less extensive account of the Athenian constitution in the fourth century than Aristotle did. Both the second and the third explanations mentioned above, on the other hand, probably contain some elements of truth. The former is usually coupled with the further assumption that Aristotle selected the material actually included with a view to its importance for the structure of the Athenian state and with the intention of using it for a more general analysis. This is probably quite correct. The latter is supported by the fact that some of the not too numerous fragments from Theophrastus' work on laws that have come down to us show clear coincidences with passages in Aristotle's treatise.[33] Hence, the uneven selection by Aristotle of the material to be included in his own treatise is often explained by the assumption that Aristotle omitted what Theophrastus wished to include in his work on Laws. This latter explanation, however, seems to be refuted by the fact that, according to what we find in the fragments of Theophrastus' work, the same material *was* used in both works.

The problem, however, cannot be solved as long as one adheres to the belief, still generally held by classical scholars and ancient historians, that Aristotle's treatise in the form in which we have it was written for a larger public. A careful comparison between its second part and certain sections of his *Politics* confirms the

[33] *Cf.* H. Bloch, in the article quoted above (note 11), pp. 371ff.

view that Aristotle selected his material with a view to its importance for his general theoretical analysis, and there are also some
sentences in the second part of the *Constitution of Athens* that show
what general problems were foremost in his mind when he wrote
it. But they are very scanty and reveal their meaning only when
taken together with the corresponding passages in the *Politics*.
While, therefore, the treatise as we have it was certainly very
useful for Aristotle and for the discussions in his school, the general
public would have been bewildered by the unevenness of the
selection of the material included in it; and one cannot believe
that Aristotle was satisfied to present his readers with a work
from which the most important material was omitted because
his disciple might publish it later in another treatise. What is
more, the second part of the treatise shows the same deficiencies
of arrangement and expression[34] as the first part.[35] It is true
that the Chapters 63ff., which nobody had been able to understand until about ten years ago, became understandable when
fragments of an ancient allotment machine were discovered
during the excavations at Athens. But it is certainly no less
significant that these chapters could not be understood until
these machines were found and that even then, because of the
carelessness of Aristotle's description, it required very considerable
ingenuity to explain the whole procedure on the basis of Aris-

[34] In the particularly detailed description, for instance, of the way in which
the jurors for the law courts were selected by lot (Chapters 63/64), Aristotle
first gives a description of the implements used in the allotment, their location, and their arrangement; then tells who is eligible for jury duty and how
those are punished who participate in the procedure without being entitled
to do so; then describes some further implements used; then describes the
first step in the allotment procedure; then supplements the description of
the implements mentioned in the first section; and then finally goes on to
describe the allotment itself. This arrangement is very confusing. It would
have been much easier for the reader if Aristotle had first discussed the
question of who is entitled to apply for jury duty and had then given an
account of the procedure of selection by lot, describing the implements used
in the procedure in the order in which, and the occasion on which, they are
used, as, incidentally, he has done in describing the second, but not in
describing the first, half of the procedure.

[35] Concerning the first part, cf. *supra*, pp. 8ff.

totle's text. To illustrate this carelessness, it is perhaps not beside the point to give just one concrete example. In describing the first step of the allotment procedure,[36] Aristotle says: "The Thesmothet draws a ticket from each chest. This man is called the 'ticket-inserter.'" On the face of it, this would mean that the Thesmothet is called ticket-inserter. In fact, however, Aristotle means to say that the man whose lot the Thesmothet draws becomes one of the ten ticket-inserters.

All this leads to the conclusion that the second part of Aristotle's treatise, no less than its first part, is a sketch that was to be used by Aristotle and his disciples, but that it was not an elaborate work destined for the general public. We, therefore, must not look for completeness in any respect nor for equally clear arrangement and formulation of the facts. At the same time, it is no longer necessary to assume that it is an excerpt from a larger work or collection, though Aristotle knew, of course, more than he wrote down. But with all the inevitable defects of a sketch of this kind, Aristotle's work is still the most important source of information that we possess concerning the history of the Athenian constitution.

A few observations may be added in conclusion. The frequent criticisms of historical statements made by Aristotle, which the reader will find in the notes to the present translation of Aristotle's treatise, might easily lead to the impression that Aristotle does not rank very high as an historian. Nothing, however, could be farther from the truth, and it is one of the purposes of this chapter of the Introduction to correct that impression. Of course, Aristotle, who, in the thirteen years between his return to Athens and his death, wrote nearly all of his most important philosophical and scientific works, did not have the time to collect, analyze, and check every bit of historical evidence that could be found anywhere, as a modern specialist might do. But there are three points which show clearly his quality as an historian. These are the use that he has made of Solon's poems and of the draft of a constitution made in 411 but never actually used, and his discussion of the position of Aristeides, in which he deviates from

[36] *Cf.* Aristotle, Chapter 64, 1/2.

what, even in his time, seems to have become a generally accepted
tradition. The first two points show that, in the search for and
the use made of first-rate historical documents, he went farther
than did Thucydides and, in fact, any other earlier historian we
know. The third point shows that he was able to see through
a faulty tradition, however well established, if the general political
situation indicated that the tradition could not be correct.

If, in other sections, Aristotle's account is less clear and less
accurate, this is due partly to the nature of the tradition which
did not and does not now admit the solution of many historical
problems, and partly to the fact that his treatise remained a
sketch which was to be used in the school but was not elaborated
for publication. Even those parts of the treatise, however, that
are historically open to criticism are valuable for the student of
the history of political philosophy because they show what Aristotle believed the constitutional development of Attica to have
been. It remains, then, to say something about the relation
between Aristotle's political philosophy and the empirical and
historical evidence that he has collected in the present treatise.

III. The Relation Between Aristotle's Treatise on the "Constitution of Athens" and His Political Philosophy

In one of Aristotle's early works, the *Protrepticus*,[1] which, in all
likelihood, was written and published when Aristotle was still
a member of Plato's Academy,[2] we find the following passage:

Just as he will not be a good builder who does not use the rule
or the other instruments of this kind,[3] but takes his measure from
other buildings; so he will not be a good lawmaker or a serious
statesman who gives his laws or administers the affairs of the
state with a view to, or in imitation of, the actions of others or
of the constitutions of actual human communities as, for instance,
those of the Lacedaemonians or of the Cretans. For a copy of

[1] Cf. *infra*, pp. 210–213.

[2] Aristotle entered the Academy in 368/7 at the age of seventeen while
Plato was absent in Sicily, and remained in the Academy until after Plato's
death in 348/7. He left only after Plato's nephew Speusippus had been
elected head of the Academy.

[3] Namely the plummet, the compass, etc. Cf. *infra*, pp. 211–212.

that which is not beautiful itself cannot be beautiful, nor can the nature of that which is not divine and stable be imperishable and stable.[4]

From this statement, it seems a far cry to the last sentences of Aristotle's *Nicomachean Ethics*, which lead over to the latest version of his *Politics*. For here he emphasizes the importance of experience for the lawmaker and the statesman and then concludes with the following words:

First, then, we shall try to review whatever valuable suggestions have been made by earlier writers [namely, in regard to the different problems of political philosophy]; then we shall attempt, on the basis of our collections of constitutions, to find out what things contribute to the preservation or the destruction of states in general and what things help to preserve or to destroy particular types of constitutions, and finally also, for what reasons some states are well governed and others the opposite. For once we have considered these problems, we shall, perhaps, be better able to discern what the best state must be like, and also how each given type of state must be ordered, and what laws and customs it should have in order to function as well as possible.

Yet the two points of view are by no means so far apart as it may seem at first sight, and it would be quite misleading to say that in the *Protrepticus* Aristotle speaks as a "rationalist" pure and simple, while in the *Nicomachean Ethics* he speaks as an "empiricist" pure and simple. To determine as exactly as possible in what respects the Aristotle of the *Protrepticus* agrees and in what respects he disagrees with the Aristotle of the *Nicomachean Ethics* is most important for a full understanding of the relation between Aristotle's historical studies and his final political theory.

The *Protrepticus* was an exhortation to the study of philosophy addressed to Themison, the king of Cyprus. Not only this fact in itself but the whole content of the treatise, of which a very considerable part has come down to us, proves beyond doubt that, at the time when Aristotle wrote it, he still believed in Plato's famous doctrine that kings should become philosophers or philosophers kings. Some years later, in his treatise on kingship which he addressed to his former pupil, Alexander the

[4] *Infra*, pp. 212–213.

Great, he wrote[5] that not only was it not necessary for a king to become a philosopher but it was a positive hindrance in his work; instead, a good king should listen to the true philosophers and be agreeable to their advice.[6] In regard to this point, then, undoubtedly Aristotle in the *Protrepticus* was still a Platonist while later he disagreed with his former master. Yet the *Protrepticus*, though unquestionably written under the strong influence of Plato and the Academy, is by no means entirely Platonic. In fact, even the mere extracts of the work that have come down to us contain an amazing number of ideas and statements which, in a slightly different wording, recur in the most fundamental sections of the theoretical works of Aristotle's most mature period.

The sentence from the *Protrepticus* quoted at the beginning of the present chapter seems to reveal Aristotle as essentially still a Platonist, since it appears to contain a direct application to lawmaking and political activity of Plato's contention[7] that only the philosopher, who looks at the eternal ideas and not at the things in space and time, which are but imperfect "imitations" of the ideas, can know the truth and guide himself and others according to the truth.[8] But the question is much more complicated.

Plato, in the beginning of the Tenth Book of the *Republic*, speaks of the craftsman who makes a couch or a table not by looking at and slavishly imitating another couch or another table, but by looking at the idea of a couch or a table and so producing something which may be different from any existing real couch or table but which is still a good couch or table, fulfilling the function or purpose of a couch or table. Certainly, instead of speaking of these pieces of household furniture, Plato

---

[5] Cf. *infra*, p. 216.

[6] It need hardly be mentioned that this sentence is almost identical with part of Kant's famous statement on the relation of kings and philosophers in *Zum ewigen Frieden, Zweiter Zusatz zum Zweiten Abschnitt*.

[7] Plato, *Republic* VI, 500b-d.

[8] The sentence is actually interpreted in this way by W. W. Jaeger, *Aristoteles* (Berlin 1923), pp. 91ff. But cf. W. Theiler, *Zur Geschichte der teleologischen Naturbetrachtung bis auf Aristoteles*, Zürich, 1925, p. 87ff. and E. Kapp, *Mnemosyne* VI (1938), pp. 185ff.

in this connection might just as well have spoken of a house. This, however, only makes it clearer that Aristotle in the *Protrepticus* did not use the theory of ideas in this form. For, if this had been the case, the sentence quoted in the beginning of the present chapter would have been formulated as follows: "Just as he will not be a good architect who does not look at the idea of a house and at its purpose, but imitates actually existing buildings; so he will not be a good lawmaker who takes actually existing constitutions as his models instead of looking at the idea of a state." Instead of mentioning the idea of the house, however, Aristotle refers to the use by the builder of exact tools, as, for instance, the plummet, the rule, and the compass; and, in the second half of the sentence, which is not very clearly formulated in Iamblichus' extract from Aristotle's *Protrepticus*, reference is made to nature rather than to the idea of the state. What does this mean? What is the meaning of "nature" in this context, and what, in the activity of the lawmaker and the serious statesman, according to Aristotle, corresponds to the exact tools of the builder?

In order to find an answer, it must first be pointed out that Plato himself never speaks of an idea of the state and that, in fact, such a concept never enters into his political philosophy. Plato does speak on various occasions of the truly wise statesman, especially in his *Politicus*,[9] which probably was written not very long before Aristotle wrote his *Protrepticus*. This truly wise statesman — one might also say the ideal statesman, though the word "ideal" is not found in Plato's terminology — according to Plato, is superior to the laws. For the laws[10] are, of necessity, always general rules which set down what should be done in certain types of cases. Since the incidents of human life, however, are infinitely varied, even the best laws are too rigid to deal adequately with this infinite variety. In order to illustrate further the relation between the truly wise statesman and the laws, Plato uses the analogy of the doctor.[11] Since the doctor

[9] *Politicus*, 292d ff., 300c-e.
[10] For this and what follows cf. *ibid*. 294a ff.
[11] *Ibid*. 295c.

cannot always be around the patient, he will prescribe the rules for the latter's treatment. The rules have to be followed strictly by the friends and relatives of the patient, as they are intelligent enough to apply the rules but do not have the doctor's true insight into the nature of the disease. The doctor himself, on the contrary, is not bound by his own prescriptions, which, like the laws, are always of a general nature and therefore hardly ever totally adequate to the infinite variety of incidents that may occur in the development of a disease. Hence, when he comes back to visit the patient, he, with deeper insight, may change the treatment in accordance with the state in which he finds him. In like manner, the truly wise statesman, who is the rarest of human beings and who, even when and where such a man may be found, cannot attend to all matters personally, will set down laws which should be strictly adhered to by those who are able to apply them and who administer the state but who do not share his deeper insight. But he himself must be free to deviate from them whenever the inevitable rigidity of the law does injustice to the claims of the individual case.

There is no room in the present introduction for a discussion of the implications, the merits and demerits, of Plato's lofty and perhaps somewhat unrealistic theory of the truly wise statesman.[12] But it is necessary for the present purpose to clarify the relation of this Platonic concept to Aristotle's concept of the activity of the true lawgiver and the serious statesman as they are found in the *Protrepticus*. Plato's truly wise statesman is above the law. But he, too, both when making laws and when deviating from them, must have a criterion for his action. This criterion, however, is not the idea of the state, but the idea of the just and of the good.

Aristotle, as is known, later rejected Plato's theory of ideas. It is possible that in the period in which he wrote the *Protrepticus*

---

[12] It should, however, be noted that in the *Politicus* the "truly wise states-man" is considered as so rare an exception that he seems to be introduced to elucidate a point of theory rather than to imply the possibility of his actual appearance on the political scene.

he was still an adherent of this Platonic theory as Jaeger tried to demonstrate.[13]   But in all the rather extensive extracts from the *Protrepticus* which have come down to us, there is no direct reference to it; and, in the section on the true lawgiver and the serious statesman, we find instead the concept of *physis* or "nature."

The term *physis* is not unfamiliar to Plato, especially in his later writings, and it is also true that it sometimes occurs in close connection with the theory of ideas.   But it is never identical with "idea."   The fact, therefore, that Plato's truly wise statesman orients himself by looking at the idea of the just and the good, while Aristotle's true lawgiver and serious statesman derives his measure from "nature," is certainly significant.

The Greek concept of *physis* has a long history which cannot be discussed in detail in the present context.[14]   One very important element in this concept was developed in early Greek medicine.   In medicine, *physis* is that which keeps the world in motion and makes things grow, and, more specifically, that which makes the human body grow and function and restores or tries to restore it to its normal strength and functions when these have been impaired or weakened by external injuries or by sickness and disease.   The doctor must study nature in all its manifestations, both in the human body and in the surrounding world, in order to be able to support it in its struggle for restoration of the body and its functions against inimical influences.[15]   The investigation

[13] In actual fact, the problem is probably a good deal more complex. There are strong indications to show that Aristotle at a rather early time and long before Plato's death began to entertain doubts concerning the validity of the theory of ideas in its Platonic form, though it was evidently much later that he freed himself completely from it and definitely attempted to refute it.

[14] For special phases of this history, cf. W. Heidel: "Περὶ φύσεως. A study of the conception of nature in the pre-Socratics," *Proceedings of the Am. Acad. of Arts and Sciences* 45 (1910), pp. 77–133, and W. Theiler, *Zur Geschichte der teleologischen Naturbetrachtung bis auf Aristoteles*, Zürich, 1925.

[15] The role of the study of nature in medicine is also discussed by Plato in the *Phaedrus* 270b ff.   In the same context, Plato speaks also of the "nature" of the soul, which must be studied by the true orator.   Here too, however,

of "nature" in this sense certainly contains a strong element of
empiricism, since it is largely based on empirical observation.
Nevertheless, it seems to contain also an element which, in a way,
transcends empirical observation, pure and simple. For the
assumption is always made that "nature" *aims* at something,
namely, perfect health, a perfect harmony and functioning of
the body which is but scarcely, if ever, realized. This concept
of "nature" is frequently found in Aristotle's writings and most
clearly illustrated by those passages in which he says that "nature
wishes to do something but cannot quite do it." [16]

Another element in the complex concept of "nature" found
in Aristotle and other philosophers was developed in the course
of what may be called the *nomos-physis* controversy. This controversy arose from the observation made by the Greeks in their
contact with other nations with different cultural traditions, that
what in one country was the most sacred law or custom might
be abhorred as impious in another country, and that, nevertheless, there appeared to exist certain moral principles which,
though not identically formulated or always applied in all respects
in the same fashion, yet, in a general way, seemed to be acknowledged as valid everywhere. From this observation the conclusion
was drawn that the laws, rules, or customs of the first kind were
man-made and owed their existence to mere "convention," [17]
while the principles of the second type were in some way based
on nature, or, as the Greeks said, existed *physei*, by nature.[18] It
was further observed that these latter principles were only partly
incorporated, and, within the various nations or political com-

nature is not identical with "idea." There is no "idea" of the soul anywhere
in Plato's writings. For the concept of "nature" in Greek medicine cf.
W. Jaeger, *Paideia*, III, p. 28.

[16] Cf. *e.g. Politics* 1255b 3.

[17] The word used for "convention" is the same as the word which means
"law": *nomos*. The difference, then, is that between laws which have merely
been set down as laws by human beings and laws or rules which have a
foundation in "nature."

[18] It need hardly be pointed out that there was also a theory according to
which the "natural law" was the rule of the stronger over the weaker. But
it is not necessary to discuss this theory in the present chapter.

munities, in very different degrees, in the positive or "written" laws, so that, for instance, in the famous funeral speech which Thucydides attributes to Pericles,[19] the greatest moral glory of the Athenians can be found in their obedience to these "unwritten laws," the violation of which brings shame upon the transgressor but is not punished by a law court.

In this form, the theory of the contrast between the conventional and the natural law or laws obviously does not preclude the possibility that the natural law could be completely and adequately incorporated in a written code, though this has never been done. Yet it is not a very far step from the theory in this form to the Platonic view that the incidents of human life are of such an infinite variety that the just and the equitable can never be formulated in general rules or laws in such a way that strict or literal application of the written law will never lead to a violation of true justice or equitableness. Plato's conclusion is that the laws of existing states are doubly imperfect; namely, both for the general reason that a formulated law is always somewhat imperfect because it is too rigid, and for the particular reason that they deviate from the ideal even more than necessary. It is then the test of the truly wise statesman as a lawgiver to make laws which come as near as possible to true justice and equity; but when called upon and able to deal with special situations and individual cases, he will still have to deviate from his own laws, on occasion, because of their inevitable imperfection.

In a way, then, it may be said that Plato continues in the tradition of the theory of natural law.[20] Yet there is a difference which is essential for a full understanding of Aristotle's position in respect to Plato, both in his *Protrepticus* and in his later writings, inasmuch as in the early beginnings of a theory of natural law, just as again later in Aristotle's *Protrepticus*, the fundamental concept is "nature," while Plato speaks of the "idea" of the just and the good. Plato's ideas are definitely beyond the world in

[19] Thucydides II, 37, 3.

[20] For an excellent discussion of this aspect of Plato's philosophy cf. the article by Joseph P. Maguire, "Plato's Theory of Natural Law" in *Yale Classical Studies*, Vol. X (1947), pp. 151–178.

space and time. The wise men must try to see them in all their
purity. "Nature," on the other hand, in the early beginnings
of a theory of natural law, just as in early Greek medicine, is
something which is common to all human beings, but it is also
characterized by its quality of always aiming at something which
is rarely, if ever, realized. Like the investigation into "nature"
in early Greek medicine, so also the investigation of "natural"
law is at the same time empirical and in a way transcendent of
empirical observation pure and simple. It is quite true that
Aristotle in the *Protrepticus* uses terms which are characteristic
of Plato's theory of ideas and which Aristotle later does not use
any longer in the same context. It is also true that he uses
"nature" in *almost* exactly the same way as Plato uses the idea
of the just and the good. The ambiguity of his position between
Plato and his own later philosophy is illustrated by the fact that,
according to one decisive passage of the *Protrepticus*, the wise
statesman must take his criteria of what is just and useful (in an
individual case) from nature itself *and from truth*. One may even
have different opinions as to how far Aristotle himself, when he
wrote the *Protrepticus*, was aware that he was on a road that led
away from Platonic philosophy. Yet, with all this, the fact that
he did *not* speak of ideas but of nature is certainly highly significant. For this deviation from Platonic philosophy,[21] or at least
from Platonic terminology, brought him nearer to the pre-
Platonic beginnings of a theory of natural law and to early Greek
medicine and medical anthropology. It made it possible for
him later to abandon Plato's theory of ideas completely and yet
to retain the fundamental principles on which his political philosophy in the *Protrepticus* was based. Above all, it opened to
him the road to the historical and empirical exploration of

---

[21] It is true that Plato himself, in the *Republic*, when discussing the happiness
or blessedness of the just man, also analyzes in a way the "nature" of the
human soul, as J. P. Maguire, *op. cit.*, has pointed out. Yet there remains
the fact that Aristotle uses the concept of nature in a somewhat different
way and in a context in which Plato would not speak simply of nature,
but of the idea of the just and the good.

political problems which he later was to undertake on so large a scale, though, at the time when he wrote the *Protrepticus*, he was obviously not yet fully aware of the usefulness of such an undertaking.

If, then, it has been shown that the step from the fundamental principles of the *Protrepticus* to the "empiricism" of the last paragraphs of the *Nicomachean Ethics* is not so great as it may seem at first sight, it can also be shown that the empiricism of the *Nicomachean Ethics* itself does not go quite so far as a superficial perusal of the sentences quoted in the beginning of the present chapter may lead the reader to expect.

At the end of the Tenth book of the *Nicomachean Ethics* (1179a 33ff.), Aristotle extemporizes a transition from his Ethics, that is, his theory of human happiness, to his Politics, that is, political science in the narrower sense. Stated in the briefest possible way, the idea is this: the mere theory of happiness is not sufficient to make the average human being qualified for happiness. What is needed are good laws providing the right kind of public education for the young and enforcement of right behavior for those who are grown up. But such laws exist for the time being only in theory, namely, in the new political science as established by Plato[22] and continued and perfected in Aristotle's school. Hence, there is the necessity — even in regard to private education[23] — of turning now to the theory of legislation and to political science in general.[24] Although it is expressly conceded that, in special circumstances, experience alone, without a general scientific foundation, gets excellent results, nevertheless, the superiority of theory over mere experience even for practical results is as strongly emphasized as it had been emphasized in the *Protrep-*

---

[22] Plato's name does not occur, but his views on education as a major if not the main objective of the art of the wise statesman and legislator are presupposed from the beginning of this whole section. It is less important, though still worth mentioning, that in 1180a 5ff. the requirement of "preambles to laws," of which Plato's *Laws* had made so much (719e and *passim*), is directly referred to and adapted to Aristotle's argument.

[23] *Nic. Eth.* 1180a 30ff.

[24] *Nic. Eth.* 1181b 13ff.

ticus;[25] and the example of the scientifically trained doctor is, at this point, used in the same way in which it is used at the beginning of the *Metaphysics*.[26] There is no indication that, in this respect, Aristotle veer changed his convictions fundamentally. Yet there is a remarkable change in tone. Whereas every line of the chapter from Aristotle's *Protrepticus* translated below[27] seems to express an enthusiastic belief that theory, accessible to none but the philosopher, can and will be the source of all that is truly good in practice, the *Nicomachean Ethics* states in a tone of resignation:

> In the Spartan state alone, or almost alone, the legislator seems to have paid attention to questions of nurture and occupations; in most states such matters have been neglected, and each man lives as he pleases, Cyclops-fashion, "to his own wife and children dealing law" [Homer *Od.*, IX 114f.]. Now it is best that there should be a public and proper care for such matters; but if they are neglected by the community it would seem right for each man to help his children and friends towards virtue, and that they should have the power, or at least the will, to do this. It would seem from what has been said that he can do this better if he makes himself capable of legislating.[28]

In other words: even if political theory is not carried into practice by the existing states according to its original meaning, it is still most essential and, under the conditions now prevailing, will have to serve as a guide for educational practice in private circles.

One of the characteristics of a theoretical science is that it can be taught.[29] Who is able to teach political theory? The way

[25] *Nic. Eth.* 1180b 7–28; for the *Protrepticus* see the following note and *infra* pp. 211–212.

[26] *Nic. Eth.* 1180b 8ff., *Metaph.* 981a 7–b 9. In the *Protrepticus* Aristotle had introduced the geometrician as compared with the practical land-surveyor, the theorist in the field of music as compared with the practical musician, the astronomer as compared with the navigator (fr. 52 in V. Rose's *Aristotelis qui ferebantur librorum Fragmenta*, Leipzig, 1886). But what we have is, unfortunately, only the negative part of the argument, namely, Aristotle's report of how opponents of theory and philosophy use examples like these. In his view, the case of the doctor may have been different.

[27] See pp. 211–213.

[28] *Nic. Eth.* 1180a 25–33 (Oxford translation).

[29] *Nic. Eth.* 1180b 35ff; *Metaph.* 981b 7–9.

in which Aristotle raises and answers this question makes it quite clear that in his mind political science was taught adequately only in his own school. He does not consider at all any kind of philosophical competition in this field, and he disposes of the possible claims of practical politicians and of the "sophists" on the political art in the orthodox Platonic way: the politicians do not teach, because they are guided by experience (*empeiria*) rather than by thought (*dianoia*); and the "sophists," who profess the political art without practising it, simply prove to be absolutely ignorant of what it takes to teach politics. Aristotle must, of course, have been fully conscious of the fact that, with regard to the claims of philosophy on political science, he was taking Plato's position; and, although he does not name Plato,[30] it is unthinkable that he intended to disregard his master in this field. But when he sums up: "Now since earlier generations have left the subject of legislation unexamined, it is perhaps best that we should ourselves study this, and the problems of political life and constitution in general, in order to complete, to the best of our ability, the philosophy of human affairs," [31] it would seem as if at the time when this was written he considered himself as the only legitimate follower of Plato in this field.

So far the trend of the argument is understandable without difficulty; there is scarcely anything in it that Plato could not have said or had not actually said. Only in the concluding sentences which outline the contents of the *Politics* do we find the emphasis already mentioned[32] on the importance of historical and empirical studies, not only for a philosophy of the political world as it actually is, but even for an understanding of the problems concerning the "best constitution."

If from here we look backwards, we must admit that Aristotle has managed somehow to prepare us for this turn of thought. When he dealt with the practical politicians, he had remarked: "Still, experience seems to contribute not a little; else they could not have become politicians by familiarity with politics; and so it

[30] But cf. *supra* p. 41 and note 22.
[31] *Nic. Eth.* 1181b 13–16.
[32] *Supra* p. 33.

seems that those who aim at knowing about the art of politics need experience as well."[33]   Much more interesting, however, is his section about the "sophists." He replaces the great old sophists, with whom Plato had dealt in his *Protagoras* and in other dialogues and passages (see especially *Republic* 492a–493d), by Isocrates, not naming him, but making him the representative of the "sophists" by an unmistakable quotation:[34]

Those of the sophists who profess the art [of politics] seem to be very far from teaching it. For they do not even know what kind of thing it is nor what kinds of things it is about; otherwise they would not have classed it as identical with rhetoric or even inferior to it, nor have thought it easy to legislate by collecting the laws that are thought well of; they say it is possible to select the best laws, as though even the selection did not demand intelligence and as though right judgment were not the greatest thing. . . .[35]

In his attempt to elucidate this point further, Aristotle comes for a second time to the example of medicine and points out that, in medicine also, the study of handbooks, however detailed their descriptions of treatments may be, is not sufficient to produce a doctor, and that, in fact, only the expert doctor, and not he who lacks his training,[36] can make use of medical books.   Then he goes on:[37]

[33] *Nic. Eth.* 1181a 9–12 (Oxford translation).

[34] Isocrates had stuck his neck out by a foolish remark about legislating. In early times, according to Isocrates (or. 15, 79ff.), when the first states were founded, it was a great thing indeed to give laws, but now it has become quite easy for anyone. After history has produced laws by the ten-thousand, a would-be lawgiver does not need any creative thinking of his own; all he has to do is to collect out of this vast number those laws which are favorably known from elsewhere. How much more difficult and important the task of Isocratean oratory!

[35] *Nic. Eth.* 1181a 12–18 (Oxford translation).

[36] Readers of the Greek text should not allow themselves to be confused by the fact that in 1180b 16ff. the man who cures himself or others δι᾽ ἐμπειρίαν (through mere experience) was supposed to be ἀνεπιστήμων ("an unscientific person" in the Oxford translation), whereas now (1181b 6) the ἔμπειροι are *opposed* to the ἀνεπιστήμονες (those who lack scientific training). The exact meaning of the words ἐμπειρία, ἔμπειρος depends entirely on the context.

[37] *Nic. Eth.* 1181b 6–12.

Now perhaps also the collections of laws and of constitutions[38] can be of good use to men capable of theory and capable of judgment concerning what is commendable or the opposite and what kinds of things are consistent with each other; on the other hand, those who go through such collections without firm training cannot possibly have sound judgment, unless they have it from nowhere [or: have it as a "gift"], but they will perhaps become better prepared, in this field, to understand [what another man says]."[39]

Aristotle's words leave no doubt that in the field of political science, just as in medicine, one has to be an "expert" first, before he can make appropriate use of the written material of the collections; not a word is said about how the expert comes to be an expert. The example of the doctor is here used only to point out, in an extreme case, that the study of books, or written material of any kind, will *not* make an expert. But while, in the case of medicine, the books had been called useless for the non-expert, Aristotle finally modifies the implications of his example with respect to beginners in the study of political science. For them a certain familiarity with the collected material is obviously considered desirable if they are to follow the lectures on "Politics" which Aristotle is going to announce.

This is important, because it is the main connecting link between the preceding discussion and the emphasis on empirical research in the announcement itself. For if we read in this announcement: " . . . then we shall attempt, on the basis of our collections of constitutions, to find out . . .; for once we have considered these problems, we shall perhaps be better able to discern what the best state must be like . . . ,"[40] etc., it is clear

[38] It is clear that Aristotle is now thinking of his own collections of constitutions, an undertaking which, of course, could not be known to Isocrates, who wrote his speech "On the Antidosis" (or. 15) in 354 B.C., when Plato was still alive and Aristotle was still a member of the Academy.

[39] εὐσυνετώτεροι, *i.e.* "of better understanding." This kind of "understanding" or "good understanding" is defined in the Sixth Book of the *Nic. Eth.* as "the exercise of the faculty of opinion for the purpose of judging *of what someone else* says about matters with which practical wisdom is concerned — and of judging soundly; for 'well' [εὖ] and 'soundly' [καλῶς] are the same thing" (1143a 13–15, Oxford translation).

[40] Fully quoted *supra* p. 33.

that Aristotle is not talking of his own way to mastership, but that he simply presupposes his own qualification to deal with the historical material as an expert; actually, he is concerned with a prospectus for his students, and what he promises is that if they have a certain preliminary acquaintance with this material *and* follow his own guidance, *they* "shall perhaps be better able to discern. . . ."[41]

For us it is very fortunate that we have such a revealing description of the part that the collections of constitutions played in Aristotle's school; and we should be careful not to misinterpret the evidence, which plainly shows so much — no more and no less — namely, that, without having become an empiricist pure and simple, Aristotle was by now thoroughly convinced of the importance of intensive and extensive historical studies.

At the same time, it cannot be denied that the whole transition from the *Nicomachean Ethics* to the contents of the *Politics* is of a rather provisional character. The need for a political theory in the narrower sense is onesidedly derived from the fact that average human nature yields only to some kind of coercion; and the amusing but almost vicious attack on one single passage from one of Isocrates' speeches can hardly claim to give a complete solution of the whole problem. We may, therefore, ask why Aristotle did not attempt to write a more satisfactory transition from his ethical to his political theory.

The difficulties which he had to face are easy to see. In earlier phases of his development, he had dealt with Ethics and Politics as strictly separate disciplines.[42] The main subject of his ethical theory is the question of the happiness of the individual. According to his theory, this happiness culminates in pure contemplation. But this is avowedly something that transgresses ordinary human

[41] Notice that in the Greek text the τάχ' ἄν of 1181b 12 is continued in the τάχ' ἄν 1181b 21.

[42] The comparatively early *Eudemian Ethics* does not claim to be part of political science, and in the likewise comparatively early first chapter of the Seventh Book of the *Politics* it is directly stated that a detailed discussion of the question of the best life is "the business of another science" (1323b 39).

nature.[43] It is realized or realizable to the degree in which an individual succeeds in developing the "divine" in human nature. Furthermore, the more an individual approaches this end, which he can never fully attain, the less he is dependent on association with other human beings.

On the other hand, a human being would not be a human being if he did not live in a community with other human beings; this is necessary for him in order to live a human life.[44] It is primarily this latter aspect of human life with which political science in its original sense is concerned. Here, then, in a way, the "end" is the state.[45] After Aristotle had decided to deal with both disciplines as parts of one comprehensive "philosophy of human affairs"[46] and to call ethics, too, "political science,"[47] a discussion of the relation of the two "ends," namely, human happiness and the state, to one another must have appeared theoretically desirable. But to engage in such a discussion on the occasion of the transition from the first to the second part, that is, from ethical theory in the narrower sense to political theory in the narrower sense, was hardly feasible. For, though Aristotle had now the advantage of being able simply to presuppose the results of his ethics concerning the question of human happiness — an advantage which he did not have when he wrote the first chapter of Book VII of his *Politics*[48] — he would have had to anticipate a large part of the work toward which he made his transition if he wished to make the relation between the two "ends" perfectly clear. What is worse, the final results of his ethical theory, as summed up in the chapters immediately preceding the transition, almost preclude an unprejudiced approach to the theory of the state.

[43] *Nic. Eth.* 1177b 26–1178a 2; but notice that Aristotle is quite aware that within the context of this part of the *Nicomachean Ethics* the opposite use of the term "human being" would make even better sense: 1178a 2–7.

[44] *Nic. Eth.* 1178b 5–7.

[45] *Politics* 1252b 30–34, 1253a 18–30.

[46] Cf. *Nic. Eth.* 1181b 15.

[47] *Nic. Eth.* 1094a 27–b 11.

[48] The whole chapter would have been superfluous; cf. also *supra* note 42.

When dealing separately, either with theoretical knowledge as the aim of the philosopher or with the normal human life in a political community, Aristotle could, in either case, begin with "nature." The first chapter of Aristotle's *Metaphysics* derives the development of theoretical wisdom from the alleged fact that "all human beings by nature desire to know," even regardless of practical results,[49] and similarly, the First Book of the *Politics* argues that "by nature all [human beings] have an impulse toward [life in] a political community,"[50] even regardless of practical results.[51] But in the Tenth Book of the *Nicomachean Ethics*, it is so strongly emphasized that a life devoted to theory is something beyond common human nature, and on the other hand, "living a human life" (ἀνθρωπεύεσθαι), applying the social virtues, is so definitely characterized as second-rate[52] that it would have been extremely difficult to proceed from here in continuous argument to Aristotle's theory that "the state is by nature clearly prior to the family and to the individual, since the whole is of necessity prior to the part,"[53] and again, "the state is a creation of nature and prior to the individual."[54]

Under these circumstances, the precarious way in which Aristotle's transition from his Ethics to his Politics reaches its aim ceases to be puzzling. For the intention was clearly to start the course itself with laying down the proper theoretical foundations, which the transition could not and was not meant to do. Still, the main advantage of the final arrangement, in which the First Book of the *Politics* is linked with the last book of the *Nicomachean Ethics*,[55] was not lost. For although the specifically Aristotelian

[49] *Metaphys.* 980a 21ff.

[50] *Politics* 1253a 29ff.

[51] This is expressly added in Book III, 1278b 20ff.; cf. *Eudemian Ethics* 1242a 8.

[52] *Nic. Eth.* 1178b 7.

[53] *Politics* 1253a 19ff. (Oxford translation).

[54] *Ibid.*, 1253a 25.

[55] Although the "announcement" at the end of the *Nicomachean Ethics* seems to point forward immediately to the Second Book of the *Politics*, it seems that the last three words found in the manuscripts of the *Nicomachean Ethics* λέγωμεν οὖν ἀρξάμενοι ("Let us then speak making a beginning") were intended to introduce "another" (or: "fresh") beginning; cf. the first words

thesis that "perfect happiness is a theoretical actiyity"[56] cannot easily enter the discussion of the state as a whole, this thesis was, in Aristotle's view, absolutely consistent with the assumption that *insofar as* we are human beings and have to live with others, happiness or the "good life" (τὸ εὖ ζῆν) can be determined only by a theory of the social virtues and closely related subjects, a task to which the largest portion of Aristotle's ethical work was devoted. The results of this part of his ethical theory are, of course, properly considered at the proper place even in the Tenth Book of the *Nicomachean Ethics*.[57] After this the political theory in the narrower sense could introduce the concept of the "good life" wherever it was needed and so far as it was needed, without special discussion.

According to the introductory paragraph of the First Book of the *Politics*, the state as an association of human beings (who always act for the sake of some good, real or imaginary) has come into being for some good; but, being the highest and most comprehensive form of human association, it is aiming at the highest good. This is an appropriate start for a course in political science; but it is no coincidence that it is made up, with due alterations of arrangement, of the same conceptual ingredients which occur in the much more explicit introduction to the *Nicomachean Ethics*.[58] Aristotle certainly would have had to be more explicit at the beginning of the *Politics*, unless the whole of the *Nicomachean Ethics* was presupposed; but, since this is obviously the case, it is not even necessary to say expressly that the "highest good" is, of course, happiness or the "good life."

We are not going to analyze the First Book of the *Politics* as a whole and may, therefore, neglect the rest of the first chapter. The theoretical foundations for dealing with the state as such

of the Second Book of the *Eudemian Ethics:* "After this, we must make another beginning and then speak about what is to follow," and similar phrases (*e.g. Nic. Eth.* 1145a 15).

[56] *Nic. Eth.* 1178b 7.

[57] *Nic. Eth.* 1178a 9ff.

[58] Chapters 1 and 2 of the *Nicomachean Ethics* (1094a 1-b 11), plus chapter 4, in which the highest practical good is identified with happiness and the "good life."

are laid in the second chapter.[59] The best way, we are told, of speculating about the state is to look at things as they grow (πράγματα . . . φυόμενα). Since individual human beings are not self-sufficient, there will, of necessity, be associations from the very beginning. Genetically, then, the associations between male and female on the one hand, and between master and slave on the other hand, come first; both associations are based on natural differentiation and, at least in the first case, on purely natural instinct.[60] The next step toward self-sufficiency is the combination of these two associations in family and household, "established by nature for the supply of men's everyday wants."[61] What follows is a combination of several families in the village, a higher form of association, which most naturally may be compared to a colony and which is the first to aim not only at the day's needs. When finally several villages combine to form a state, the limit of possible self-sufficiency is reached; and so the state is the perfect association (κοινωνία τέλειος): "it comes into being for the sake of bare existence, but when it has come into being, it *is* for the sake of the good life."[62]

At this point Aristotle draws the conclusion that *every* state exists "by nature," taking now for granted that the earlier forms of association are "by nature," and assuming that complete self-sufficiency is the final cause of the whole progress toward it. Thus he is able to identify self-sufficiency (and the state in which it is realized) with the "end" at which nature was aiming from the beginning.[63]

The rest of the chapter, in which Aristotle draws the further conclusion that it is by nature that man is a political being (more

[59] *Politics* 1252a 24–1253a 39.

[60] *Politics* 1252a 26ff.

[61] *Ibid.* 1252b 13 (Oxford translation).

[62] *Ibid.* 1252b 29ff.

[63] In order to make this plausible, Aristotle appeals to his general philosophy of nature and for once must use the word "nature" as directly equivalent to "end": "now nature is an end; for what a thing is like when the development has come to its end, that we say is its nature, as in the case of 'man,' 'horse,' 'house.' " (οἰκία is here "house," not "family," cf. *de part. an.* 646a 17, b4.)

than any gregarious animal), but that the state is by nature
prior to the individual, etc., is now comparatively easy to understand. But there seems to remain one difficulty. It is clear that
the discussion concerns the state in general and that the conclusions drawn claim to be valid for any state as such. Yet,
while it could be said of the state in general that it "has, so to
speak, reached the limit of all self-sufficiency,"[64] it certainly
would not make sense to contend that the state as such "has
reached the limit of all good life"; besides, from the contents of
the second chapter, it is not at all clear how the "good life"
suddenly enters the argument.

In order to understand this, one has to go back to the introductory paragraph at the beginning of the book, part of which
may now be quoted in an accurate translation: "If all communities aim at some good, the state or political community, which
is the highest of all, and which embraces all the rest, aims at a
good in a greater degree than any other, and at the highest
good."[65] For the purpose of following Aristotle's intentions, it
does not matter whether or not we approve of the way in which
the thesis that the state aims at the highest good is here presented
to us; at any rate, the fact that this thesis had been proposed
from the very beginning explains the only seemingly unwarranted
assertion within the second chapter. For we have already seen[66]
that the "highest good" is happiness or the "good life," and we
cannot fail to realize now that in Aristotle's theory the assertion,
"the state is for the sake of the good life," has exactly the same
meaning as the thesis, "the state aims at the highest good"; and
this can, of course, be generally true, even if the "good life" is
actually not reached or reached only to a small extent.[67]

We cannot go into a more detailed interpretation of the second
chapter of the *Politics;* so much should be clear by now that
Aristotle's general theory of the state, as displayed in this chapter,

[64] *Politics* 1252b 28ff.

[65] *Ibid.*, 1252a 4–6 (Oxford translation).

[66] *Supra*, p. 49 and note 58.

[67] A passage in Book III of the *Politics* (1278b 24–30) shows that Aristotle
was inclined to interpret even the striving for bare existence (which in 1252b
29f. is opposed to the good life) as a striving for happiness.

cannot be fully understood without going back to the introductory paragraph at the beginning of the *Politics*, which, in turn, as we have stated earlier,[68] is closely related to the first chapters of the *Nicomachean Ethics*. But if we now compare the second chapter of the *Politics* directly with the introduction to the *Nicomachean Ethics*, an interesting change in the philosopher's orientation can be observed. In the introduction to the *Nicomachean Ethics*, it is not "nature" that appears to be concerned with the state and the good life, but rather political art and science; the word "nature" does not even occur. In the second chapter of the *Politics*, the political art is not entirely forgotten, as its last section[69] proves, but, with this exception, the importance of "nature," and what nature is aiming at, as the basis for an understanding of the state, is so strongly emphasized[70] that the state itself and the task of dealing theoretically with political communities is seen in a new light. So long as not only ethics but political theory, too, is dominated by the concept of the best life, the attitude toward the actually existing states is necessarily more or less critical; but, if "nature" pervades political life in all its forms, and if, consequently, *any* state "is" (after it has come into being) for the sake of the good life, a much more positive attitude toward all these forms appears to be possible and theoretically justified.

It is in this way that Aristotle's political theory finally attempted to become completely free from those remnants of Plato's theory of ideas[71] which could be discovered in his *Protrepticus*. Still, the theory lends itself to the construction of an ideal state, that is, the state in which the good life is realized as far as humanly possible; and, in fact, the end of the *Nicomachean Ethics* does promise another discussion of the best state. But there is now a shift of emphasis. The very sentence in which Aristotle promises the new discussion of the best state shows that the "ideal" state

[68] *Supra*, p. 49.

[69] *Politics* 1253a 30–34.

[70] Notice that the noun "nature" occurs twenty times.

[71] Already the *Eudemian Ethics* had replaced the "idea" of the good by the highest practical good, and so does, of course, the *Nicomachean Ethics*.

is no longer the sole or even the principal subject of political philosophy. At least of equal importance seems now the question of what rules, laws, regulations, and institutions are most suitable to any given kind of constitution. This change of emphasis as against the *Protrepticus* becomes still clearer if one looks at the *Politics* itself. It is, of course, not possible within the present introduction to analyze in detail the origin and composition of the whole work as it has come to us. But modern scholars have proved beyond reasonable doubt that its last two books, which contain an obviously uncompleted sketch of the best constitution, were written considerably earlier than the rest of the work.[72] It is possible that Aristotle intended to replace these books later by a more elaborate discussion of the same subject. But it is hardly a mere coincidence that he never did replace them and that by far the most important sections in the work as we now have it are the First Book, in which he discusses the anthropological, sociological and economic foundations of political life, and Books IV to VI and parts of Book III, in which he discusses the various possible forms of government and the question of how they can be made to function well and to be as stable as possible. It is also significant that in the Second Book he analyzes and criticizes Plato's ideal state and the earlier utopias of Phaleas of Chalcedon and Hippodamus of Miletus on the same level as the actually existing constitutions which had evoked special admiration.

It is interesting to observe that the considerations which seem to have led to this change of emphasis in some way go back to Plato himself; not so much to his theoretical writings, to be sure, as to his actual attitude when he came in contact with practical politics. For in the few cases in his life in which Plato had an opportunity to exercise his influence in practical politics, as in the case of his friend Dion in Sicily, in the case of his former students Erastus and Coriscus in Scepsis, and in the case of the latters' political friend Hermias of Atarneus, he did not advocate

---

[72] *Cf.* W. Jaeger, *Aristoteles* (Berlin, 1923), pp. 271ff. Quite recently some attempts have been made to refute Jaeger's theory in this respect. But the arguments are not convincing.

the introduction of his ideal state, whether it be the ideal state of his *Republic* or that of his *Laws*, but a much more modest change and adjustment of existing political institutions. In his *Republic* and his *Laws*, on the other hand, Plato describes not only the political and social institutions of his best and his second best state, respectively, but also their geographical location in regard to climate, distance from the sea, distance from other political communities, the upper and lower limits of their population, etc., conditions which obviously cannot all be met by an existing state but only by a state which is to be newly founded by a certain number of selected colonists in a specifically selected location. The evident conclusion from this, stated to some extent by Plato himself in his *Laws*,[73] is that in existing states the political and social institutions must, at least to some extent, be adapted to those existing conditions which cannot be altered.

There is another factor of equal importance. This is the question of whether and how far a change toward the good may be brought about by force. Again one must distinguish, to some extent, between Plato's theoretical and his practical attitude. It is very well known that Plato did not have a very high opinion of Athenian democracy, though, after he had seen the "happy life" in the cities of southern Italy, he was forced to admit that, at least comparatively speaking, Athenian democracy was not quite as bad as he had thought it was when he had not known anything but Athens.[74] In any case, he never advocated or participated in an attempt to bring about a change in the Athenian constitution by force, but, on the contrary, expressed the conviction that, for the citizens of a state, resort to force in order to change its constitution was as great a crime as it was for the son to do violence to his parents. This aversion to violent change or revolution is also revealed by the fact that, wherever he did make an attempt to bring about a change of political institutions in the direction of his political ideals, he addressed himself to men already in power who could make such a change in a legal way and without the use of force and violence. This

[73] *Laws* V, p. 746a-c.
[74] Cf. *infra*, Plato's *Seventh Epistle*, pp. 223–224.

is also the reason for his association with the younger Dionysius. There is, indeed, the one important exception that he finally did give his blessing to his friend Dion, when the latter set out to overthrow the tyranny of the younger Dionysius by force, and that he supported him by his moral authority. But even in this case, where the object of the revolution was a man who at one time had aroused some hope but later had turned into a real tyrant, according to Plato the worst possible type of ruler, and where the leader of the revolution, Plato's most intimate friend, had been personally wronged by the ruler, it is obvious that Plato for a long time was very hesitant and reluctant to give his approval.

Again Plato's attitude in theory was somewhat different, that is, very characteristically for Plato, somewhat less mild and moderate than his practical attitude. Yet the difference is not a fundamental one. Rather one may say that two opposite tendencies stand out very clearly. On the one hand, there is the conviction, most definitely stated in the *Politicus*,[75] that the truly wise statesman is entitled to do what he knows to be just and good, whether his action be sanctioned by law or not and whether he can bring about what is just and good by persuasion or whether he has to do it by force. Yet, on the other hand, in the *Laws* the superiority of persuasion to force is firmly upheld, and Plato establishes the principle that no law should merely set down a rule that has to be obeyed, but that, on the contrary, every law should have a long introduction which explains to the citizen why such a rule has been set down and why the rule is just.[76] The reason is that even the justest law cannot function properly if it is not understood and if its application, therefore, causes resentment among the citizens.

Though Aristotle does not discuss the question of the application of force in political life so frequently and in such definite terms as Plato does, it is quite clear from his emphasis on the *stability* of constitutions and government, which is a characteristic of his whole *Politics*, that he was even more averse to violent

[75] *Politicus* 293a.
[76] *Laws* 722d ff.

political changes than Plato was. For "stability" of a constitution or a government to Aristotle does not mean unchangeability, but it does mean that a government is of such a nature that it is not likely to be overthrown or even to be attacked by a rebellious or revolutionary movement from within.

If these principles are accepted, it is clear that in a theory which wishes to provide guidance to the practical statesman under variable conditions, the problem of the ideally best state must recede into the background.[77] The construction of such an ideal state may then still serve a useful purpose, inasmuch as it helps to clarify the general direction in which the true good of a political community is to be found. But, for all practical purposes, it will be much more important to find an answer to the question of what specific form this ideal will assume under particular geographic, social, economic, and generally historical circumstances. There will also be the question of what means can or may be used to bring a state, even if it were by only a little, nearer to this specific goal. For it is now acknowledged that, with the exception of the case of absolute tyranny, which, according to Aristotle and Plato, is no government and no real political community at all, a violent overthrow of the existing form of government produces more harm than good.

[77] The new conception of a generally applicable political theory is discussed at length in the first chapter of Book IV of the *Politics*. Although it is true that, toward the end of Aristotle's life, it must have become more and more clear that those men who were to dominate Greek political life from now on would pay little attention to his political theory, and although the transition from Ethics to Politics at the end of the *Nicomachean Ethics* contains one passage in which Aristotle seems to concede defeat with regard to "most of the (existing) states" (1180a 26ff., cf. *supra* p. 42), he was far from changing his theory, as this same passage shows. It is also true that Aristotle's political theory, even though only many centuries later and through indirect channels, has had a much more far-reaching influence on actual political institutions than Plato's. That Aristotle's own disciples believed in the practical applicability of their master's political philosophy is attested by the fact that his disciple Demetrius of Phaleron under Macedonian domination officially assumed the title of lawgiver (νομοθέτης) in Athens and attempted to reform the Athenian state in agreement with Aristotle's principles (cf. Sterling Dow and A. H. Trevis: "Demetrius of Phaleron and His Lawgiving" in *Hesperia* XII (1943) pp. 144ff.).

It was after the discussion of these problems had become a
main interest of Aristotle's political theory that the historical
study of a large variety of actual political institutions acquired
an infinitely broader significance than it could have had for him
when he wrote the *Protrepticus*. At that time, Aristotle had had
only contempt for legislators who, unlike Plato, found their
political ideal in existing constitutions, such as the Spartan or
Cretan, and who tried to form their laws after such models.[78]
In contrast, especially Books IV to VI and parts of Book III of
the *Politics* could never have been written without the help of
the enormous enterprise of a collection of all political constitutions which, as far as could still be found out, had existed anywhere in the Greek and in some of the most important non-Greek
political communities.

When Aristotle wrote the history of the Athenian constitution
as an integral part of this undertaking, two different courses
were open to him. He could either insert his positive and negative evaluations of the political institutions and actions into the
history itself, whenever an occasion presented itself, or merely
give an account of the historical facts, reserving the critical
discussion of these facts for his systematic and theoretical work.
It is clear that, for the most part, he followed the second course.
Yet value judgments are not altogether absent from his historical
treatise. They are found in Chapters 22–41[79] and become more
and more frequent toward the end of that section, which deals
with the development of radical democracy and the oligarchic
reactions against this development down to the restoration of
democracy in 403 B.C.

Aristotle was not an Athenian citizen. He could not make
and did not think of making an attempt to take an active part
in Athenian political life. All direct value judgments in the
Constitution of Athens refer to a period preceding his first stay in
Athens. Most of them concern a period in which Plato, accord-

[78] *Infra*, p. 213.

[79] Aristotle's defense of Solon's personal integrity and his evaluation of
the personal character of Pisistratus and his sons are intended to establish
factual truth and do not belong to the kind of value judgments mentioned
above.

ing to his own testimony,[80] took a passionate interest in Athenian politics, while the remainder refers to the most important steps that led to the political conditions prevailing in Plato's youth. Therefore, the question may be asked how far these value judgments were influenced by Plato's experiences with, and his attitude toward, the Athenian democracy, and how far they are the natural application of Aristotle's own political theory to the various phases of the development of Athenian institutions.

There can be no doubt that neither Plato nor Aristotle had a favorable opinion of Athenian democracy as it existed in the latter part of the fifth century. This unfavorable judgment applies not only to the development of the Athenian democracy after the death of Pericles, that is, that period which is also condemned by the historian Thucydides, but extends also, though in a somewhat milder form,[81] to Pericles' own leadership, which is greatly admired by Thucydides. If, on the whole, Aristotle's judgment of Athenian democracy may appear less severe than Plato's, one must not forget that if Plato in the *Politicus*[82] considers good democracy the least good of the good, he at the same time considers bad democracy the least bad of the depraved forms of government. What is more, we learn from Plato's *Seventh Epistle* that, before he went to Sicily, Plato despised Athenian democracy and considered it hopeless. But when he had seen the "so-called happy life" of the Greek cities of southern Italy, he had to admit that Athenian life and Athenian democracy were far from being the worst of the forms of human, political, and social life.[83] In spite of the differences in their general political theory, Plato and Aristotle, therefore, seem largely to agree in their evaluation of Athenian democracy as it existed in the last quarter of the fifth century. But Aristotle, in the *Constitution of Athens*, is more specific in regard to the historical details and the various phases of the development.

It is certainly significant that Aristotle does not criticize the

[80] *Cf.* Plato, *Seventh Epistle*, *infra* pp. 221–222.
[81] *Cf.* Plato, *Gorgias* 515e ff., Aristotle, *infra*, Chapters 27–28.
[82] *Politicus* 303a.
[83] See *infra*, pp. 223–224.

democratic reforms of Solon, whom, on the contrary, he seems to admire very much, nor even the much more radical reforms of Cleisthenes, though there can be hardly any doubt that these reforms opened the way for the development toward an ever less restricted majority rule, the latter phases of which Aristotle greatly deplores. The first note of criticism is struck in Chapter 25, where Aristotle says that, for seventeen years after the Persian Wars, under the supervision of the Areopagus, the political order remained essentially the same, though the situation was slowly degenerating. What he has in mind becomes clear from what follows. He deplores the reduction of the powers of the Areopagus, which had been a conservative and aristocratic element in the state.[84] He also obviously looks with disfavor on the conversion of the Athenian Sea Confederacy into an Empire ruled by Athens and on the change in the political attitude of the "people" which resulted from this political act. He attributes the responsibility for these unfortunate innovations to Ephialtes and Pericles, and also, to a considerable extent, to Aristeides, though the latter, in ancient literature in general, was rather considered a conservative and at the same time was admired for his personal integrity and disinterestedness which made him die a poor man after he had been a leader of his country for many years. Even Plato, who, in the *Gorgias*, attacks so many other great men of Athens, has only praise for Aristeides. The case of Aristeides seems to indicate that in his historical judgments Aristotle is not entirely dependent on Plato.

Aristotle admits[85] that, in spite of these unfortunate steps, the state was still in a "fairly" good condition as long as Pericles was

[84] Since the Areopagus consisted of the former Archons and since until 487/6 the Archons had been selected ἐκ προκρίτων, *i.e.* from candidates previously selected by vote, and not by lot, it is possible that at the time when its prerogatives were abolished, there were still some members of the Areopagus who had been selected by this older procedure. Above all, it was only some years after the reduction of the power of the Areopagus that the archonship became accessible to the Zeugitae. In 462, therefore, the members of the Areopagus probably still belonged to the two highest property classes.

[85] Chapter 28, *infra*, p. 98.

the leader of the democratic party. But after his death, things went rapidly from bad to worse, owing to the rise of demagogues who were not gentlemen, as all the political leaders of the earlier time had been, but men of bad manners, who shouted on the public platform, who reviled their opponents, who, in their speeches, played on the emotions of their audience instead of appealing to their intellect and understanding, and who, generally speaking, catered to the wishes of the masses in order to promote their own selfish interests rather than the good of the community. He praises the leaders of the conservative or anti-democratic party of the time of Pericles and the earlier part of the Peloponnesian War, Thucydides, the son of Melesias, and Nicias.[86] He also praises the initiators of the oligarchic constitution of 411, but not the way in which the men who had come to power in 411 postponed the actual application of the moderate oligarchic constitution in order to keep control of the government in their own hands.[87] Of the outstanding men of the last decade of the Peloponnesian War, his favorite is Theramenes, the leader of the moderate wing of the anti-democratic party. He defends[88] Theramenes against the accusations of his enemies, who called him a turncoat,[89] a man who belonged to all parties and tried to overthrow all constitutions, by pointing out that, on the contrary, Theramenes worked for the good of any established government as long as it did not transgress the fundamental laws, but was always willing to incur the enmity of those in power in defending the law of the country against their encroachments upon it.

To sum up, then, one may say that Aristotle admired the democratic reforms of Solon and did not criticize the further democratization of the Athenian constitution by Cleisthenes and his immediate successors, but that, in regard to the period from the end of the Persian Wars to the beginning of the Decelean War, he favored the leaders of the conservative or oligarchic

---

[86] Cf. *ibid.*, p. 99.

[87] Cf. Chapters 32–33, *infra*, pp. 104f.

[88] Cf. Chapter 28, *infra*, p. 99.

[89] "Cothurnus," a shoe that could be worn on either foot.

party as against the leaders of the democratic party and, in regard
to the last phase of the Peloponnesian War, the leaders of the
moderate wing of the conservative party as against the radicals
on both sides. The shift of his preference from the democratic
leaders of the period before the Persian Wars to the conservative
leaders of the succeeding period can be easily explained on the
assumption that he shared to some extent the opinion of the men
quoted by him in Chapter 29, namely, that the constitution of
Cleisthenes was not yet fully democratic. It must, however, also
be pointed out that, in spite of his opposition to unrestricted
democracy, Aristotle, on several occasions,[90] praises the leniency
of the Athenian *demos* and extols especially the moderation of
the democratic leaders who restored democracy after the overthrow of the Thirty, in contrast to the violence, cruelty, and
disregard of the laws of their oligarchic predecessors.

In order to see all this in the correct perspective, one must be
aware of the characteristic features of the Athenian democracy
of the second half of the fifth century, by which it differed from
all the various and again widely differing political forms which
are currently designated by this name. One of the most striking
features of the Athenian democracy consisted in the fact that
since the earlier eighties of the fifth century practically all public
functionaries of the state, with the exception of the military
commanders, were selected, not by vote, but by lot. It must
further be observed that Aristotle, though he does not consider
a state in which the public functionaries are elected by vote an
oligarchy, does regard election by vote as an aristocratic feature
in a constitution, because in such an election naturally only
those men who are known through some distinctive qualities
have a chance of being elected, so that the chances are not exactly
the same for everybody. It was a natural consequence of the
institution of selection by lot that the official civil magistrates
who were responsible to the people for the administration of
affairs were not the actual political leaders, but that the political
leadership was in the hands either of one of the commanding

[90] *Infra*, Chapters 22, 4 and 40, 2/3; cf. also *Politics*, 1281a 39ff. and 1282a
15ff.

generals or of orators who succeeded in gaining the decisive
influence in the assembly of the people but had no official
responsibility at all.

The second decisive peculiarity of Athenian democracy in the
same period is the almost completely unrestricted power to decide
absolutely everything by a simple majority of votes, a power
which the assembly of the people seems to have claimed toward
the end of the fifth century. It is true that there must have
existed at that time the so-called *graphé paranomon*, which made
it possible to try and to punish a speaker who had proposed a
measure which was in conflict with the laws of the country.
But there is also evidence to show that occasionally the assembly
claimed it as part of the sovereignty of the people, not only to
usurp the functions of the law courts, but even to violate established rules of procedure, if the majority of the assembly expressed
the will to do so. [91]

A third point was the custom of the law courts, which consisted
exclusively of laymen, not only to interpret the law very freely
and to decide the cases brought before them more according to
the general impression produced by the conflicting parties than
on the basis of a careful investigation of the facts, but also to mete
out punishment according to their arbitrary judgment in cases
for which no provision had been made in the established law.

Under a system like this, a clearly conceived, steady, and
consistent policy of any kind was possible only if, and only as
long as, there existed a political leader of such personal influence
and authority that the assembly in most cases would follow his
advice and leadership. During the lifetime of Pericles, therefore,
the natural consequences of the system did not become completely visible, though even Pericles not infrequently had to

[91] The outstanding example is, of course, the condemnation of the generals
of the battle of the Arginusae by the assembly of the people. On this occasion, as Xenophon, *Hellenica* I, 7, 11ff., informs us, several people protested
that the procedure was illegal, and Socrates, who happened to be president
of the Council on that day, refused to put the question to a vote. But the
people shouted that "it would be terrible if anyone should try to prevent
the people from doing what it wished to do," and the generals were actually
condemned and executed.

struggle very hard to retain his leadership, and though it is not certain whether Pericles did not, in order to retain his hold on the majority of the people, sometimes make political decisions which he would not have made otherwise and which he did not like to make.

After the death of Pericles, Cleon tried for some time to continue the policy of Pericles, especially in regard to the war and the relation to the other members of the Sea Confederacy who were now considered as little, if anything, more than "subjects" of Athens. But he continued this policy with much cruder and more violent methods. When Cleon also had died, there followed a period of complete political irresponsibility. For if a decision which had been taken turned out to have bad consequences, those who had voted for it could always claim that they had been misled or deceived by the orators who had spoken in favor of the measure, while the orators could claim that they had no responsibility because they had no authority. They had merely expressed their opinion, and nobody had been compelled to follow it. There can be no doubt that this government by irresponsible advisers and chance majorities contributed largely to the crushing defeat which Athens suffered at the end of the Peloponnesian War, although at the end of the first part of that war the advantages had been all on the Athenian side in spite of the terrible and unforeseeable losses that Athens had suffered through the plague of the years 430, 429, and 426.

In the fourth century, the absolute sovereignty of the people was somewhat restricted through the introduction of a more elaborate law code and the prescription of a very strict and complicated procedure for the repeal of old, and the creation of new, laws. At the same time, the *graphé paranomon* was now used ruthlessly against those who made proposals for decrees of the assembly which, if accepted, would have violated an established law. Nevertheless, the tendency of demagogues to win favor with the masses "by giving the people presents out of the people's own pockets" and to cater to the immediate desires of the people rather than to promote the long-range interests of the community was still very prevalent; and again the people had finally to pay for it by succumbing to a foreign power, this time to Macedonia.

In view of all this, one can hardly say that Aristotle is wrong when he says[92] that in a democracy like this the people is a monarch—a composite monarch to be sure, but still a monarch whose rule may be just as arbitrary as that of a tyrant—the demagogues playing the same role with the people as the flatterers and courtiers with the king or tyrant, since by their advice they mean above all to serve their own personal interests and not those of their master whom they advise. Against the evils of such a system, Aristotle advocates in the first place a rule of law, that is, of long-range law which cannot be changed by arbitrary decision of single-chance majorities.   Secondly, he wishes a democracy to be tempered by aristocratic or oligarchic elements. In this connection, however, it must again be pointed out that election by vote, instead of selection by lot, of representatives of the people (in the Council) and of public functionaries was, in ancient tradition, considered as something not purely democratic and that, likewise, any kind of checks and balances, the like of which form the very foundation of what in modern times is mostly called democracy — though not, of course, by the totalitarian tyrannies, which also call themselves democracies — is not democratic in the sense of the absolute sovereignty of the majority of the people as conceived in the last decades of the fifth century.   Apart from this Aristotle himself makes the very judicious observation that those institutions and measures might, in a truer sense, be called democratic which make a democracy stable and lasting, than those which are more democratic in the sense of an abstract ideal of democracy but which, by their very nature, will inevitably lead to the downfall of the democratic state itself.[93]

There are also in Aristotle's works some other observations on various forms of less "democratic" but more stable democracy which are obviously based, at least in part, on a study of Athenian democracy; for instance, the observation that democracy functions best in a preponderantly rural and agricultural community.

[92] *Politics* IV, 1292a 11ff.
[93] *Politics* VI, 1320a 2ff.

For, Aristotle says,[94] in such a community people will not have the time to meddle as a body in all political affairs. They will, by necessity, leave the conduct of ordinary political affairs to the elected magistrates and will assemble only for the purpose of elections, for the checking of the magistrates, and for major decisions. At the same time, in a mainly agricultural community, there will be but few people without property, a situation which also makes for stability in a state. This theory is certainly connected with the observation, made in the *Constitution of Athens*,[95] that the evils of Athenian democracy began with the influx of a large part of the rural population of Attica into the city, in consequence of the conversion of the Athenian Sea Confederacy into an empire. The observation in itself seems true enough, although, under somewhat different circumstances, the consequences of a change of this kind may not always be exactly the same.

That, on the other hand, Aristotle in his analysis of the democratic form of government was not exclusively dependent on Athenian history is demonstrated by the fact that he compares the "customary" leniency of the Athenian *demos* with the rougher and more cruel methods of other democracies, and, likewise, by the fact that he makes direct reference to the democratic regimes in Rhodes, Cymae, Heracleia, Megara, etc., in the *Politics*.

Aristotle's analysis of the general anthropological, psychological, economic, and political foundations of the state, the most magnificent part of his political theory, rests on a much broader basis than a study of Athenian history could have provided; only very faint traces of the influence of this particular study can be found in his general theory. In those chapters, however, especially of Books III, IV, V, and VI of the *Politics*, in which Aristotle deals with the problems of democracy — the advantages and disadvantages of different forms of democracy, the ways and means of making a democracy more stable, and the causes which may lead to its decay and destruction — the influence of Athenian history on his criticisms and suggestions

[94] *Politics* VI, 1318b 9ff.
[95] *Infra*, p. 94.

and, above all, also on his terminology is very strong, much stronger obviously than that of other historical studies which he has made. For a full understanding, therefore, of these sections of Aristotle's *Politics*, and, likewise, of those sections of Plato's works in which Plato deals with the problems of democracy, a careful study of Aristotle's *Constitution of Athens* is indispensable.

The Constitution of Athens

The Constitution of Athens

1. . . . . With Myron acting as accuser, a court, selected from the nobility and sworn in upon the sacrifices, passed a verdict to the effect that a sacrilege had been committed.[1] Thereupon, the bodies of the guilty were removed from the tombs, and their family was exiled forever. On account of these events, Epimenides of Crete purified the city.[2]

2. After that,[a] there was civil strife for a long time between
2 the nobility and the common people. For the whole political setup was oligarchical, and, in particular, the poor together with their wives and children were serfs of the rich. They were called Pelatae[b] and Hectemori ["sixth-parters"], for it was at this rent[c] that they cultivated the land of the wealthy. All the land was in the hands of a few, and if the serfs did not pay their rent, they and their children could be sold into slavery. All loans were contracted upon the person of the debtor, until the time of
3 Solon, who was the first to become a leader[d] of the people. The hardest and most hateful feature of the political situation as far as the many were concerned was their serfdom. But they also nursed grievances in all other respects, for they had, so to speak, no share in anything.

3. The ancient political order that existed before Draco was as follows:[3] The magistrates were selected from the noble and the wealthy. At first, they governed for life; later, for periods
2 of ten years. The most important and the earliest offices were those of the King, the Polemarch, and the Archon.[4] Of these,

a) This obviously refers to the Cylonian affair itself, not to the purification of Athens by Epimenides, which is usually dated in the time of Solon.

b) Usually explained to mean *clients*, but the exact meaning is doubtful.

c) That is, one sixth of the produce.

d) The Greek word is προστάτης. In later times leadership of the people became almost a permanent institution (cf. Chapter 28), but it was never an official position.

the office of the King was the earliest, for it had come down from
ancestral times.   Secondly, there was introduced the office of
the Polemarch, which was added because some of the kings
turned out unfit for war; this, by the way, is why Ion was sent
3 for in an emergency.   Last was the office of the Archon.   Most
authorities say that this office was introduced under Medon, but
some say under Acastus.   They offer as evidence the fact that
the nine archons swear to execute the oaths "as under Acastus,"
which seems to indicate that under his rule the descendants of
Codrus gave up the kingship in return for the prerogatives given
to the Archon.[5]   Whichever of the two accounts is true, the
chronological difference is not very great.   At any rate, that the
office of the Archon came last is indicated by the fact that the
Archon is not, like the King and the Polemarch, in charge of
any of the ancestral functions, but only of those that were added
later.   And this is the reason why the archonship became great
only in more recent times, having been increased in importance
by these added functions.[6]
4   The Thesmothetae were not elected until many years later,
when the elections to the magistracy already had become annual.
The Thesmothetae had as their duty to record the laws and to
keep them for cases of litigation.   This office, having been introduced at a comparatively late date, was the only one of the chief
magistracies which was never held for more than one year.
5   Chronologically, then, this order of precedence the magistracies had over one another.   Not all the nine Archons had their
official residence together.   The King occupied what is now called
the Bucolium, near the Prytaneum (as indicated by the fact that
even now the union and the marriage of the King's wife with the
god Dionysus[a] takes place in that building), while the Archon
resided in the Prytaneum and the Polemarch in the Epilyceum.
The latter building had originally been called Polemarcheum,
but, after Epilycus, during his polemarchy, had rebuilt it and
fitted it out, it was called Epilyceum.   The Thesmothetae lived
in the Thesmotheteum.   However, at the time of Solon, all the
Archons came together in the Thesmotheteum.   Then also, the

a) A religious ceremony forming part of the festival of the Greater Dionysia.

Archons passed the final judgment in lawsuits and did not, as now, hold only the preliminary hearings. Such was the estab-
6 lished order in regard to the magistracy. The Council of the Areopagus had the task of watching over the laws; in fact, it controlled the greater and most important part of the life of the community[7] as the only and final authority in regard to the punishment of public offenders and the imposition of fines. It must be observed that the selection of the Archons was based on considerations of birth and wealth, and that the Areopagus consisted of former Archons. This fact explains also why this[b] is the only office which has continued to be held for life down to the present day.

4. In outline, such was the first political order. Not much later,[8] in the archonship of Aristaechmus,[a] Draco enacted his
2 laws. His constitutional order[9] was the following: Full political rights had been given to those who provided themselves with full military equipment; and these elected the nine Archons and the Treasurers from persons who possessed an unencumbered property of not less than ten minae, the minor magistrates from those who owned full military equipment, and the Generals (*strategoi*) and the Commanders of the cavalry (*hipparchoi*) from those who declared an unencumbered property of not less than one hundred minae[b] and legitimate sons over ten years old. These officers [that is, the newly elected Generals and Hipparchs] were to be held to bail by the Prytanes,[10] as were the Generals and Hipparchs of the preceding year until the completion of their audit. The Prytanes were to accept as securities four citizens from the same class as that to which the Generals and
3 Hipparchs belonged.[11] The Council[c] was to consist of four hundred and one chosen by lot from those possessing full rights

b) That is, the membership in the Areopagus.

a) This Archon had not been known before the discovery of Aristotle's treatise. But the traditional date of Draco's legislation is 621 B.C.

b) Cf. Introduction, Chapter 2, p. 17.

c) Here, as elsewhere, Aristotle seems to take it for granted that there always existed an "Assembly of the People," and a "Council" different from the Council of the Areopagus.

of citizenship. This Council and the other magistrates[d] were chosen by lot from those citizens who were more than thirty years old. The same man could not become a magistrate twice until all other citizens had had a turn. Then the whole procedure of casting lots would begin again. If anyone of the Councilmen failed to attend when there was a session of the Council or of the Assembly of the People, he had to pay a fine of three drachmae if he was a Pentacosiomedimnus,[e] two drachmae if he was a

4 Knight, and one drachma if he was a Zeugites. The Council of the Areopagus was the guardian of the laws and also kept watch over the magistrates so as to take care that they ruled according to the laws. Anyone who had been wronged could file complaint with the Council of the Areopagus indicating the

5 law which had been violated by the wrong done to him. But loans were secured on the person of the debtor, and the land was in the hands of a few.

5. This being the political order and the many being serfs of

2 the few,[12] the common people rose against the upper class. When the civil discord had become violent and the two opposing parties had been set against each other for a long time, they chose, by mutual agreement, Solon as their mediator and Archon[a] and entrusted the state to him. This happened after he had composed the elegy[b] that begins:

I observe, and my heart is filled with grief when I look upon the oldest land of the Ionian world as it totters.[13]

In this poem he fights for both parties against both parties. He tries to distinguish the merits and demerits of the one and

d) That is, the "minor" magistracies, which in the preceding paragraph have been distinguished from the Archons and Treasurers, on the one hand, and from the generals and commanders of the cavalry, on the other.

e) For an explanation of these and the following terms see *infra* Chapter 7.

a) The traditional date of Solon's archonship is 594 B.C., but cf. Chapter 14 and Appendix, note 33.

b) At the time of Solon, the art of reading and writing was practiced for only very limited purposes; a political pamphlet, in order to be effective, had to be conceived in poetic form; in this way it could be easily memorized and transmitted.

of the other, and, after having done so, he exhorts both of them together to end their present dispute.

3 Solon was by birth and renown one of the most distinguished men of the country, but by wealth and occupation he belonged to the middle class.[14] This can be inferred from many facts and is also confirmed by Solon's own testimony in the following passage of a poem in which he exhorts the wealthy not to set their aims too high:

> You who are plunged into a surfeit of many goods restrain the strong desires in your breast, let your proud mind be set on moderate aims.
> For we shall not submit to you, and not everything will turn out according to your wishes.

And, in general, he attaches the blame for the conflict to the rich; and, accordingly, he says, in the beginning of the poem, that he was always afraid of "love for money and an overbearing mind," implying that these had been the cause of the conflict.

6. As soon as Solon had been entrusted with full powers to act, he liberated the people by prohibiting loans on the person of the debtor, both for the present and for the future. He made laws and enacted a cancellation of debts both private and public,[15] a measure which is commonly called *seisachtheia* [the shaking-off of burdens], since in this way they shook off their
2 burdens. In regard to this measure, some people try to discredit him. For it happened that when Solon was about to enact the *seisachtheia*, he informed some of his acquaintances[16] of his plans, and when he did so, according to the version of the adherents of the popular party, he was outmaneuvered by his friends; but, according to those who wish to slander him, he himself shared in the gain. For these people borrowed money and bought a great extent of land; and a short time afterwards, when the cancellation of debts was put through, they became very rich. It is said that this was the origin of those who later were con-
3 sidered to be of ancient wealth. However, the version of the friends of the people appears much more trustworthy. For it is not likely that in all other respects Solon should have been so

moderate and public-spirited that, when it would have been in his power to subdue all others and to set himself up as a tyrant, he preferred to incur the hostility of both parties and valued his honor and the common good of the state higher than his personal aggrandizement, and that yet he should have defiled himself by
4 such a petty and unworthy trick. Now, that he did have that opportunity [that is, of setting himself up as a tyrant] is proved by the desperate situation of the state at that time; he himself mentions the fact frequently in his poems, and it is universally admitted. Hence, one must regard the accusation as completely unfounded.

7. Solon set up a constitution and also made other laws.[17] After that, the Athenians ceased to make use of the laws of Draco with the exception of those relating to murder. The laws were inscribed on the Kyrbeis[a] and placed in the portico of the King, and all swore to observe them. The nine Archons, however, regularly affirmed by an oath at the Stone[b] that they would dedicate a golden statue if they ever should be found to have transgressed one of the laws; and they still swear in the same
2 fashion down to the present day. He made the laws unalterable for one hundred years and set up the political order in the following way:
3   He divided the population, according to property qualifications, into four classes as they had been divided before — namely, Pentacosiomedimni, Knights, Zeugitae, and Thetes.[c] He distributed the higher[18] offices, namely, those of the nine Archons, the Treasurers, the Poletae,[d] the Eleven,[e] and the Colacretae[f] so that

a) Wooden tablets set up on pillars revolving around an axis.

b) This stone is also mentioned and described in Chapter 55.

c) These terms are explained a little below in the present chapter.

d) Officials who farmed out public revenues, sold confiscated property, and drew up all public contracts. See also Chapter 47.

e) The superintendents of the State Prison.

f) A very ancient office connected with the administration of finances. The specific duties assigned to the Colacretae seem to have changed again and again in the course of time. They are still mentioned in the last decade of the fifth century. But there is no evidence of the existence of the office after the restoration of democracy in 403 B.C.

they were to be held by men taken from the Pentacosiomedimni, the Knights, and the Zeugitae, and assigned the offices to them in proportion to their property qualifications.[19] To those who belonged to the census of the Thetes, he gave only a share in the 4 Assembly of the People and in the law courts. A person belonged to the census of the Pentacosiomedimni if he obtained from his own property a return of five hundred measures of dry and liquid produce, both of them reckoned together. If he had an income of three hundred measures, or, as others say, if he was able to keep horses, he was rated a Knight; and as confirmation of the latter explanation they adduce the name of the class ["Knights"] as being derived from the fact mentioned, and some ancient votive offerings. For on the Acropolis there is a statue of Diphilus[20] with the following inscription:

Anthemion, the son of Diphilus, has dedicated this statue to the Gods, when from the status of a Thes he had been raised to the status of a Knight.

And a horse stands beside him in testimony of the fact that the status of a Knight means this [that is, the ability to keep a horse].[21]

In spite of this, it is more probable that this class also, like that of the Pentacosiomedimni, was distinguished by measures. To the census of the Zeugitae[g] belonged those who had an income of two hundred measures (liquid and dry). The rest belonged to the census of the Thetes and had no share in the magistracies. Consequently, even today when the superintending officer asks a man who is about to draw the lot for an office to what census class he belongs, nobody would ever say that he is a Thes.

8. Solon established the rule that the magistrates were to be appointed by lot out of candidates previously selected by each of the four Tribes.[22] In regard to the nine Archons, each Tribe made a preliminary choice of ten, and among these they cast the lot. Hence the custom still survives with the Tribes that each of them first selects ten by lot and then they choose, again

g) The word "Zeugites" is derived from *zeugos*, which means a yoke, in this case probably a team of oxen.

by lot, from these men.[23] A confirmation of the fact that the magistrates were to be selected by lot from the respective property classes mentioned is the law concerning the Treasurers, which is still in use down to the present day. This law orders that the Treasurers are to be chosen by lot from among the Penta-cosiomedimni.[24]

2 Such, then, was Solon's legislation in regard to the nine Archons. For, in the ancient times, the Council of the Areopagus called upon suitable persons and appointed, according to its own independent judgment, for one year to the various offices whom-

3 ever it found fit for the respective tasks. There were four Tribes, as before, and four Tribe-kings. Each Tribe consisted of three *trittyes*, and there were twelve *naucrariai* to each Tribe. The Naucraries were presided over by the Naucrari who were appointed to supervise the receipts and expenditures. Hence the expressions, "the Naucrari shall levy . . . " and "the Naucrari shall spend from the Naucraric fund," are frequently found in those Solonian

4 laws which are no longer in force. Solon also established a Council of Four Hundred, one hundred from each Tribe. Yet he still made it the task of the Areopagus to watch over the laws, just as in the preceding period it had been the guardian of the political order; and this Council [that is, the Areopagus] still supervised the greater and more important part of public life and, in particular, chastised offenders, with full power to impose punishment and fines. It deposited the money exacted through fines in the Acropolis without having to indicate the reasons for the imposition of the fine. It also tried those who had conspired to deprive the people of their political rights, Solon having

5 enacted a law of impeachment for such cases. Finally, seeing that violent political dissensions frequently arose in the city but that some citizens, out of a tendency to take things easy, were content to accept whatever the outcome of the political struggle might appear to be, Solon made a special law for persons of this kind, enacting that whoever, in a time of political strife, did not take an active part on either side should be deprived of his civic rights and have no share in the state.

9. This, then, was the order established by Solon in regard to the public offices. The three most democratic features of his constitution appear to be the following: first, and most important, the law that nobody could contract a loan secured on his person; secondly, the rule that anyone who wished to do so could claim redress on behalf of a person who had been wronged; thirdly (and, according to the prevailing opinion, this more than anything else has increased the political power of the common people), the right of appeal to a jury court. For when the people have a right to vote in the courts, they become the masters of
2 the state. Moreover, since the laws are not written down in clear and simple terms, but are like the one about inheritances and heiresses, disputes over interpretation will inevitably arise, and the court has the decision in all affairs, both public and private. Some people believe that Solon deliberately made the laws obscure so that the people would be masters of the decision. But this is not likely. The reason is rather that he was not able to formulate the best principle in general terms. It is not fair to interpret his intentions on the basis of what is happening in the present;[a] it should be done on the basis of the general character of his constitution.

10. As far as his legislation is concerned, these appear to be its democratic features; but, even before his legislation, he had effected the abolition of debts and afterwards[25] the augmentation
2 of the measures, the weights, and the coin. For it was under his administration that the measures became larger than those of Pheidon, and the mina, which formerly had had a weight of seventy drachmae, was increased to a full hundred.[26] The original type of coin was that of the double drachma. He also introduced trade weights corresponding to the coinage at the rate of sixty-three minae to the weight of a talent, and proportional parts of the three additional minae were apportioned to the stater and the other units of weight.[27]

a) Namely, when the unclear wording of the laws on inheritances and heiresses caused innumerable lawsuits.

11. After Solon had established the political order described above, many people came to him and plagued him with all sorts of criticisms and questions in regard to his laws. So, since he did not wish to change them nor to become an object of invidious attacks if he stayed, he went on a journey to Egypt with the object of doing some business and of seeing the country at the same time; and, at his departure, he announced that he would not be back for ten years. For, he said, he did not consider it right for him to interpret the laws, as he would inevitably be called upon to do if he stayed, but that, in his opinion, every

2 citizen should rather be careful to obey them to the letter. Moreover, it happened that many of the nobles had become his enemies because of the cancellation of debts, and that both parties were alienated from him because the settlement had turned out contrary to their expectations. For the common people had believed that he would bring about a complete redistribution of property, while the nobles had hoped he would restore the old order or at least make only insignificant changes. Solon, however, set himself against both parties, and while he would have been able to rule as a tyrant if he had been willing to conspire with whichever party he wished, he preferred to antagonize both factions while saving the country and giving it the laws that were best for it, under the circumstances.

12. That this was Solon's attitude is generally acknowledged, and it is also confirmed by the following passages from his own poems:

To the common people I have given such honor and privilege as is sufficient for them, granting them neither less nor more than their due.

For those possessed of power and outstanding through wealth I had equal regard, taking care that they should suffer no injury.

Firmly I stood, holding out my strong shield over both of them, and I did not allow either party to triumph over the other in violation of justice.

2 In another passage he makes clear in what way one should deal with the common people:

The people will follow the leaders best if it is neither given too much license nor restrained too much.

For satiety breeds insolence when too great prosperity comes to men lacking right judgment.

3 Again, in another place, he speaks of those who wished to redistribute the land:

Those who gathered, setting their minds on plunder, nourished excessive hopes.

Everyone of them expected to win great riches, and believed that I was wheedling with smooth words but would finally come out with a revolutionary plan.

Idle were their expectations. Now they are irate against me and they look at me askance as if I were their enemy.

This they should not do. For, with the help of the Gods, I have accomplished what I promised.

Other things I did not vainly undertake.

I find no pleasure in achieving anything by the forceful methods of a tyrannical regime, nor would it please me to see the noble and the vile[28] have an equal share of the rich soil of our fatherland.

4 Again, about the cancellation of debts and about those who formerly had been slaves but then were freed in consequence of the *seisachteia*, he says:

Which of the aims because of which I gathered the people did I abandon before I had accomplished it?

My best witness before the tribunal of posterity will be the great mother of the Olympian Gods, black Earth.

For I removed the markstones of bondage[a] which had been fastened upon her everywhere; and she who had then been a slave is now free.

I brought home to Athens, to their fatherland, many Athenians who, lawfully or unlawfully, had been sold abroad, and others who, having fled their country under dire constraint of debts, no longer spoke the Attic tongue — so wide had been their wanderings.

I also restored to freedom those who here at home had been subjected to shameful servitude, and trembled before their masters.

a) These are the stones (ὅροι) set up on the lands of the indebted farmers to indicate that the land, which could not be sold outright, was mortgaged, together with its owners, to the creditor.

These things I accomplished by the power which I wielded,
  bringing together force and justice in true harmony, and I
  carried out my promise.
I enacted laws for the noble and the vile alike, setting up a
  straight rule of justice for everybody.
Yet, if another man, of evil intent and filled with greed, had held
  the goad as I did, he would not have held the people back.
For if I had been willing to do what pleased the enemies of the
  people at that time, or again what *their* opponents planned for
  them,[b] this city would have been deprived of many of her sons.
For this reason I had to set up a strong defense on all sides, turning around like a wolf at bay in the midst of packs of hounds.

5 And again, reproaching both parties for the attacks which they
  afterwards directed against him, he says:

If I must express publicly my just rebuke, I have to say that the
  common people would never have seen in their dreams what
  they now enjoy. . . .
And those who are privileged and powerful might well praise
  me and call me their friend;[29]

for, he says, if someone else had obtained such an exalted office,

He would not have held the people back and would not have
  rested until, by shaking up the state, he would have got the
  butter from the milk for himself.
But I set myself up as a barrier between the battleline of the
  opposing parties.

13. These, then, were the reasons for which he went abroad.
After Solon's departure, the state was still torn by internal dissensions. Yet, for four years, they kept the political peace. But
in the fifth year after Solon's archonship, they were unable to
appoint the Archon because of the party strife; and another four
years later they again skipped the appointment of the Archon
2 for the same reason. Then, still within the same period,[30]
Damasias was elected Archon, and he ruled for two years and
two months, until he was expelled from his office by force. Then,

b) What Solon means is that if, instead of taking his position between the
two parties, he had sided either with the enemies of the common people or with
their opponents, that is, with the revolutionary leaders of the common people
itself, there would have been civil war and bloodshed in either case.

because of their dissensions, they decided to elect ten Archons,
five from the nobility of birth, three from the farmers, and two
from the craftsmen.[31] From this, incidentally, it is clear that
the Archon had the greatest power. For the dissensions arose

3 always in regard to this office. In general, however, they continued in a condition of internal disorder. Some people found
reason for discontent in the cancellation of debts; for they had
been reduced to poverty by this measure. Others were dis-
satisfied with the political order because it had undergone such
radical changes. Still others participated in the party strife
because of their personal rivalries with one another.

4 There were three parties. First, there was the party of the
Shore, which was led by Megacles, the son of Alcmeon. This
party seemed to follow a middle road. The second party was
that of the Plain; their aim was oligarchy, and Lycurgus was
the leader. The third party was that of the Highlanders, which
was headed by Pisistratus, who was considered a champion of

5 the common people. Affiliated with this party were also those
who had lost money owed them, for they had now become poor;
and those who were not of pure descent, for they were appre-
hensive [concerning their rights of citizenship].[32] This latter
observation is confirmed by the fact that, after the overthrow of
the tyrants, the Athenians revised the citizen roll on the ground
that many had assumed citizen rights without being entitled to
it. The different parties derived their names from the parts of
the country in which they had their lands.

14. Pisistratus, who was considered as the outstanding advocate
of the common people and who had distinguished himself in the
war against Megara, inflicted a wound on himself, and then,
under the pretense that he had suffered this injury from the
hands of his political opponents, he persuaded the people to
grant him a bodyguard, on a motion presented by Aristion.
With the help of these so-called "club bearers," he rose up
against the people and occupied the Acropolis, under the Archon
ship of Comeas,[a] in the thirty-second year[33] after Solon's legisla-

a) 561/60 B.C.

2 tion. It is said that, when Pisistratus asked for the bodyguard, Solon opposed the demand and said that he [that is, Solon] was wiser than some and braver than others. For, he said, he was wiser than those who were not aware that Pisistratus was aiming at tyranny, and braver than those who were aware of it but kept silent. But when he did not convince them by what he said, he brought his armor out and placed it in front of his door saying that he had come to the aid of his fatherland as far as was in his power (for he was already a very old man), and that he called on all others to do likewise.

3 This time, then, Solon had no success with his exhortations. And Pisistratus, having seized the government, administered the state in a constitutional rather than in a tyrannical fashion. But his rule had not yet taken root; and the parties of Megacles and Lycurgus made common cause and drove him into exile in the sixth year after his first accession to power in the archonship of

4 Hegesias. In the twelfth year after this,[34] however, Megacles, being hard-pressed in the party struggle, opened negotiations with Pisistratus and, having reached an understanding that he [Pisistratus] would marry his daughter, brought him back by a rather primitive device. He first spread the rumor that the goddess Athena was bringing back Pisistratus. Then, having picked out a tall and beautiful woman by the name of Phya (according to Herodotus she was from the Attic deme of Paeania; according to others she was a Thracian flower-girl from the deme Collytus), he dressed her up so that she looked like the goddess and brought her into the city together with Pisistratus. And so, Pisistratus drove into the city on a chariot, the woman standing at his side, and the citizens fell down in worship and received him with awe![b]

15. His first return to power occurred in the way described. But when, in the seventh year after his return from exile, he was exiled again — for he did not hold his rule for a long time, and slipped out of the country when he became afraid of a combination of both parties because he had refused to consummate

b) Cf. Herodotus I, 60.

2 the marriage with the daughter of Megacles — he first participated in the establishment of a colony at a place by the name of
Rhaecelus, near the Gulf of Thermae. From there he went to
the region around Mount Pangaeus. There he raised money
with which he hired mercenaries and went again[35] to Eretria
in the eleventh year. It was then that he made an attempt for
the first time to recover his rulership by force, an undertaking
in which he was supported by many allies, especially the Thebans
and Lygdamis of Naxos and, further, the Knights of Eretria, who
held all the political power in that city.

3 When he had been victorious in the battle of Pallene and
had captured the city of Athens and confiscated the weapons of
the people, he had, at last, the tyranny firmly in his hands. He
4 also took Naxos and established Lygdamis as ruler. The manner
in which he disarmed the people was this: He held a military
review in full armor at the Theseum and began to address the
assembled crowd. Then, after he had spoken for a short time,
when the people said they could not hear him, he told them to
come forward to the gateway of the Acropolis so that his voice
would carry better. While he continued to talk and talk, some
men appointed for the purpose collected the arms and locked
them up in the buildings adjoining the Theseum. Then they
came to Pisistratus and informed him that it had been done.
Upon hearing this, Pisistratus finished the rest of his speech and
then told the crowd what had happened to their arms, adding
that they should not be surprised or distressed, but should go
home and take care of their private affairs, since in the future
he would attend to all the business of the state.

16. In this way the tyranny of Pisistratus was first established,
2 and these were the vicissitudes which it underwent later. As
said before, Pisistratus administered the state in a moderate
fashion, and his rule was more like a constitutional government
than like a tyranny. For he was benevolent and kind, and readily
forgave those who had committed an offense; he even advanced
money to the poor to further their work so that they could make
3 a living by farming. In doing this he had a twofold purpose:

first, that they might not stay in the city but live scattered all over the country; secondly, that they might be moderately well off but fully occupied with their own affairs so that they would have neither a strong desire nor the leisure to concern themselves

4 with public affairs.   Another incidental consequence was that his income was increased by the thorough cultivation of the land. For he exacted a tax of ten percent on the produce.

5   For the same general purpose, he also set up judges in the demes[a] and frequently made the tour of the country himself in order to inspect everything and to settle private disputes, so that the people would not have to come to the city and meanwhile

6 neglect their farmwork.   It is said that, during one of these inspection tours of Pisistratus, there occurred the famous story of the farmer from the Hymettus Mountain who cultivated the piece of land which was later called "the Taxfree Farm." Pisistratus saw a man who was working hard to dig a piece of land which was, so to speak, nothing but stones.   He became curious and ordered his attendant to ask the man how much he got out of the land.   The man answered: "Just so many aches and pains; and of these aches and pains Pisistratus ought to take his ten percent."   He gave this answer without knowing that he spoke to Pisistratus.   Pisistratus, however, liked his frankness and his

7 industriousness and freed him from all taxes.   And so, in general, Pisistratus did not impose any heavy burdens on the people as long as he ruled, but kept everything in a peaceful state both externally and internally, so that it became a common saying that the tyranny of Pisistratus had been the Golden Age.   For later, when his sons succeeded in the rulership, the tyranny

8 became much more severe. But most important of all the qualities mentioned was his popular and kindly attitude.   For in every respect it was his principle to regulate everything in accordance with the laws without claiming a special privilege for himself. Once, when he was summoned to appear before the Areopagus on a charge of homicide, he even appeared in person to defend himself.   But the man who brought the charge against him

9 became afraid and stayed away.   For these reasons he remained

a) That is, the country districts.

in power for a long time; and even when he was expelled, he reconquered the power easily. For the majority both of the nobles and of the common people were in his favor. The former he won over through his friendly intercourse with them, the latter through the help which he gave them in their private
10 affairs; and he always proved fair to both of them. On the other hand, as to the Athenians themselves, it should be observed that in that period their laws concerning tyranny were also very mild. This is especially true of the law regarding specifically the establishment of a tyranny. For it reads as follows: "This is the law and the ancestral rule of the Athenians. Whoever conspires to set up a tyranny, or helps to set up a tyranny, shall lose his citizenship, and so shall his whole family."

17. So Pisistratus grew old in the possession of sovereignty and died from an illness in the archonship of Philoneus, having lived for thirty-three years after the time when he had first set himself up as a tyrant. Of this time he spent nineteen in the
2 possession of power, the rest in exile.[36] On the basis of these facts it is quite clear that those talk nonsense who say that Pisistratus was loved by Solon and that he was general in the war against Megara for the possession of Salamis. For this is quite impossible, considering their respective ages, as one can easily see from a calculation of the years during which each lived and of the date on which each died.
3   After the death of Pisistratus, his sons held on to his rule and continued to conduct the public affairs in the same fashion. There were two sons from his legitimate wife, Hippias and Hipparchus, and two from his Argive consort,[37] Iophon and
4 Hegesistratus, the latter with the surname Thettalus. For Pisistratus took a wife from Argos, by the name of Timonassa, the daughter of an Argive, Gorgilus. This Timonassa had previously been the wife of Archinus of Ampracia, a man belonging to the Cypselid family. This marriage promoted Pisistratus' friendly relations with the Argives, so that one thousand Argives fought on his side in the battle of Pallene, having joined him under the leadership of Hegesistratus. According to some

authorities, Pisistratus married the woman from Argos during his first exile; according to others, while he was in the possession of power.

18. Hipparchus and Hippias found themselves [after the death of Pisistratus] in control of the state through their rank and their age. Hippias, however, being the elder of the two, a born statesman and wise and self-controlled, was the real ruler. Hipparchus, on the other hand, preferred the lighter side of life,[a] was always engaged in love affairs, and liked music and poetry. (It was he who brought Anacreon, Simonides, and 2 other poets to Athens.) Thettalus was much younger, and violent and overbearing in his conduct; and this was the origin of all the evils which befell them.[38] He fell in love with Harmodius, and when he was unable to win his friendship, he could not control his anger. He gave vent to his bitterness in many ways; and finally, when Harmodius' sister was going to be a basket bearer at the festival of the Panathenaea, he prevented her from participation, at the same time insulting Harmodius as effeminate. This provoked Harmodius and Aristogeiton to such wrath that they perpetrated their famous deed, with the help of many 3 accomplices. While they were lying in wait for Hippias on the Acropolis at the Panathenaean festival (Hippias receiving the procession at its end, and Hipparchus supervising its start), they saw one of those who were in the conspiracy approach Hippias in a friendly fashion. Since they believed that he was betraying the secret and wished to accomplish at least something before they would be arrested, they went down into the city and killed Hipparchus while he was organizing the procession near the Leocoreum. They did this without waiting for their fellows, and so they spoiled the whole plot.

4 Harmodius was killed on the spot by the bodyguards. Aristogeiton was caught later and was tortured for a long time. Under torture he accused a great many who belonged to the aristocracy

a) The Greek words παιδιώδης ἦν are almost an equivalent of "he was a playboy."

of birth and were supporters of the tyrants. At first the investi-
gators had been unable to find any trace of the conspiracy; for
the story that Hippias ordered the men who marched in the
procession to give up their arms and then searched out those who
carried daggers is obviously untrue, since at that time they did
not carry weapons in the processions, this being a custom intro-
5 duced in later times by a popular decree.[39] Now the supporters
of the popular party say Aristogeiton deliberately denounced
the friends of the tyrants so that they [that is, the tyrants] would
commit an impious act and at the same time weaken themselves
by killing their innocent supporters; whereas some say Aristogeiton
did not invent a fictitious story but betrayed his actual accom-
6 plices. Finally, in any case, when he was unable to find relief
through death, in spite of all his efforts, he declared that he
would reveal the names of many more persons; and, having
persuaded Hippias to give him his right hand as a pledge, he
reviled him for having given his hand to the murderer of his
brother. In this way he stirred Hippias to such a fit of rage
that, unable to control himself, he drew his dagger and killed
Aristogeiton.

19. Following this, as a natural consequence, the tyranny
became much harsher. In taking revenge for his brother by
putting many to death and driving others into exile, Hippias
2 became distrusted and hated by all. About three years after
the death of Hipparchus, when the situation in the city became
bad for him, he began to fortify the Munichia harbor with the
intention of taking up residence there. But while this work was
still going on, he was expelled by Cleomenes, the king of the
Lacedaemonians, because the Laconians had received one oracle
after the other ordering them to overthrow the tyranny. The
3 reason for this had been the following: The exiles, whose leadership the Alcmeonidae had assumed, were unable to bring about
their return by their own strength and failed in all their attempts.
In one of these unsuccessful attempts, they fortified a place called
Lipsydrium, out in the country above Mount Parnes. They

were joined there by some people from the city. But the tyrants conquered the place; and that is why later, after the fiasco, people were wont to sing, as one of their drinking songs:

> Ah, Lipsydrium, betrayer of friends,
> What men did you destroy!
> Brave men in battle and noble of birth
> Who proved at that time from what stock they were bred.

4 Then, failing in all other attempts, the Alcmeonidae contracted to rebuild the temple of Delphi,[a] and in this way they acquired ample funds to win the support of the Laconians. At the same time, the Pythia, whenever the Lacedaemonians consulted the oracle, urged them to liberate Athens until she finally brought the Spartans around to it, although the Pisistratidae were connected with them by ties of hospitality.[40] The friendship between the Pisistratidae and the Argives had no less a share in causing
5 the sudden decision of the Laconians.[b] Accordingly, they first sent out Anchimolus by sea at the head of an army. But he was defeated and killed, in consequence of the help given to the enemy by the Thessalian Cineas who appeared on the scene with a thousand cavalry. The Spartans were stirred to great anger by this event and sent their king, Cleomenes, with a bigger army by land, who defeated the Thessalian cavalry when they tried to block his way into Attica, shut up Hippias within the so-called Pelargic wall, and began to besiege him with the help of the Athenians.
6 While he was keeping the place under siege, it happened that the sons of the Pisistratidae were captured while they tried to make their way out of the city. When these children had been captured, they [that is, the Pisistratidae] concluded an agreement on condition that their children would not be harmed and that they themselves would have five days to remove their private properties from the country. Then they surrendered the Acropolis to the Athenians under the archonship of Harpactides,[c] having

a) The temple of Delphi had burned down (cf. Herodotus II, 180).
b) The Spartans and the Argives were traditional enemies.
c) 511/10 B.C.

held the tyranny for about seventeen years after the death of their father, or for forty-nine years altogether if one adds the time of rule of their father.[41]

20. After the overthrow of the tyranny, Isagoras the son of Tisander, a former supporter of the tyrants,[42] and Cleisthenes from the family of the Alcmeonidae pitted their respective political strengths and influences against each other. When Cleisthenes was defeated in the political clubs,[43] he won the support of the common people by promising to give the state into their hands.
2 So Isagoras, seeing his power waning, called upon Cleomenes, with whom he was connected by ties of hospitality, to come up again and persuaded him "to drive out the curse," for the Alcmeonidae were believed to be among those who were under
3 a curse.[44] When, as a result of this, Cleisthenes secretly fled the country, Cleomenes arrived with a small force and expelled as accursed seven hundred Athenian families.[a] This done, he tried to dissolve the Council[45] and to make Isagoras, with three hundred of his supporters, master of the city. But when the Council put up a resistance and the crowd began to gather, Cleomenes and Isagoras with their troups and adherents fled to the Acropolis. There the common people of Athens besieged them for two days. On the third day, however, they permitted Cleomenes and his men to withdraw under a truce, and called
4 back Cleisthenes and the other exiles. After the political power had come into the hands of the people in this way, Cleisthenes became their chief and "the leader of the people."[b] For it could hardly be denied that it was the Alcmeonidae who played the most important part in the overthrow of the tyrants, since they almost incessantly made political trouble for them. Even before the Alcmeonidae, however, Cedon had made an attack on the tyrants, on account of which he, too, was celebrated in a drinking song:

a) The word for "family" used by Aristotle in this passage means the family in the narrower sense, namely, the family belonging to one household, and not the family in the larger sense, in which this word designates all those who consider themselves as the descendants of the same noble ancestor.

b) See *supra*, p. 69, note d.

> Pour wine also in honor of Cedon, boy, and let him not be
> forgotten
> If to drink a toast to the good and the brave is the right thing
> to do.

21. For these reasons the common people trusted Cleisthenes.
So then, being the leader of the people, in the fourth year after
the overthrow of the tyranny, in the year of the archonship of
2 Isagoras,[46] he distributed the whole population into ten tribes
instead of the previous four, with the aim of mixing up the
population so that a greater number would share in the administration of the state [that is, would be admitted to citizenship].[47]
This is the origin of the proverbial saying: No tribe-investiga-
tion! It was directed against those who wanted to check on
3 family backgrounds.[48]   Then he established a Council of Five
Hundred instead of the existing one of Four Hundred, taking
fifty from each tribe, whereas previously there had been one
hundred [from each of the previous four tribes].   The reason he
did not distribute them into twelve tribes was that he wished to
avoid a division according to the already existing Trittyes.   For
the four tribes consisted of twelve Trittyes; hence, a completely
new mixture of the population could not have been obtained
4 from such a division.[49]   At the same time, he divided the whole
country into thirty parts (composed of demes[50]), ten from the
city quarters, ten from the shore district, and ten from the
interior.   These parts he called Trittyes and assigned three of them
by lot to each tribe, in such a way that each tribe would have
one portion from all the main regions of the country.   He made
those who lived in each of the demes fellow-demesmen, so that
they would not, by addressing one another by their fathers'
names, expose the newly enrolled citizens, but would call them
by the names of their demes.[51]   This is the reason the Athenians
speak of one another by the names of their demes.
5   He also established Demarchs with the same functions as those
of the former Naucrari,[52] replacing the naucraries by the demes.
He named some of the demes after the localities, others after
their founders.   For not all of them were still connected with
6 their localities.[53]   But he let everybody retain his family connec-

tions,[a] his membership in a brotherhood, and his family rites according to ancestral custom. He assigned to the tribes as eponymous heroes[b] ten "Archegetae,"[54] who had been selected by the Delphic Oracle from a previously chosen group of one hundred.

22. After these reforms the political structure became much more democratic than it had been under Solon. This development was in part also due to the facts that the Solonian laws had fallen into disuse under the tyranny until they were eventually obliterated and that Cleisthenes enacted new ones with the aim of winning the people's favor. Among these was the law about ostracism.

2   In the fifth year after the introduction of this order, under the archonship of Hermocreon,[55] they imposed for the first time on the Council of Five Hundred the oath which they still swear at the present time. Furthermore, they began to elect the generals by tribes, one from each tribe. The [Archon] Polemarch, however, was the supreme commander of the whole army.[56]

3 When, in the twelfth year after these innovations, in the archonship of Phaenippus, they had won the victory at Marathon, and when two more years had passed after that battle, and the common people gained greater self-confidence, they employed for the first time the law concerning ostracism. This law had been enacted because of their suspicion against those in power, for Pisistratus had established himself as a tyrant when he was both

4 a popular leader and a general. The first to be ostracized was one of the relatives of Pisistratus, Hipparchus, the son of Charmus, of the deme of Collytus; and it had been chiefly on this man's account that Cleisthenes had introduced the law, since he wanted to drive him out of the country. For the Athenians, with the customary leniency of the democracy, had permitted the supporters of the tyrants to remain in the city,[57] as far as they had not personally taken part in their wrongs at the time of the civil disorders. The acknowledged head and leader of these men was

a) Here the family in the larger sense is meant; cf. *supra*, p. 89, note a.
b) That is, the heroes from whose names the names of the tribes are derived.

5 Hipparchus. In the year immediately following, in the archon-ship of Telesinus,[a] they selected, for the first time since the tyranny, the nine Archons by lot through the tribes, from among five hundred candidates previously elected by the demesmen.[58] Previously, the archons had all been elected by vote.[b] In the same year Megacles, the son of Hippocrates, from the deme

6 Alopece, was ostracized. In this way they continued for three years to ostracize the supporters of the tyrants, who had been the reason for enacting the law. But in the fourth year they began to remove others also — whoever appeared to be too influential. The first of those to be ostracized, though he had nothing to do with the tyrants, was Xanthippus, the son of Ariphron.

7   In the third year after these events, in the archonship of Nicodemus,[c] when the mines in Maroneia came to light[59] and the state had a surplus of one hundred talents from their exploita-tion, some men proposed to distribute the money among the people, but Themistocles prevented this. He did not say for what purpose he wished the money to be used, but proposed that they should lend one talent to each of the one hundred most wealthy citizens of Athens, and then, if the way in which the money had been employed met with the approval of the people, the expenditure should be charged to the state; if not, they should get the money back from those to whom it had been lent. When he was granted the money on these terms, he had one hundred triremes built, each of the hundred citizens building one of them. With these triremes they fought at Salamis against the barbarians.

   At this time Aristeides, the son of Lysimachus, was ostracized.

8 But three years afterwards, in the archonship of Hypsechides,[d] because of the approach of Xerxes' army, they called back all

a) 487/6 B.C.

b) This statement must be restricted to the period after the overthrow of the tyranny down to 487–6; otherwise, Aristotle would be contradicting here his own words about the Solonian constitution in Chapter 8, 1 (see Chapter 8, and Appendix, note 22).

c) 483/2 B.C.

d) 481/0 B.C,

the men who had been ostracized. For the future it was made a rule that those who had been ostracized must <not>[60] take their residence this side of Geraestus[e] and Scyllaeum.[f] Otherwise, they were to lose their citizenship forever.

23. By this time, then, the state had made great progress, having become gradually consolidated with the advance of democracy. After the Persian wars the Council of the Areopagus again acquired strength and was again in control of the public life.[61] They acquired this leadership, not by any formal decree, but in consequence of the fact that it had been responsible for the battle of Salamis. For when the generals did not know how to deal with the emergency and made a public proclamation saying that everybody should care for his own safety, the Council provided sufficient money to distribute eight drachmae to each man and so prevailed upon them to man the ships. For this

2 reason the people held it in high repute, and during this period the public order in Athens was in an excellent state.[62] For in this period the Athenians were not only well trained for war, but also had a good reputation throughout Greece and obtained the leadership at sea[63] against the will of the Lacedaemonians.

3 At this time Aristeides, the son of Lysimachus, and Themistocles, the son of Neocles, were the leaders of the people.[64] The latter had the greatest renown for military skill, while the former was famous as a statesman and as the most upright man of his time. For this reason they used the one as a general, the other

4 as a counselor. Though they were political rivals, they collaborated in the reconstruction of the walls of the city. But it was Aristeides who instigated the defection of the Ionians from the alliance with Sparta, having availed himself of the opportunity offered by the fact that the Laconians had fallen into bad repute

5 through Pausanias.[65] For this reason it was also Aristeides who first assessed the contributions to be paid by the allied cities in the third year after the battle of Salamis, in the archonship of Timosthenes.[a] He also administered to the Ionians the oath

e) The southeasternmost point of the island of Euboea.

f) The easternmost point of the Argolis.

a) 478/77 B.C.

by which they swore to have the same enemies and the same friends as the Athenians. It was in confirmation of this oath that they cast the heavy pieces of iron into the sea.[b]

24. After this, when the Athenian state was growing in self-confidence and in the accumulation of much wealth, he [that is, Aristeides] advised the Athenians to seize the leadership[66] and to give up their residence in the countryside to come to live in the city.[67] For they would all have their livelihood there, some by participating in military expeditions, some by doing garrison service, and still others by participating in public affairs; and 2 in this way they would keep hold of the "leadership." They followed this advice and placed themselves in control of the empire;[68] and from then on they got into the habit of treating their allies, with the exception of Chios, Lesbos, and Samos, as if they were their masters. These three they used as guards of the Athenian empire and, therefore, left their constitutions untouched and allowed them to rule over whatever subjects they happened to have.

3   They also made it possible for the masses to live comfortably, as Aristeides had proposed. For out of the income derived from the contributions made by the allies[69] and from internal levies more than two thousand persons were maintained. For there were six thousand judges,[70] one thousand six hundred bowmen, one thousand two hundred cavalry men, five hundred Councilmen, five hundred guards of the dockyards plus fifty guards on the Acropolis, about seven hundred state officials at home and about seven hundred abroad.[71] In addition, when later they went to war, there were two thousand five hundred heavy-armed soldiers, twenty guard-ships,[a] and other ships carrying the guardians, that is, two thousand men chosen by lot.[72] Finally, there were the Prytaneum,[b] the orphans, and the jail-keepers. All these persons received their livelihood from the state.

b) Cf. Herodotus I, 165.

a) That is, a number of about four thousand men, since there were normally a crew of two hundred to one trireme.

b) This means, in fact, the citizens who had done special service to the

25. This, then, was the way in which the people obtained their livelihoods.   For seventeen years following the Persian Wars, the political order remained essentially the same under the supervision of the Areopagus, although it was slowly degenerating.   But as the common people grew in strength, Ephialtes, the son of Sophonides, who had a reputation for incorruptibility and loyalty to the constitution, became leader of the people and

2 made an attack upon that Council [that is, the Areopagus]. First he eliminated many of its members by bringing suits against them on the ground of administrative misconduct.   Then, in the archonship of Conon,[a] he deprived the Council of all those prerogatives which it recently had acquired[73] and which had made it the guardian of the state, and gave some of them to the

3 Council of Five Hundred, some to the [Assembly of the] people, and some to the law courts.   He did this with the assistance of Themistocles, who was himself a member of the Areopagus and was about to be tried for treasonable collaboration with Persia. For this reason Themistocles wished the Areopagus to be broken up, and therefore he told Ephialtes that the Council [that is, the Areopagus] was about to have him arrested, while at the same time he told the members of the Areopagus that he was going to reveal to them certain persons who were conspiring to overthrow the constitution.   Then he led the deputies of the Areopagus to a place where Ephialtes could be found, as if he were going to reveal to them the conspirators who had assembled there, and

4 talked to them with a great show of seriousness.   When Ephialtes saw this, he was stricken with fear and took refuge at an altar, wearing only his undergarment.[b]   Of course, everybody was surprised at these happenings; and at the next meeting of the Council of Five Hundred, and later, before the Assembly of the People, Ephialtes and Themistocles denounced the Areopagitae again and again until they succeeded in depriving the Areopagus

state and who were honored by being entertained at public expense at the Prytaneum, that is, the City Hall.

a) 462/61 B.C.

b) That is, the appropriate attire of a suppliant.

of its power. ... ^cand not much later Ephialtes also was done away with, being assassinated by Aristodicus of Tanagra.[74]

26. In this way, then, the superintendence of the life of the community was taken away from the Council of the Areopagus. Following these events, the public order was further weakened by the efforts of popular leaders to stir up the common people. For it so happened that at this time the better people[75] had no real chief, since their leader Cimon, the son of Miltiades, was rather young[76] and had only recently begun to take an active part in politics, and since a great many of them had perished in war.[77] For since in those times the expeditionary forces were made up from the roll of citizens,[a] and since they were led by inexperienced generals who had been selected on the basis of the reputations of their families, the result was always that two or three thousand of those who had participated in the expeditions perished. In this way the ranks of the better men, of both the wealthy and poorer classes, were depleted.

2   In all other respects, they changed the administration, not paying the same attention to the laws as before; but the election of the nine Archons was left untouched except insofar as[78] it was decreed, in the sixth year after Ephialtes' death, that the Zeugitae should be included in the preliminary choice of candidates from among whom the Archons were selected by lot. The first of that class to hold the archonship was Mnesitheides. Before that time all the Archons had been chosen from the Knights and the Pentacosiomedimni, while the Zeugitae held only the lower magistracies, except that occasionally the constitutional regulation may have been neglected.

3   In the fifth year after these events, in the archonship of Lysicrates,[b] the thirty so-called "local justices"[c] were reestablished. Two

c) The "also" in the last sentence of this chapter seems to indicate that the first part of this sentence is missing in the papyrus. It probably contained a reference to the later fate and the death of Themistocles.

a) That is, it did not, as in later times, consist largely of foreign mercenaries.

b) 453 B.C.

c) See *supra*, Ch. 16, 5 and *infra*, Ch. 53, 1.

years later, in the archonship of Antidotus,[d] in consequence of the increasing number of citizens, it was decreed, on a motion of Pericles, that a person should not have the rights of citizenship unless both of his parents had been citizens.

27. After this,[79] when Pericles started on his career as a popular leader and first earned renown, though still a rather young man, by prosecuting Cimon on his audits as a general, the constitution became even more democratic. He took away some of the powers of the Areopagus, and, what is most important, he turned Athens' aspirations definitely toward its sea power. As a result of these changes, the masses gained still greater self-confidence and took more of the control of the state into their own hands.[80]

2 In the forty-ninth year after the battle of Salamis, in the archonship of Pythodorus,[a] the Peloponnesian War broke out. During this war the population was shut up in the city and became accustomed to being paid from public funds while on their military campaigns; and so, partly of their own will, partly without even noticing it, the common people chose to administer the state themselves.

3 Pericles was also the first to introduce payment for service on the law courts, a measure by which he tried to win popular favor to counteract the influence of Cimon's wealth. For Cimon, who possessed a truly regal fortune, performed the regular public services[81] in a magnificent manner, and, in addition, supported a good many of his fellow demesmen. For anyone of the deme of Laciadae who wished to do so could go to him every day and receive a reasonable maintenance; and his whole estate was unfenced so that anyone who liked could help himself to the fruit.

4 Pericles' resources were quite unequal to such lavish liberality. So he followed the advice of Damonides of Oea, who was generally believed to have been the instigator of most of Pericles' measures,

d) 451 B.C.
a) 432/31 B.C.

and was later ostracized for that reason. This man had advised
Pericles to "offer the people what was their own,"[82] since he
was handicapped as far as his own private means were concerned;
and, in consequence of this, Pericles instituted pay for the judges.
Some people blame him on this account and say that the law
courts deteriorated, since after that it was always the common
men rather than the better men who were eager to participate
5 in drawing the lot for duty in the law courts. Also, after this
corruption ensued; and Anytus was the first to set an example,
after his command at Pylos, for he bribed the judges and was
acquitted when he was prosecuted by some because he had lost
Pylos.[b]

28. As long as Pericles was the leader of the people, the state
was still in a fairly good condition, but after his death everything
became much worse.[83] For then the people first chose a leader
who was not in good repute with the better people, while, in
the earlier period, the political leadership had always been in
2 the hands of the latter. For the first leader of the people, in the
very beginning, was Solon, the second one was Pisistratus, both
of whom belonged to the aristocracy of birth. After the overthrow
of the tyranny, it was Cleisthenes from the noble family of the
Alcmeonidae; and he had no political rival after Isagoras and
his adherents had been exiled. After this Xanthippus was the
leader of the people, and Miltiades the leader of the aristocracy.
Then Aristeides and Themistocles [were the popular leaders.][84]
After these, Ephialtes was the leader of the people, and Cimon,
the son of Miltiades, of the wealthy class. Then Pericles was the
leader of the common people, and Thucydides,[a] a relative of
Cimon, head of the other party.
3   After the death of Pericles, Nicias, who later died in Sicily,
became the leader of the aristocratic party, and Cleon, the son
of Cleaenetus, the leader of the people. This man, more than
anybody else, appears to have corrupted the people by his violent

b) This was in 409 B.C., twenty years after the death of Pericles. Anytus
was one of the leaders of the moderately conservative party (Chapter 34, 3).
He was also one of the accusers of Socrates.

a) Thucydides, the son of Melesias, not the historian.

methods. He was the first who shouted on the public platform, who used abusive language and who spoke with his cloak girt up about him, while all the others used to speak in proper dress and manner. After this, Theramenes, the son of Hagnon, was the leader of the other party, and Cleophon, the owner of a lyre factory, the leader of the people. The latter was also the first to introduce the distribution of two obols.[85] This distribution continued for some time. Then Callicrates of the deme Paeania abolished it, being the first to promise that he would add another obol to the two. Later, however, both of these leaders were condemned to death. For the people, even if they allow themselves to be deceived for some time, later begin to hate those who have induced them to do something improper.[86]

4 After Cleophon there was an unbroken succession of popular leaders who distinguished themselves above all by their brazenness and by their eagerness to cater to the wishes of the masses, having nothing in mind but their most immediate interests.

5 The best Athenian statesmen, after those of the early period, seem to have been Nicias, Thucydides, and Theramenes. In regard to Nicias and Thucydides, there seems to be almost universal agreement that they were not only true gentlemen but also statesmen, and that their attitude toward the city as a whole was the attitude of a father. But in regard to Theramenes, opinion is divided, because he happened to live in a time when public affairs were in a turmoil. But, if one tries not to judge lightly, it seems clear that he did not, as his detractors say, overthrow all constitutions, but that, on the contrary, he worked for the good of any established government as long as it did not transgress the [fundamental] laws, and that, in this way, he showed that he was able to serve the state under any kind of political setup, which is what a good citizen should do, but would rather incur enmity and hatred than yield to lawlessness.

29. Now as long as the fortune in the war was equally balanced, they retained the democracy. But when, after the disaster in Sicily,[a] the Lacedaemonian side became stronger through the

a) In the fall of the year 413 B.C.

alliance with the Persian king, they were compelled to abolish the democracy and to establish the constitution of the Four Hundred. The speech initiating this resolution was made by Melobius, and the resolution itself was drafted by Pythodorus of the deme Anaphlystus. What chiefly won over the masses to support the resolution was the belief that the king of Persia would be more likely to take part in the war on their side if they had an oligarchical constitution.

2　　The text of the resolution of Pythodorus was as follows: that the people should elect, in addition to the already existing emergency committee of ten,[87] twenty others from those over forty years of age, and that these men together, after having sworn an oath to draft such measures as they considered best for the state, should then put down in writing proposals for the salvation

3 of the country. Furthermore, they resolved that whoever wished to do so should be free to submit proposals of his own so that then they could choose what was best of all the proposals. Cleitophon supported the motion of Pythodorus in all respects, but added the proposal that the elected committee should also investigate the ancient laws which Cleisthenes had enacted when he established the democracy,[88] so that, after having acquainted themselves with those measures, they might then deliberate as to what the best course would be. The implication was that the constitution of Cleisthenes was not really democratic but similar to that of Solon.[89]

4　　The committee, when elected, first proposed that it should be obligatory for the chairman of the Council to put to a vote all proposals made for the preservation of the state. Furthermore, they abolished the indictments for unconstitutional proposals,[90] and all impeachments and citations,[b] so that all Athenians who wished could freely give their advice in regard to the intended changes. They also ordered that if anyone should impose punishment on another man or should summon him, or bring him to court for this reason, such a person was at once to be indicted and

---

b) With the last two expressions Aristotle refers to indictments or summons for conspiracy to overthrow the constitution.

to be brought before the generals, and that the latter were to hand him over to the Eleven[c] for capital punishment.

5   After this, they established the following principles for the new political order: that the public revenue was to be used only for the war; that the public officials, with the exception of the nine Archons and the Prytanes in office, should serve without pay for the duration of the war; that these officials should each receive three obols a day; that, for the rest of the administration, the whole state should be entrusted, until the end of the war, to those of the Athenians who were most capable of serving the state with their persons and their property, to the number of not less than five thousand.[91] These men should also be empowered to conclude treaties with whomever they wished.   To effect this the people should elect from each tribe ten men over forty years of age who would have the task of drawing up the list of the five thousand, after having sworn a solemn oath over a full and perfect sacrifice.

30. These were the proposals drafted by the selected committee. When these proposals had been ratified, the five thousand elected[92] from their own number one hundred men who were entrusted with the task of drawing up the constitution.[93]   The commissioners so selected drew up and made public the following plan:

2   Those [that is, of the five thousand] over thirty years of age were to be members of the Council, on an annual basis, without payment.[94]   To this Council were to belong the generals, the nine Archons, the Hieromnemon,[a] the Taxiarchs,[b] the Hipparchs,[c] the Phylarchs,[d] the commanders of the garrisons, the ten Treasurers of the Sacred Funds of the goddess Athena and the other gods,[e]

---

c) The superintendents of the State Prison, see *infra* Chapter 52, 1.

a) A recorder whose exact functions are not known in detail (cf. *Politics* VI, 1321b 34–40). He is not identical with the representative of Athens at the Amphictyonic Council who had the same name.

b) See *infra*, Chapter 61, 3.

c) See Chapter 61, 4. (d) See Chapter 61, 5.

e) For the existence of a joint board of the Treasurers of Athena and of the other gods, cf. Andocides, *de mysteriis* 77.

the Hellenotamiae,[f] the Treasurers in charge of all other secular funds, twenty in all, the ten Commissioners of the sacrifices,[g] and ten overseers.[h] The Council was to appoint these men from a larger number of candidates selected by it in a preliminary election[95] and chosen from among its own members of the current year. All the other officials were to be selected by lot and not from the members of the Council. The Hellenotamiae, who actually managed the finances, were not to take part in the sessions of the Council.[96]

3 There were to be, in the future, four Councils, to be formed from the men of the age indicated; and that section of them which would obtain a place on the Council by lot was to serve as Councilors; but the others, too, were to be assigned to each term[97] respectively. The hundred men[98] were to divide themselves and the others as equally as possible into four sections and were to determine by lot who were to belong to each section;

4 and for one year. . . . (?)[99] The Councilors were to make resolutions that seemed best to them in regard to a safe and sound administration of the revenue and expenditures, and in regard to all other affairs, to the best of their ability; and, if they wished to confer about some matter with a greater number, each member was to be entitled to bring with him as an associate member whomever he wished from the same age group. The Council was to have a sitting every fifth day, unless there was need for

5 more frequent meetings. The lot for the Council was to be cast by the nine Archons.[100] The votes on divisions in the Council were to be counted by five men chosen by lot from the members of the Council; and from their number one was to be chosen every day by lot and entrusted with the task of putting the proposals to the vote. The five men selected were also to cast the lot among those who wished to appear before the Council, first concerning matters of religion, second for the heralds, third for the embassies, fourth for other matters; but, as to matters of war, the generals were to be free to bring them up for discussion

f) The collectors and administrators of the contributions paid by the other members of the Athenian Sea Confederacy.

g) Cf. *Politics* 1322b 22ff. h) Cf. *ibid.* 1322b 19ff.

whenever necessary without having to cast the lot for precedence.
6 Furthermore, a Councilor who would not come to the Council house at the time previously announced was to pay a drachma for each day, unless he obtained leave of absence from the Council.

31. This constitution they drafted for the future.[101] But for the immediate present, they drafted the following political order: Four hundred men should form the Council according to the ancestral order,[102] forty from each of the tribes, elected from bodies of candidates over thirty years old previously selected by their tribesmen.[103] These men were to appoint the magistrates, to lay down the rules concerning the oath which they were required to take, and to take such measures in regard to laws 2 and to the audit of public accounts as seemed best to them. The laws in regard to the political constitution which would be laid down were to be observed and it was not to be permitted to change them or to enact others.[104] For the present, the generals were to be elected from the whole number of the five thousand, but the Council, after it had been constituted,[105] was to hold a military inspection in full armor and to select ten men plus a secretary for them; and the men thus chosen were to hold office with full powers during the coming year and to consult 3 with the Council if the need arose. Furthermore, they[106] were to elect one Commander of the Cavalry and ten Phylarchs. But, in the future, the Council was to elect these magistrates according to the regulations drafted.[107] Regarding all offices except the office of the Councilors and that of the generals, it was not to be permitted either to these officials[108] or to anybody else to hold the same office more than once. And, for the time after the immediate present, in order to make provision that the Four Hundred be distributed over the four terms,[a] namely, when the ordinary citizens[109] will be admitted to serve in the Council together with the others, the hundred men are to divide them [that is, the Four Hundred] into sections.[110]

32. This, then, was the political order drafted by the hundred men who were elected by the five thousand.[111] When these

a) Cf. Chapter 30 and Appendix, note 97.

proposals had been ratified by the people[112] under the chairmanship of Aristomachus, the Council of the year of the archonship
of Callias[a] was dissolved on the fourteenth of the month Thargelion
before it had completed its term of office, and the Four Hundred
entered on their office on the twenty-first of the same month.
The regular new Council selected by the lot[b] was to have entered
into office on the fourteenth of Scirophorion.[113]

2   In this way the oligarchy was established under the archonship
of Callias, about one hundred years after the expulsion of the
tyrants.   The chief promotors of this constitutional change were
Pisander, Antiphon, and Theramenes, all of them men of good
family and renowned for their outstanding political insight and
3 well-balanced judgment.   When this political order came into
being, the five thousand were only nominally chosen.[114]   But
the Four Hundred, together with the ten who had been entrusted
with full powers, entered the Council house and ruled the city.[115]
They also sent an embassy to the Lacedaemonians and proposed
to make an end of the war on the basis of the *status quo*.   But when
the latter were not willing to listen except on the condition that
the Athenians abandon their maritime supremacy, they [that is,
the new rulers] gave up the attempt.

33. The constitution of the Four Hundred lasted for about
four months.   As one of their number, Mnesilochus held the
office of Archon for two months[a] in the year of the Archon
Theopompus, who held the office for the remaining ten months.
When they were defeated in the naval battle off Eretria and when
the whole of Euboea with the exception of Oreos revolted,[b] the
Athenians were more embittered by the revolt than by anything
that had happened before, for they drew more support from

a) 412/11 B.C.
  b) This is the Council which, if there had been no change in the constitution,
would have been selected by lot to succeed the regular Council of 412/11.
  a) It seems that Callias was allowed to remain in office until the end of the
year, while the new Archon for 411/10, who had been elected according to the
new constitutional procedure, was ejected after the restoration of the democracy
and replaced by Theopompus.
  b) See Thucydides VIII, 95.

Euboea than from Attica itself. And, in consequence, they abolished the rule of the Four Hundred, entrusted the government to the five thousand capable of doing military service with full equipment,[116] and decreed at the same time that there was to be no pay for any public office.

2   The chief promotors of the dissolution of the new rule were Aristocrates and Theramenes, who disapproved of the attitude of the Four Hundred. For the latter had decided everything by themselves and had never referred anything to the five thousand. It would appear that in this period Athens had a good form of government, when, in a time of war, the government was in the hands of those able to serve with full equipment.[c]

34. These men, then, were quickly deprived of their political power by the people of Athens.[117] In the sixth year after the overthrow of the Four Hundred in the archonship of Callias of the deme of Angele,[a] after the naval battle of the Arginusae, it happened that the ten generals who had won the victory in the battle were all condemned[118] by a single division [in the Assembly of the People], though some of them had not even taken part in the battle and others had been picked up from the sea by other vessels.[b] This vote was the work of agitators who deceived the people by stirring up public anger. Moreover, when the Lacedaemonians offered to evacuate Decelea[c] and to make peace on the basis of the *status quo*, some were very anxious to accept, but the majority would not listen to the proposal, since they were misled by Cleophon, who came into the Assembly drunk and wearing his breast plate,[d] and spoke against the conclusion of peace, declaring that he would never agree to it unless the

2 Lacedaemonians surrendered all the cities.[e] This was a great

c) Cf. Thucydides VIII, 97, 2.

a) 406/05 B.C.

b) The generals were put on trial because, on account of a storm, they had not stayed to pick up the survivors from vessels that had been sunk.

c) A fortified place in Attica north of Athens which the Spartans had occupied and from which they ravaged the country.

d) That is, in military attire.

e) This probably means those which they had conquered in the war.

blunder; and it did not take long before they realized their mistakes. For in the following year, in the archonship of Alexias, they met with disaster in the naval battle at Aegospotami, as a result of which Lysander[f] became master of the city and established the rule of the Thirty.

3   This happened in the following way. The peace had been concluded on the condition that they would return to "the ancestral constitution."[119] On this basis the popular party tried to preserve the democracy; those of the nobles who belonged to the political clubs and the exiles[g] who came back after the conclusion of the peace aimed at an oligarchy, while those who did not belong to the clubs but otherwise were considered as belonging to the best classes really wanted the ancestral constitution.[120] To this last class belonged Archinus, Anytus, Cleitophon, Phormisius, and many others. Their leader was Theramenes. When, however, Lysander sided with the oligarchs, the people were intimidated and felt compelled to vote for the oligarchy. The motion was drafted by Dracontides of Aphidna.

35. In this way the rule of the Thirty was established, in the archonship of Pythodorus.[a] When they had become masters of the city, they paid no attention to the other regulations concerning the constitution which had been passed.[121] They did appoint five hundred Councilmen and also made appointments for the other magistracies from among persons previously selected from the Thousand.[122] They associated with themselves ten governors of the Piraeus and eleven superintendents of the prison, and, furthermore, appointed three hundred lash bearers as their attendants. In this way they kept the city under their control.

2   At first they showed moderation in dealing with their fellow citizens and pretended to be aiming at the ancestral constitution. They took down from the Areopagus the laws of Ephialtes[b] and

f) The famous Spartan general.

g) After the overthrow of the rule of the Four Hundred some of the leaders of the oligarchic party had gone into exile.

a) 404/03 B.C.

b) Cf. *supra*, Chapter 25, 2.

Archestratus about the Areopagitae. They abolished those of the Solonian laws which were controversial[c] and also abolished the arbitrary power of the judges [to interpret the laws]. In doing this, they claimed to correct the constitution by removing ambiguities. For instance, the right of giving [by will] one's property to whomever one wished[123] was made absolute; and the troublesome clauses by which it was limited (unless he be insane or not in full possession of his mental powers because of age or under the influence of a woman) were removed so that there might be no opening for sycophants. They applied the same principle to other matters.

3   This is what they did in the beginning. They made away with the professional denunciators ["sycophants"] and those mischievous and low politicians who curried favor with the people for the sake of their own evil aims. The citizens were delighted with these measures and believed that they did all these things
4 out of the best intentions. But when they had acquired a firm hold on the state, they did not keep their hands off any kind of citizens but put to death persons who were distinguished by wealth or birth or reputation. For they intended to remove anyone whose influence they might have reason to fear, and, at the same time, wished to get hold of their possessions. In fact, after a short time, they had done away with more than one thousand five hundred persons.

36. Theramenes, however, became indignant over the way in which the city was slowly going to pieces and exhorted the Thirty to cease such wanton conduct and to give the better classes their share in the government. At first, they merely opposed his suggestions; but when his counsel became known among the people, and the masses took the side of Theramenes, they were afraid that he might become the leader of the people and overthrow their despotic rule. So they started to make a list of three thousand people[124] on the pretense that they would give them a share
2 in the government. But Theramenes attacked them again on the ground of this measure, first, because, having promised to

c) Cf. *supra*, Chapter 9, 2 and Aristotle *Rhet.* 1354a 31ff.

let the "better people" participate, they admitted only three
thousand, as if all merit were confined within that number;
secondly, because they were attempting to do two things which
were entirely inconsistent with each other, namely, to establish a
government based on force and yet weaker than its subjects.[125]

The Thirty, however, paid no attention to these criticisms,
and for a long time they postponed the publication of the list
of the Three Thousand and kept the names of the persons included
to themselves; in fact, whenever they did decide to publish it,
they at once began again to remove the names of some who had
previously been included and added the names of some who
were not on the list.[126]

37. At the beginning of the winter, Thrasybulus, together with
the exiles,[a] occupied Phyle.[b] When the Thirty were defeated
in an expedition which they had led against [the exiles], they
decided to disarm the others[c] and to do away with Theramenes.
This they contrived in the following way: They laid two laws
before the Council and ordered the Council to pass them.[127] The
first of these laws gave the Thirty full powers over life and death
of all citizens who were not on the list of the Three Thousand;
the second prohibited anyone from participating in political
rights who either had taken part in the demolition of the fortifications of Eetionea[d] or had in any way been in active opposition
to the Four Hundred who had set up the previous oligarchic
regime. Theramenes had done both, so that, when the laws had
been passed, Theramenes was deprived of his political rights[128]
2 and the Thirty had full power to put him to death.   When
Theramenes was out of the way, they disarmed all people except

a) That is, the democrats who had fled when the oligarchy of the Thirty
was established.

b) A place north of Athens in the Parnes Mountains.

c) That is, all those Athenians who did not belong to the Three Thousand
(Xenophon, *Hellenica* II, 3, 20).

d) A fortification which the Four Hundred had begun to build for the pro-
tection of the Piraeus. Since the moderate party led by Theramenes suspected
that the oligarchs might hand this harbor over to the Spartans, they incited the
people to tear down the fortifications. Cf. Thucydides VIII, 91ff

the Three Thousand,[129] and from then on became ever more cruel and wicked.

They also sent an embassy to Sparta to denounce Theramenes and at the same time asked for military assistance. Upon this request, the Lacedaemonians sent Callibius as harmost[e] with about seven hundred men; and he, upon his arrival, occupied the Acropolis.

38. Following this, the exiles from Phyle occupied Munichia[a] and defeated the force sent by the Thirty to rescue the place. After this skirmish, the men from the city retreated. On the following day, they assembled in the market place and deposed the Thirty. Then they elected ten citizens with full powers to bring the war to an end. These men took over the government but did not do anything to achieve the ends for which they had been elected. On the contrary, they sent to Sparta in order

2 to ask for help and to borrow money. When those admitted to full citizenship showed their indignation over their actions, they [the Commission of Ten] were afraid lest they might be deprived of their office. They, therefore, decided to intimidate the others — in which action they were successful — and arrested one of the most outstanding citizens, Demaretus, and put him to death. From then on they had the power firmly in their hands, being supported by Callibius and the Peloponnesian forces which were in Athens, and also by some of the Knights. For some of this group of citizens were most anxious to prevent a return of the exiles from Phyle.

3 When, however, the party which was in possession of the Piraeus and of Munichia[b] gradually gained the upper hand,

e) This is a special term used by the Spartans. It designates a man who has the mission of "establishing order" in a city which was allied with Sparta or subject to its rule. In actual fact, however, a harmost often had the function of a military governor.

a) The name of a hill overlooking the harbor of Athens and of the bay and harbor southeast of the hill. From Xenophon's account (*Hellenica* II, 4, 11ff.) it appears that Thrasybulus had occupied the hill after having made an attempt to occupy the Piraeus.

b) After their victory on the hill of Munichia, the democrats had occupied the Piraeus, since the whole people went over to their side, they [that is, the Three Thousand] deposed the board of Ten which they had elected originally and elected another board of Ten consisting of men who enjoyed the highest reputation.[130]   Thus the end of the civil strife was actually brought about while these men were in power and were sincerely doing whatever they could to help.

The most active members of this board were Rhinon of the deme Paeania[131] and Phayllus of the deme Acherdus.   For these men, even before the arrival of Pausanias, had undertaken missions to the men in the Piraeus, and after his arrival they did
4 everything to promote the return of the exiles.   For it was the Spartan king Pausanias who brought the peace and the reconciliation to completion, together with the ten mediators[132] who arrived later from Sparta and whom he himself had requested to come.   Rhinon and his associates were praised because of their good will toward the people.   Though they had been entrusted with their duties under the oligarchy, they handed in their accounts under the democratic regime.   Yet no one, either of those who had remained in the city or of those who returned from the Piraeus, brought any charge against them.   On the contrary, Rhinon was at once elected General because of his aforementioned activities.

39. This reconciliation was effected in the archonship of Eucleides[a] on the following terms: Those of the Athenians who had remained in the city[b] and now wished to leave it were to have Eleusis[c] as residence, retaining their full civil rights, having their own independent administration and enjoying their own
2 revenues.   The temple of Eleusis was to belong to both parties in common, and under the superintendence of the Ceryces and

a) 403/02: according to Plutarch (*de gloria Atheniensium* 349F) in the third month of that year, that is, in September, 403.

b) That is, who had not joined the democrats when the latter were holding the Piraeus.

c) Those of the Thirty who were still alive when their regime was overthrown had fled to Eleusis (Xen. *Hell.* II, 4, 24), the famous place to the west of Athens where the mysteries were celebrated.

the Eumolpidae[d] according to the ancestral custom. But those settled at Eleusis were not to be permitted to go into the city, and those in the city were not to be permitted to go to Eleusis, except that both parties were to be free to do so for the celebration of the mysteries. The settlers at Eleusis were to contribute to the defense fund from their revenues in the same way as the other Athenians.

3   Those of the prospective settlers who were going to acquire a house at Eleusis were to try to persuade the owner [to sell it]. But if they could not come to an agreement, both parties were to choose three appraisers each and the owner was to receive whatever price these appraisers assessed. Those of the people of Eleusis whom the new settlers were willing to accept were to be allowed to stay and live together with them.

4   The final registration date for those who wished to emigrate [to Eleusis] was to be ten days from the date on which the peace was sworn; the last term for their actual emigration was to be twenty days from that date, if they were living in the city. But if they were abroad, the same number of days was to be counted from the day of their return.

5   No one of those who had settled at Eleusis was to be permitted to hold any office in the city unless and until he had registered for taking up his residence again in the city. Trials for homicide, that is, cases in which a man had killed or wounded someone with his own hands, were to be conducted according to the ancestral custom.

6   There was to be a complete amnesty in regard to the past [political] events, except for the Thirty, the Ten,[133] the Eleven, and those who had been governors of the Piraeus; and the amnesty was to extend even to them if they were willing to render account. The former governors of the Piraeus were to render account before a court consisting of men who had taxable property in the Piraeus, and those who had ruled in the city, before a court consisting of people who had taxable property [in the

----

d) The two noble families which of old had been connected with the Eleusinian mystery cult.

city].[134] Then, after satisfying all these legal requirements,[e] those who wished might emigrate. Finally, each party was to repay separately the loans which it had contracted for the war.

40. When the reconciliation had been effected, those who had taken an active part in the civil war on the side of the Thirty were still full of fear, and many of them were inclined to change their residence but waited with their registration until the last moment, as people usually do. Now, when Archinus saw how many there were, he wished to hold them back. He did this by cutting off the last days allowed for the registration so that many were compelled to stay, much against their will, at least until

2 they regained courage. In this case, Archinus appears to have acted as a true statesman; and also when he preferred a charge of unconstitutionality against the decree proposed by Thrasybulus by which full rights of citizenship were given to all those who had participated in the return from the Piraeus, though some of them were notoriously slaves. There was still a third occasion at which he appears to have shown his statesmanship. When one of those who had participated in the return began to take up complaints in violation of the amnesty, Archinus took him before the Council and persuaded the Councilmen to have him executed without trial. He achieved this by telling them that now was the moment when they must show whether they were willing to save the democracy and to live up to their oaths. For if they were going to let this man off, they would encourage others to act as he did; but if they executed him, they would set a warning example. This was actually the result. For when he had him executed, nobody ever dared to violate the amnesty again. In fact, it appears that their attitude both in private and in public in regard to the past disturbances was the most admirable and the most statesmanlike that any people have ever shown in such

3 circumstances. For, apart from having wiped out all considerations of guilt in regard to the past events, they even refunded at common expense the money which the Thirty had borrowed from the Lacedaemonians for the war, though the agreement

e) "... after satisfying all these legal requirements" is Sandys' interpretation of the Greek οὕτως ("so, 'in that way.' ").

said that the two parties, namely, that of the city and that of the Piraeus, should pay their own debts separately. For they thought that this was the way to start the restoration of concord and harmony, while in other countries the democrats, if they come to power, do not even think of making any contributions out of their own money, but, on the contrary, seize the land for
4 redistribution. They also brought about a reconciliation with those who had settled at Eleusis[135] in the third year after their emigration, in the archonship of Xenaenetus.[a]

41. The events last mentioned happened at a somewhat later date. But immediately after the people had become masters of the state,[136] they established the constitution which is still in force, in the archonship of Pythodorus. . . .[137] And the people seemed to have a just claim to the control of the state since they had effected a return by their own efforts.

2 This was the eleventh of the changes of the constitution. The first change[138] of the original state of things occurred when Ion and his companions came to dwell with them.[139] For it was at this time that they were grouped together in the four Tribes and that the Tribe-kings were first established. The second change, and the first after this which implied something of a constitutional order,[140] was the one which happened under Theseus. This was a slight deviation from the pure monarchy. After this came the constitution which prevailed under Draco, in which, for the first time, they drew up a code of laws. The third was the one under Solon, after the civil disturbances, from which democracy had its beginnings. The fourth was the tyranny under Pisistratus. The fifth was the constitution of Cleisthenes after the overthrow of the tyrants, a constitution more democratic than that of Solon. The sixth was the one after the Persian War, when the Council of the Areopagus had the leadership. The seventh was the one which followed this constitution;[141] it had been anticipated to some extent by Aristeides,[142] but was brought to completion by Ephialtes when he deprived the Areopagus of his power. Under this constitution, the greatest mistakes were

a) 401/00 B.C.

committed by the nation under the influence of the demagogues and for the sake of the domination of the sea. The eighth was the establishment of the Four Hundred. After this, the ninth was the restored democracy. The tenth was the tyranny of the Thirty and the Ten. The eleventh was the one which came into being after the return of the exiles from Phyle and the Piraeus, from which date [?] it continued to exist until it reached its present form, all the time adding to its grasp of arbitrary power for the people.[143] For the people have made themselves masters of everything and administer everything through decrees of the Assembly and decisions of the law courts, in which they hold the power. For even the juridical functions of the Council have passed into the hands of the people. In this they appear to be right. For a small number of judges can be more easily corrupted by money and favor than the many.

3   At first, they refused to allow payment for attendance at the Assembly of the People. But when the people did not come and the Prytanes had tried many things to induce the people to attend for the sake of ratification of proposals by their vote, Agyrrhius first introduced a fee of one obol; afterwards, Heracleides of Clazomenae,[144] with the surname "King," a fee of two obols; and then again Agyrrhius[145] a fee of three obols.

42. The present constitutional order is as follows: the right of citizenship belongs to those whose parents have been citizens. They are enregistered on the rolls of the demes at the age of eighteen. When they come up for enrollment, their fellow demesmen decide by vote under oath the following: first, whether they appear to have reached the legal age[146]—and if they do not appear of the right age, they return to the state of boys; secondly, whether the candidate is freeborn and of such parents as the law requires. If they [their fellow demesmen] decide that he is not free,[147] he appeals to the law court and the demesmen choose five men from among themselves as his accusers; and if it appears that he has no right to be enrolled, the city sells him into slavery,

2   but if he wins, the demesmen are compelled to enroll him. After this the Council examines those who have been enrolled, and if

someone appears to be younger than eighteen years, the Council fines the demesmen who enrolled him. When the young men (*epheboi*) have passed this examination, their fathers assemble by tribes and, after having taken an oath, elect three of their fellow tribesmen over forty years of age whom they consider the best and the most suitable to supervise the young men. Then out of these men the people elect by vote one from every tribe as guardian (*sophronistes*), and, from the other Athenians, they elect

3 a superintendent (*kosmetes*) for all of them. These men then call the young men together and first make the circuit of the temples. Then they proceed to the Piraeus, and one part takes garrison at Munichia, the other at Acte.[a] The Assembly also elects two trainers for them and special instructors who teach them to fight in full armor and to use the bow, the javelin, and the catapult.[b] They [the people] pay the guardians one drachma each for their keep and the young men four obols each. Each guardian receives the allowance for all those of his tribe, buys all the necessary provisions for their common upkeep (they have their meals

4 together by tribes), and also takes care of all other matters. This is what they do in the first year. In the following year, when there is an Assembly of the People in the theatre, the young men give a public display of their military drill before the people. Then they receive shield and spear from the state, and from then on they patrol the country and are stationed at the guardposts.

5 While they are in service for their two years, their uniform is a military cloak, and they are free from taxes. And, so that they will have no pretext for requesting a leave, they cannot be sued at law or bring suit against someone else. Exceptions are only cases of inheritance, of unmarried heiresses,[c] and of a man's

a) A broad hilly peninsula south of the Piraeus harbor and included in the fortifications.

b) This compulsory training of the *epheboi* was introduced by the Athenian statesman Lycurgus, probably in 335 B.C.

c) An orphaned girl could be claimed in marriage by her nearest male relative; and if her father had left an estate, this estate went to the sons born of such marriage. If the girl was poor, the nearest of kin was obliged either to marry her or to provide her with a dowry.

having to take over a priesthood hereditary in the family.[d] When the two years are over, their place is with the other citizens.

43. So much for the rules about the enrollment of citizens and about the young men of military age. All the officials for the ordinary administration are chosen by lot, with the exception of the Treasurer of the military funds, the Treasurers of the theatre fund,[a] and the Superintendent of the water supply. These latter officials are elected by vote and hold their office from one Panathenaean festival[b] to the celebration of the next Panathenaean festival. All the military officers are also elected by vote.

2   The Council is selected by lot and consists of five hundred members, fifty from each tribe. Each of the tribes holds the presidency ["Prytany"] in turn, the sequence being determined by lot; the four on which the lot falls first hold the presidency for thirty-six days each, and the remaining six for thirty-five days each. For they have a lunar year.[148]

3   Those who belong to the presidency [the Prytanes] first dine together in the Tholus;[c] they receive money from the state[d] for this purpose. Then they convoke the Council and the Assembly of the People: the Council every day except on holidays, the Assembly of the People four times in each presidency. They draw up [for publication on the notice-boards] the agenda for the Council and announce the special program and the meeting-

4   place for each day. Likewise, they make the announcements for the meetings of the Assembly of the People. There is one principal meeting in which they have to confirm the magistrates in their office if they appear to govern properly,[e] and in which

d) "Family" in the larger sense, as in Chapter 21.

a) The fund from which the citizens, upon application, received the two obols which they had to pay for admission to the theatre performances at the Dionysiac festivals.

b) The Panathenian festival was celebrated toward the end of the month Hecatombaeon, the first month of the Attic year (July). The other officials entered upon their offices at the beginning of this month.

c) A round building near the Buleuterium or Council Hall.

d) Cf. *infra*, Chapter 62, 2.

e) Cf. *infra*, Chapter 61, 2.

they deal with the food supply and with the defense of the country. It is also on these particular days that those who wish to introduce impeachments[149] may do so, that the inventories of confiscated property, and also legal claims for the right of succession to inheritances and of marrying an heiress[f] are read, so that nobody may be in ignorance of any vacancy in an estate.

5   In the sixth prytany, in addition to the matters mentioned, they also decide by vote whether there is to be a vote on ostracism or not,[g] and receive complaints against malicious accusers,[h] Athenians or metics, but not more than three of either kind. Finally, they consider the cases of persons who have failed to perform a promise made to the people.

6   They have another meeting [in each prytany] for the hearing of petitions. In this meeting anyone who wishes to do so can speak to the people on any matter, whether private or public, after having placed the token of the suppliant[i] [that is, on the altar].

The two other meetings are assigned to all other kinds of business, and the law orders that three questions concerning sacred matters, three connected with heralds and embassies, and three concerning secular matters[150] be dealt with. Sometimes they also do business without a preliminary vote. Both heralds and embassies are first received in audience by the presidents of the Council (prytanes), and those who bring written messages hand them over to the presidents.

44. The Prytanes have a chairman (*epistates*) who is chosen by lot. He holds the chairmanship for one day and one night, and he cannot hold it for a longer time; nor can the same man hold it twice. This chairman keeps the keys of the sanctuaries where the treasure and the public records are kept. He also has the public seal. He is obliged to stay in the Tholus and have with

f) Cf. *supra*, p. 115, note c.

g) That is, they decided whether there was a *prima facie* case for ostracism or not. If the ayes prevailed, a day for the actual vote on the ostracism was fixed in the eighth prytany.

h) "Sycophants."

i) An olive branch bound with white wool.

2 him one-third of the Prytanes, chosen by himself. When the Prytanes convoke the Council or the Assembly of the People, this chairman appoints by lot nine presiding officers (*prohedroi*),[a] one from each tribe, except the one which holds the prytany for the time being; and then he appoints, again by lot, one of them as their chairman (*epistates*). Then he hands the agenda to them.

3 When they have received the agenda, they see to it that an orderly procedure is followed; they bring forward whatever belongs to the order of the day, count the votes, and direct all other business. They also have the authority to dismiss the meeting. Nobody can be chairman more than once a year, but he can be one of the presiding officers (*prohedroi*) once in every prytany.

4   The election of the Generals, the Commanders of the Cavalry, and the other military officers takes place also in the Assembly of the People in whatever way the people see fit. These elections are held after the sixth prytany by the first board of presidents (*prytaneis*) in whose term the omens are favorable.[151] But about these elections, there also has to be a preliminary deliberation in the Council.

45. In previous times the Council had had the power of imposing fines, imprisonment, and death. Once, when the Council was handing over a certain Lysimachus to the executioner and Lysimachus was already sitting waiting for the executioner, Eumelides of Alopece rescued him,[152] saying that it was not permissible to put a citizen to death without the decision of a law court. Then, when a trial in a law court took place, not only Lysimachus himself was acquitted and afterwards was called by the nickname "the one who escaped the stick," but also the people took away from the Council the power of imposing the death penalty or imprisonment or fines, and made a law that whenever the Council passes sentence on a person for an offense or imposes a punishment on him, the Thesmothetae shall bring

a) This was obviously an innovation of the fourth century. In the fifth century the prytanes and *their* chairman had acted as presiding officers in the Assembly of the People.

the sentence or penalty before the law court, and what the jury-men decide shall be the final judgment in the matter.[a]

2 The Council investigates most of the magistrates, especially those who have something to do with the administration of public funds. Their judgment is not final but subject to revision[153] by the law court. Private citizens also have a right [to take the initiative and] to lay information [with the Council] against any of the magistrates for disobeying the laws. But in such cases, too, there is the benefit of revision in the law court if the Council passes a verdict of guilty.[154]

3 The Council also examines the Councilmen and the nine Archons for the following year. And in earlier times its decision to reject a person was final, but now his rejection is reviewed in the law court.

4 In these matters, then, the Council does not have final juris-diction. On the other hand, it holds a preliminary deliberation on everything that is brought before [the Assembly of] the people, and the people cannot vote on a decree unless it has previously been discussed by the Council and has been placed on the agenda by the Prytanes. For if anyone brings in a bill in violation of these rules, he is liable to an action for illegal proposal.[b]

46. The Council supervises the upkeep of the triremes, which are on hand, and of their rigging and of the ship-sheds; and it also has the new triremes and quadriremes[a] built for which the people have voted, and has the riggings and the ship-sheds made which go with them. But it is the people who choose the master-builders for the ships by vote. If these builders[155] do not hand over the vessels to the new Council in a completed state, they cannot receive the customary reward. For they receive the reward under the following Council. The Council undertakes

a) Concerning the law courts see *infra*, Chapters 63ff.

b) γραφὴ παρανόμων; cf. Appendix, note 90.

a) Quadriremes were built for the first time shortly after 330 B.C. Quin-queremes are mentioned for the first time in 325 B.C. Hence, the present treatise appears to have been written before 325. Cf. also Introduction, p. 5.

the construction of the triremes by appointing from its own midst ten men as commissioners for ship construction.

2   The Council also inspects all the public buildings, and, if it comes to the conclusion that someone is in default, it reports him to the people and, after having passed a verdict on him,[156] hands him over to the law court.

47. The Council also collaborates with the other magistracies in the greater part of the administration.   There are in the first place the Treasurers of Athena, chosen by lot, one from each tribe.   They are chosen from the Pentacosiomedimni according to the law of Solon — for this law is still in force — but he who is designated by the lot holds the office even if he is very poor.[157] These Treasurers take over, in the presence of the Council, the statue of Athena, the [golden] figures of Nice,[a] the other precious articles of the sacred treasure,[b] and the money.

2   Secondly, there are the ten Poletae,[c] chosen by lot, one from each tribe.   They farm out all the public contracts.   In the presence of the Council and together with the Treasurer of the military fund and the administrators of the theatre fund, they offer for lease the mines and the taxes, and ratify [the leases] for the person whom the Council has selected by vote.   They also sell, in the presence of the Council, the estates of persons exiled by the Areopagus[d] and of the others [namely, whose goods have been confiscated?], but in this case the sale must be confirmed by the nine Archons.[158]   And they write down on whitened tablets[e] the mines which were let out, both those in working condition, which are leased for a period of three years, and those

a) There had been ten such statues of Nice, or Victory, at the beginning of the Peloponnesian War, eight of which were melted down and made into gold coin toward the end of that war.   Later the number was again increased.

b) These included necklaces, bracelets, golden wreaths, etc.

c) Literally "vendors."   From the succeeding description of their functions, they might be designated as commissioners of public contracts.

d) A person accused of wilful murder before the Areopagus was allowed to go into exile in order to avoid the death penalty.   But his property was confiscated; and whenever a decree was passed permitting the return of exiles, those "fleeing from the Areopagus" were always exempted.

e) Wooden boards with a coat of chalk.

obtained as concessions,[159] which are leased for ten[f] years,[160] and the taxes, which are leased for one year, together with the name of the man who has taken a lease and the sum which he is
3 paying. These tablets they hand over to the Council. They write down separately (a) on ten lists those who have to pay their installments in each prytany, (b) on three other lists those who have to pay three times a year, making a separate list for each of the three dates of payment, and (c) on still another list those who have to make their payments in the ninth prytany. They draw up a list of the lots and houses which have been confiscated and are sold by order of a law court; for these, too, are sold by them. In the case of houses, the purchase price must be paid in full within five years, in the case of lots of land, in ten years. The installments are paid in the ninth prytany.
4 The Archon King[g] places before the Council the leases of sacred precincts listed on whitened tablets. These leases are also for ten years, and the payments are made in the ninth prytany so that in that prytany the greatest revenue is collected.
5 As has been said, the tablets on which the payments are listed as they become due are placed before the Council; after that, the public clerk[h] is in charge of them. And whenever payments are due, this clerk takes from the shelves those tablets on which the sums are listed which on that day must be paid and [after payment] must be canceled on the list, and hands them over to the Receivers. The other tablets are kept separately so that they may not be canceled out before payment is made.

48. There are ten Apodectae ["Receivers"] collectors of public revenue, one chosen by lot from each tribe. These men take the tablets and cancel, in the presence of the Council in the Council hall, the sums of money which have been paid; then they return the tablets to the public clerk. If someone has failed to pay an instalment due, his name remains on the list, and the debtor will have to pay double the amount of the arrears or face imprison-

f) The number is half destroyed and not certain, but seems to have been ten.

g) See Appendix, notes 4–6, and *infra*, Chapter 57.

h) A state slave.

ment.   The Council has full powers according to the laws to exact the money in such cases or to inflict imprisonment.

2   They [the Receivers] receive, then, all the instalment payments and apportion the money among the magistrates on the first of two successive days; and on the second day they bring the report of the apportionment, written on a wooden tablet, to the Council chamber and read it there.   At the same time, they place these questions before the Council: whether anyone knows of any person, public official or private individual, who is guilty of any malpractice in regard to the apportionment.   If someone is suspected of bad practices, the Council votes on the question of his guilt.

3   The Council selects also by lot ten Accountants (*logistai*)[a] from its own members.   These men have to check the accounts of the magistrates during each prytany.

4   They also select by lot one Examiner (*euthynos*) from each tribe, and two associate examiners for each of the Examiners. These men, together with their associates, have to sit during the regular market hours at the statue of the eponymous hero[b] of each tribe.   And if any citizen wishes to prefer a charge, either of a public or of a private nature, against any of the magistrates who have rendered account before a law court, within an interval of three days after he has rendered his account, he must write on a whitened tablet his own name and the name of the man he accuses, the offense with which he charges him, and the fine

5   which he considers appropriate.   This he gives to the Examiner, who takes the tablet and examines it.   If the Examiner finds the charge well founded, he hands it, if it is a private suit, to the local judges[c] who introduce [to the law courts] the matters

a) These λογισταί , which are selected from the Council, are to be distinguished from the λογισταί mentioned in Chapter 54, 2, who are taken from the general body of citizens and who audit the accounts of all officials at the end of their terms.

b) That is, one of the heroes from which the tribes derived their names. The statues of these heroes were erected on the northern slope of the Areopagus, south of the Tholus and the Council Hall.

c) Concerning these local judges or judges in the demes see *supra*, Chapter 16, 5 and *infra*, Chapter 53.

relating to the tribe concerned, and if it is a public matter, he hands in a written report to the Thesmothetae. When the Thesmothetae have received the charge, they bring the account of this magistrate again before the law court; and the decision of the court is final.[161]

49. The Council also examines the horses; and if anyone has a good horse but does not seem to take good care of it, he is punished by taking away his allowance for its feed.[a]   Horses which cannot keep up with the squadron, or will not keep in line but are unsteady, are branded with the sign of a wheel on the jaw, and a horse so marked is disqualified. The Council also inspects the mounted scouts (*prodromoi*)[b] to find out which are fit for their kind of service, and if it rejects one of these scouts, he has to give up serving on horseback. It also inspects those who fight on foot together with the cavalry, and if it votes against someone, he ceases to receive pay.

2   The cavalry is recruited by the ten Commissioners of Enlistment (*katalogeis*), who are elected by vote in the Assembly of the People. They give the list of those whom they have selected for this service to the Hipparchs and Phylarchs,[c] and these men take the list and bring it before the Council. And they open the tablet on which the names of the cavalrymen are listed under seal;[d] and then they strike out the names of those cavalrymen previously enrolled who declare under oath that they are no longer physically able to serve and call up those who have been newly enrolled. If someone of the latter swears that he is not able to serve in the cavalry either for reasons of health or because of lack of money,[162] they let him go.   But if he does not make such a declaration under oath, the Councilmen decide by vote whether he is fit for service in the cavalry or not.   If they decide that he is fit, they enter his name on the tablet; and, if they decide against him, this man, too, is dismissed.

a) The men serving in the cavalry received a daily allowance for the upkeep of their horses.

b) The light cavalry, which served also as advance guard and mounted scouts.

c) Concerning the Hipparchs and Phylarchs see *infra*, Chapter 61, 4, 5.

d) That is, those who are already doing cavalry service.

3   In former times the Council also passed judgment on the
models and [?] on the robe (*peplos*),[163] but now this is done by
the law court which the lot designates.   For the Councilmen
were suspected of favoritism in passing judgment [in this matter].
The Council, together with the Treasurer of the military funds,
also supervises the manufacture of the images of Nice [Victory][e]
and the prizes at the Panathenaean festival.

4   The Council also examines the invalids.   For there is a law
which orders that those whose property is less than three minae
and who are so completely disabled physically that they cannot
do any work shall, after having been examined by the Council,
receive two obols daily for their support from the public funds.
The Treasurer for the invalids is selected by lot.

   The Council collaborates also with the other magistrates in,
one may say, most of their functions.[164]

   50. These then are the matters which are attended to by the
Council.   Ten men are selected, also by lot, as Commissioners
for the maintenance of the sanctuaries.   These men receive
thirty minae from the Apodectae[a] and take care of what is most
2 necessary for the upkeep of the sanctuaries.   There are also ten
City Commissioners (*astynomoi*); five of them hold office in the
Piraeus harbor, the other five in the city.   They keep control
over the flute-girls, harp-girls, and lyre-girls, and see to it that
they are not hired for more than two drachmae; if several persons
are anxious to hire the same girl, they cast the lot between them
and assign her to the winner.   They also see to it that none of
the dung-collectors deposits the dung within ten stadia[b] of the
city walls.   They prevent people from encroaching with their
buildings on public roads, from constructing balconies protruding
into the road, from making drain-pipes with a discharge into
the street from above, and from having windows opening into
the street.   And they remove the corpses of people who die in
the streets, having state slaves at their disposal.

e) Cf. *supra*, Chapter 47, note a.
a) Cf. *supra*, Chapter 48.
b) Ten stadia are approximately one mile.

51. Market-inspectors (*agoranomoi*) are selected by lot, five for the Piraeus and five for the city. The laws make it their duty to supervise all articles offered for sale and to see to it that they
2 are pure and unadulterated. Commissioners of weights and measures (*metronomoi*) are appointed by lot, five for the city and five for the Piraeus. They have to inspect all weights and measures and see to it that the sellers use fair weights and meas-
3 ures. There also used to be ten Corn Commissioners (*sitophylakes*), chosen by lot, five for the city and five for the Piraeus. But now there are twenty for the city and fifteen for the Piraeus. These men see to it that the unground grain which is in the market is sold at a fair price, that the millers sell barley flour at a price corresponding to that of the barley, that the bakers sell their loaves of bread at a price corresponding to that of the wheat, and that the loaves have the full weight fixed by these officials. For the law orders that they fix the weight.
4 They select by lot ten Supervisors of the Trade Exchange (*emporion*) whose duty it is to supervise the trading places and to see to it that two-thirds of the grain which is brought by sea to the corn emporium is brought up to the city.

52. They also appoint by lot the Eleven whose duty it is to take care of the prisoners in the state prison. These men punish with death the robbers, kidnappers, and thieves who are brought before them, in case they confess;[a] but, if they deny the charge, they bring them before the law court. If they are acquitted, they let them go, and if they are not acquitted, they have them executed. It is their duty to bring before the law court the lists of farms and houses alleged to be public property, and to hand them over to the Poletae[b] if the court decides that they belong to the state. They also bring in informations (*endeixeis*);[c] for these,

a) The death penalty was obligatory in these cases, and if the culprit confessed, the case did not have to be taken to a court. But this does not mean that the Eleven did not conduct an investigation.

b) See *supra*, Chapter 47, 2 and note c.

c) The ἔνδειξις was a special kind of information brought against persons who claimed or made use of political rights to which they were not entitled, too, are brought before the court by the Eleven, though in some cases it is up to the Thesmothetae to bring in the informations.

2   They also select by lot five men as Introducers (*eisagogeis*), who introduce the law cases which are to be decided within a month, each one acting for two tribes. The following cases are "monthly" in this sense: if someone does not pay a dowry which he is obliged to pay, if someone has borrowed money at an interest of a drachma in the mina[d] and does not pay, and if someone borrows capital from another person in order to start a business in the market.[e] Furthermore, prosecution for assault, and cases arising out of friendly loans (*eranoi*),[f] out of partnerships, in regard to slaves, draft animals, trierarchies,[g] and transactions

3   with banks, are thus introduced. These are the cases for which the Introducers are competent, bringing them in within the month. But in cases for and against the tax-farmers,[h] the competence is with the Apodectae;[i] and if the amount concerned is ten drachmae or less, these men can decide the case themselves. All other cases of this kind they bring before the law court as cases to be settled within the month.

for instance, exiles who had returned without permission, debtors of the state who accepted a magistracy or acted as jurymen on a law court, etc.

d) A drachma in the mina, that is, one percent a month or twelve percent annually. This was considered a reasonable rate of interest. Loans at a higher interest were not forbidden, but if the interest was higher, the creditor could not make use of the more expeditious procedure of the "monthly" cases.

e) Namely, "and does not pay the instalments when due."

f) "Eranos" is the term for a loan without interest to which several persons contributed in order to help a friend. Such loans were supposed to be paid back in instalments, and recourse could be had to the law courts if the instalments were not paid when due.

g) The Trierarch had to take care of the upkeep of his trireme. At the end of his year of office, he had to hand over the ship to his successor. All sorts of lawsuits could naturally arise, either if the predecessor did not hand over his ship in a reasonably good condition, or if the successor failed to take over at the beginning of his term, etc.

h) The taxes were not collected directly by employees of the state, but by businessmen who agreed to pay the state a fixed sum of money and then collected the taxes from the individuals. See *supra*, Chapter 47, 2.

i) See *supra*, Chapter 48.

53. The Forty[a] are also selected by lot, four from each Tribe; and the other lawsuits are brought before this board. Formerly, there had been only thirty men who gave judgment going from deme to deme. After the oligarchy of the Thirty, however, their number was increased to forty. Up to án amount of ten drachmae, they decide a case all by themselves. But when the value of the claim exceeds this sum, they hand the case over to the

2 Arbitrators.[165] The Arbitrators then take it up; and, if they are unable to bring the parties to an agreement, they make a decision. If then their decision is satisfactory to both parties and they abide by it, the case ends there. If, however, one of the two parties appeals to the law court, they put the testimony of the witnesses, the challenges, and the text of the laws applying to the case into [two] receptacles, one for the documents of the plaintiff, one for those of the defendant. Then they seal them up and attach to them the decision of the Arbitrator written on a tablet. Having done this, they hand them over to the four

3 judges who handle the cases of the tribe of the defendant. These judges take them and bring them before the law court: if the claim is one thousand drachmae or less, before a court of two hundred and one jurors; and if it is more than one thousand drachmae, before a court of four hundred and one. It is not permitted to use laws or challenges or evidence other than those [received] from the Arbitrator, which have been placed [by him] into the receptacles. People become Arbitrators in the sixtieth

4 year of their lives. Their age is apparent from the Archons and the eponymous heroes.[166] For there are ten eponymous heroes of the tribes[b] and forty-two of the age groups (*helikiai*). Formerly, the *epheboi*[c] were registered on whitened tablets under the name of the Archon in whose year they were registered and of the eponymous hero of the citizens who served as Arbitrators in the preceding year. But now they are inscribed on a bronze pillar which is erected in front of the Buleuterium next to the epony-

a) They have the same functions as the "judges in the demes," first instituted by Pisistratus and mentioned in Chapter 16, 5. Cf. also Chapter 26, 3.

b) Cf. *supra*, Chapter 21, 6.

c) Cf. Chapter 42.

5 mous heroes. The Forty take the last of the eponymous heroes[d] and distribute the arbitration cases among the men listed under his name, determining by lot in which case each of them is to act as Arbitrator. And it is obligatory for everyone to carry through the arbitration which has been assigned to him by lot. For the law orders that anyone who does not serve as Arbitrator after having reached the proper age shall be deprived of his civil rights, unless he happens to hold another public office in that year or to be abroad. These are the only persons who are 6 free from this service. If a person is wronged by an Arbitrator, he can indict him before the body of Arbitrators; and if the latter find him guilty, he is deprived of his civil rights according to the laws. An Arbitrator, however, also has the right to appeal, 7 if condemned. The eponymous heroes are also used in the case of military expeditions. When men liable to military service are sent on an expedition, a notice is put up which says that the classes from such and such an Archon and eponymous hero to such and such an Archon and eponymous hero are to participate in the expedition.

54. The following public officials are also selected by lot: the five Commissioners of Roads (*hodopoioi*), who, with the help of 2 state slaves, have to keep the roads in good condition; and ten Auditors and ten Assistant Auditors, to whom all those who have held a public office must render account. For these are the only officials who audit the accounts of the officials subject to this examination (the *euthyna*) and who place the account before the law court.[167] If they prove that someone has embezzled money, the jurymen condemn him for theft, and he has to pay ten times the sum he has been found guilty of taking. If they show that someone has been bribed and the jury finds him guilty, they estimate the value of the bribe, and he has to pay this amount tenfold. If they find him guilty of maladministration of funds, they estimate the amount, and he has to pay simply that amount if he pays it before the ninth prytany; if not, the amount is

d) That is, the class or age group designated by the name of the last of the eponymous heroes.

doubled [namely, for which he has been found guilty]. But where a man has to pay ten times the amount, the amount is not doubled [that is, if he does not pay up before the ninth prytany].

3 They also select by lot the so-called Clerk of the Prytany, who is in charge of the documents and keeps the record of the decrees which are passed. He checks the transcription of all other public documents and attends the sessions of the Council. In former times, he was elected by show of hands, and they used to elect the most distinguished and trustworthy men. In fact, his name is inscribed on the pillars with the records of alliances, grants of proxeny,[168] and grants of citizenship. But now he is selected by 4 lot. They also select another secretary by lot for the recording of laws. He attends the sessions of the Council and makes copies 5 of all the laws. In addition, the people elect by show of hands a clerk whose duty it is to read documents to the people and to the Council, and this man has no other function but that of reading the documents.[169]

6 The people also select by lot ten Commissioners of Sacrifices, called the "*hieropoioi* for expiatory sacrifices," who make the sacrifices prescribed by oracle and who, when it is necessary to obtain favorable omens from sacrifices for an enterprise, make 7 these sacrifices with the collaboration of soothsayers.[170] The people further select by lot ten other Commissioners of Sacrifices, who are called "annual *hieropoioi*." They make certain sacrifices and make the arrangements for all those religious festivals which are celebrated every fifth year,[a] except the Panathenaean festival. The following are the festivals celebrated every fifth year: (1) the mission to Delos[b] — there is also a festival celebrated every seventh year which takes place there — (2) the Brauronia,[c] (3)

a) That is, once in every period of *four* years, since the Greek count is always inclusive.

b) This included the sending of a ship (cf. Plato, *Phaedo* 58c; Xenophon, *Memorabilia* IV, 8, 2) with an official delegation, with a boys chorus, and with gifts for the temple of Apollo. The festival on the island itself included gymnastic competitions and horse races. See also *infra*, Chapter 56, 3.

c) A festival in honor of Artemis, celebrated in the Attic village Brauron.

the Heracleia,[d] (4) the Eleusinia,[e] and (5) the Panathenaean festival.[f] None of these is celebrated in the same [year? place?].[g] But now another festival of this kind has been added, the Hephaestia, which was first introduced in the archonship of Cephisophon.[h]

8   They also elect by lot an Archon for Salamis and a Demarch for the Piraeus, who hold the Dionysian festivals in these two places and appoint the Choregi.[i] In Salamis the name of its Archon is added in public documents.

55. These magistrates, then, are selected by the lot and have the functions mentioned. As to the nine Archons, the way in which they were appointed in the beginning has already been described.[171] At the present, they [that is, the Athenians] select six Thesmothetae by lot and in addition a secretary for them; and also the Archon, the King, and the Polemarch,[172] one of them

2   in turn from each tribe.[173] These magistrates, with the exception of the secretary, are first examined in the Council of Five Hundred; the secretary is examined only in the law court, like the other officials; for all officials, whether they be selected by lot or elected by show of hands, enter upon their offices only after they have passed an examination as to their qualifications.[174] The nine Archons, however, are examined both before the Council and then again in a law court. In former times, a man who had been rejected by the Council could not become an Archon. But now the verdict is referred to the law court, and the latter has the final decision as to the qualification.

3   The questions asked in this examination are: "Who is your father and to what deme does he belong? And who is your

d) A festival in honor of Heracles, celebrated at Marathon.

e) A special festival different from the well-known Eleusinia, which were celebrated every year.

f) Concerning the Panathenaean festival cf. *infra*, Chapter 60.

g) Aristotle says merely "in the same." The most natural interpretation would be "in the same year." But then there must be something wrong with the text as translated above. So far no satisfactory explanation or restoration of what Aristotle intended to say seems to have been found.

h) 329/28 B.C.

i) The Dionysian festivals were connected with theatrical performances. As to the Choregi see *infra*, Chapter 56, 3ff.

father's father, and your mother, and your mother's father, and to what demes did they belong?" Then they ask whether he has an ancestral Apollo and a household Zeus[a] and where their sanctuaries are, whether he has family tombs and where they are, whether he treats his parents well and pays his taxes, and whether he has served on the military expeditions [that is, to which his group had been called up[b]]. Having asked these questions, [the examiner] says: "Call the witnesses to these state-

4 ments." Then, when he has presented his witnesses, [the examiner] asks: "Does anyone wish to bring a charge against this man?" And if there is an accuser, both the charge and the defense are heard. Then the examiner has the Council vote by show of hands, or the law court by ballot. If nobody brings a charge, he puts the matter to the vote at once. In former times one judge only used to cast his ballot into the voting-urn [that is, in this latter case], but now all the judges have to vote about the candidates so that, if a dishonest man has got rid of his potential accusers,[c] it is still in the power of the judges to

5 reject him. After having passed the examination in this way, they [that is, the Archons] betake themselves to the stone on which are the pieces of the victims, the same stone on which the Arbitrators also take their oath before pronouncing their decisions, and on which people called as witnesses swear that they have no evidence to give.[175] Mounting on this stone, the Archons swear that they will govern justly and according to the laws, that they will not accept gifts on account of their office, and that, if they do, they will set up a golden statue.[176] After having taken this oath, they go from that place to the Acropolis and there take the same oath again. After this they enter upon their office.

56. The Archon, the King, and the Polemarch take each two assessors of their own choice; these are examined in the law court before they actually become assessors, and they have to render account[a] at the end of their term.

a) This was one of the prerequisites of Athenian citizenship in the period of democracy.

b) Cf. *supra*, Chapters 42, 49, and 53.

c) By bribing them or putting pressure upon them.

a) Cf. *supra*, Chapter 54, 2.

2   As soon as the Archon enters upon his office, he proclaims
through the public herald that whatever a person possessed before
he entered upon his archonship he will have and possess until
3 the end of his term.   Then picking out the wealthiest men from
the whole body of Athenians, he appoints three Choregi[177] and
assigns them to the tragic poets. In former times he also appointed
five for the comic poets; but now the tribes provide the Choregi
for them.   Then he receives the Choregi who are presented by
the tribes, namely, those for the men's choruses and the boys'
choruses, and the comic choruses at the Dionysia,[b] and for the
men's choruses and the boys' choruses at the Thargelia.[c] (For
the Dionysia there is one chorus for each tribe, for the Thargelia
one chorus for every two tribes, each of the two providing the
chorus alternatively with the other.)   Having met them, the
Archon makes provision for exchanges of property[178] and reports
claims for exemptions [that is, to a law court], as, for instance, if
someone says that he has already performed this liturgy, or that
he should be exempt because he has performed another liturgy
and because the time during which he should be exempt after
this service is not yet over, or that he is not of the required age.
For the Choregus of a boys' chorus must be over forty years
of age. He also appoints Choregi for the festival at Delos and
a chief of the deputation on the thirty-oared boat that carries
4 the young men to that island.[d] He organizes processions: the
one celebrated in honor of Asclepius when the initiated keep
watch in the temple, and the one at the great Dionysia. The
latter he organizes together with ten Supervisors (*epimeletai*).
Formerly, the people elected those ten Supervisors by show of
hands, and they had to pay the expenses of the procession out

b) The Great Dionysia or City Dionysia celebrated in the spring (9.–13.
Elaphebolion, which corresponds approximately to the end of March), at which
the main theatrical contests, especially of tragic tetralogies, took place; to be
distinguished from the Country Dionysia or Rustic Dionysia, mentioned *supra*,
in Chapter 54, which were celebrated in December.

c) A festival in honor of Apollo, celebrated in May, at which singing contests
between choruses, but no theatrical performances, took place.

d) See *supra*, Chapter 54, 7 and p. 129, note b.

of their own money; but now the people select by lot one from
each tribe, and they receive one hundred minae from the public
5 funds for the expenses.   He [the Archon] also arranges the procession of the Thargelia and the one in honor of Zeus the Savior.
He also presides over the contests at the Dionysia and the
Thargelia.   These, then, are the festivals which he organizes.

6   There are a number of criminal and civil lawsuits which come
before the Archon; he conducts a preliminary investigation and
then brings the matter before a law court: namely, action for
ill-usage of parents[e] (in this case anyone can act as prosecutor
without having to fear a penalty),[f] for ill-usage of orphans (these
actions can be brought against the guardians), for ill-usage of
an heiress[g] (these actions can be brought against the guardians
and the relatives with whom she lives), for mismanagement of
the estate of an orphan (these actions also are brought against
the guardians), for insanity (if someone accuses a person of
squandering his property in an insane state of mind), for appointment of distributors (if someone does not agree to a partnership
in the use of property held in common), for the establishment of
a guardianship, for the decision between rival claims to a guardianship, for the exhibition of property or documents,[h] for enrollment as a guardian, and for the decision of claims to inheritances
7 and heiresses.   He also takes care of orphans, heiresses, and
widows who, after the death of their husbands, declare that they
are with child; and he has power to impose fines on those who
commit an offense against persons of those categories or to cite
them before a law court.   He also leases out the houses of orphans,
and of heiresses until an heiress reaches the age of [four]teen,[179]
and takes security for the property leased.   Also, if the guardians

e) "Ill-usage of parents" included neglect to take proper care of them; cf.
Xenophon *Memorabilia* II, 2, 13.

f) In most cases the prosecutor had to pay a penalty if he received less than
one fifth of the votes of the jury.

g) Cf. *supra*, Chapter 42, 5 and p.115, note c.

h) Such actions would be brought if a person was in possession or was suspected to be in possession of property or of documents which another person
claimed as his own or which another person had a right to inspect.

fail to provide the proper maintenance for the children, the Archon exacts it from them.

57. The Archon, then, has to attend to the matters mentioned. The King, first of all, takes care of the mysteries.[a] He does this together with the Supervisors whom the people elect by show of hands, two from the whole body of the Athenian citizens, one from the Eumolpidae, and one from the Ceryces.[b] Secondly, he organizes the Lenaean Dionysia.[c] This festival consists of a procession and a contest. The procession is organized and supervised by the King in collaboration with the Supervisors. The contest is arranged and presided over by the King. The King also holds all the torch-race contests,[d] and, generally speaking,

2 he administers all the ancestral sacrifices. Indictments for religious offenses are brought before him; likewise, disputes concerning hereditary priesthoods. He gives the decisions in regard to all conflicting claims concerning religious privileges[e] which arise between families and between priests. All actions for homicide are brought before him, and he is the one who proclaims that a

3 person is excluded from all customary religious rites.[180] The trials for homicide and infliction of wounds, if a man kills or wounds someone intentionally, including murder by poison, and, likewise, trials for arson, take place in the Areopagus. For these only are held before that Council, while involuntary homicide, attempt at homicide, killing of a slave, a metic, or a foreigner, are offenses which are tried by the court at the Palladium. If, however, a person admits that he has killed someone but claims that he had a right to do so, as, for instance, when he has surprised an adulterer in the act, or if he has killed a fellow citizen in war, by mistake, or in a gymnastic contest, then the trial takes

a) The famous Eleusinian mysteries.

b) See *supra*, Chapter 39, 6 and p. 111, note d.

c) A Dionysian festival celebrated in late January in the district called Limnae. Some of Aristophanes' comedies were produced at this festival.

d) Torch-race contests were held at various festivals in Athens, the Panathenaea, the Thesea, Promethea, etc.

e) The text is not quite clear, but Aristotle seems to refer to religious functions which were connected with special honors for those performing them.

place in the Delphinium. If a man who has gone into exile after an offense which admits of reconciliation is charged with homicide or the infliction of bodily injury, he is tried in the precinct of Phreatus and makes his defense from a boat anchored near the 4 shore.[181] These cases, with the exception of those which are brought before the Areopagus, are tried by Ephetae (?)[182] selected by lot. They are introduced by the King, and the court sits within a sacred precinct in the open air, and, when he hears a case, the King takes off his crown. At all other occasions the defendant is debarred from all sacred places, and it is not even lawful for him to enter the market place. But, on the occasion of his trial, he enters the sacred precinct and makes his defense. When the King does not know who committed the offense, he institutes proceedings against "the person who did the deed."[f] The King and the Tribe-kings conduct prosecution of inanimate things and animals also.[g]

58. The Polemarch makes the sacrifices to Artemis the Huntress and to Enyalius.[a] He arranges the funeral games for those who have been killed in war and the offerings in memory of Harmodius 2 and Aristogeiton. Private lawsuits which are brought before him are those in which metics, *isoteleis*, and *proxenoi* are involved.[183] It is his duty to accept these cases, to divide them into ten groups, and to assign to each tribe one group by lot; and it is the duty of the jurors of each tribe to hand them over to the Arbitrators. 3 However, the Polemarch himself introduces cases against aliens who are accused of acting without their patron or of not having a patron, and also trials concerning estates and heiresses; and, in general, all those actions which, in the case of citizens, are introduced by the Archon, are, in the case of resident aliens, introduced by the Polemarch.

59. The Thesmothetae have, first of all, the function of fixing the days on which the law courts are to sit; then, of assigning the law courts to the magistrates.[184] For, as the Thesmothetae assign

f) That is, against "unknown"; cf. also Appendix, note 180.
g) Concerning this strange custom cf. Plato's *Laws* 873e.
a) That is, Ares.

them, so the magistrates have to use them [that is, for the decision

2 of the actions which they have to take to a court]. They, furthermore, bring before the people: (1) impeachments (*eisangeliai*),[185]
(2) proposals that a man be removed from public office by a vote
of the people (*katacheirotoniai*),[186] (3) proposals that a man be
censured by the people (*probolai*), (4) indictments for a motion
conflicting with the laws (*graphai paranomon*),[a] (5) indictments for
proposing laws contrary to the interests of the state, (6) indictments against *prohedroi*[b] and their chairman, and (7) the accounts

3 (*euthynai*)[c] presented by the generals. It is also the Thesmothetae
before whom are brought all the indictments in which a money
deposit must be paid in [by the prosecutor], namely, indictments
for usurpation of civic rights by an alien, for bribery in connection with the usurpation of civic rights (if a man escapes an
indictment for usurpation of civic rights by bribery), for dishonest
prosecution,[187] for bribery, for fraudulent entry of a person as
a public debtor, for having falsely appeared as a witness to a
summons, for having conspired not to erase or to reenter in
the public records the name of a public debtor who has paid all
that was due, for not having entered the name of a public debtor,[d]

4 and for adultery. They also introduce before the law courts the
preliminary examinations (*dokimasiai*)[e] of all magistrates, the
appeals of those whose claims to citizenship have been rejected
by their demes,[f] and the condemnations handed on by the

5 Council.[g] They also introduce certain private actions, namely,
those concerning commerce and mining, and also actions against
slaves for slandering a free man. They distribute the law courts
both for private and criminal actions among the magistrates by

6 lot.[h] They handle the ratification of international commercial

a) See Appendix, note 90.

b) See *supra*, Chapter 44, 2f.

c) See *supra*, Chapter 54, 2 and Appendix, note 167.

d) These indictments for false entry of public debtors were, of course, directed
against the officials entrusted with this function.

e) Cf. *supra*, Chapter 55, 2.

f) Cf. *supra*, Chapter 42.

g) Cf. *supra*, Chapter 45, 1.

h) See section 1 of this Chapter and Appendix, note 184.

agreements[188] and bring before the law courts the actions which are brought in on the basis of such agreements. They also introduce prosecutions for false testimony instituted by the Areopagus.

7 All the nine Archons, together with the Clerk of the Thesmothetae,[i] select by lot the jurors, each of them selecting those of his own tribe.

60. These are the rules concerning the nine Archons. They [that is, the people] also select by lot ten Commissioners of Games (*athlothetai*), one from each tribe. These men, after having passed the preliminary examination, retain their office for four years. They arrange the Panathenaean procession,[a] the musical contest, the gymnastic contest, the horse race; they provide, together with the Council, the robe for Athena[b] and the prize

2 vases;[c] they also give the olive oil to the contestants. This olive oil is collected from the sacred olives. The Archon levies it from the owners of the farms on which the olive trees grow, three-quarters of a pint from each plant. In former times the state used to sell the fruit; if anyone dug up or cut down a sacred olive tree, he was taken before the Areopagus; and if the Areopagus found him guilty, the penalty was death. Ever since the owner of the farm has been paying the olive oil as a tax, the law has nominally remained in force, but the trial [for its violation] has gone out of use. The oil is now a state charge on the property

3 and is not taken from the individual trees.[d] After the Archon has collected the oil that is due in his year, he hands it over to the Treasurers at the Acropolis; and the Archon is not allowed to go up to the Areopagus before he has handed over the full amount to the Treasurers. The Treasurers keep the oil in the

i) Cf. *supra*, Chapter 55, 1 and note 173.

a) Cf. *supra*, Chapter 54, 7.

b) Cf. *supra*, Chapter 49, 3 and note 163.

c) The prize in the athletic contests was a vase filled with oil, and a garland from the sacred olive trees.

d) That is, though nominally three quarters of a pint are to be taken from each tree, in actual fact, a fixed amount of oil has to be contributed by the estate, even if the number of trees in the estate may have changed since the time when that amount was fixed.

Acropolis for the rest of the time. But at the Panathenaean festival, they measure it out to the Commissioners of Games; and the latter give it to those who have won in the athletic con-
4 tests. The prizes are, for the winners in the musical contests, in silver [money] and gold decorations; for those who have won the contest in physical fitness and beauty (*euandria*),[e] a shield; but for the winners in gymnastic contests and horse races, olive oil. . . .[f]

61. The people also[189] elect by show of hands all the military officers. First of all, they elect ten Generals, in former times one from each tribe, but now from the whole body of citizens; they also assign their duties to them by vote. One becomes commander of the heavy-armed infantry and leads them when they go on a foreign expedition. Another one becomes chief of the home defense; he stays in the country and is in command of all operations when there is war within the borders of the country. There are two for the Piraeus, one of them for Munichia,[a] the other for Acte;[b] and these together are in charge of the defense of the Piraeus. There is one who superintends the symmories;[190] he nominates the Trierarchs and arranges the exchanges of property[c] and brings before the courts the requests for decisions in cases of disagreement concerning these obligations. The remaining Generals are dispatched to whatever business may have to
2 be attended to at the moment. In each prytany a vote is taken to determine whether their conduct of military affairs appears satisfactory;[d] and if they [the people] vote against someone's confirmation in office, he is tried in a law court. If he is found guilty, they fix his punishment or fine; but if he is acquitted, he resumes his office. When on active duty, the Generals have power to have a man arrested for breach of discipline, to discharge

e) This was a contest of military and graceful bearing under arms and on horseback.
f) See Appendix, note 189.
a) See *supra*, p. 109, note a.
b) See *supra*, p. 115, note a.
c) See Appendix, note 178.
d) Cf. *supra*, Chapter 43, 4.

him publicly from the army, and to impose a fine. But they usually do not impose fines.

3   The people also elect by show of hands ten Taxiarchs, one from each tribe. These command their fellow tribesmen and appoint the company commanders (*lochagoi*).

4   They also elect by show of hands two Hipparchs from all the citizens [that is, without regard to the tribes]. These command the cavalry, each taking five tribes. They have the same powers that the Generals have in regard to the heavy-armed infantry. They, too, have to be confirmed in office by a regularly repeated vote.

5   They also elect by show of hands ten Phylarchs, one from each tribe, who command the sections of the cavalry in the same way in which the Taxiarchs command the sections of the infantry.

6   They also elect by show of hands a Hipparch for Lemnos who has charge of the cavalry in Lemnos.[e]

7   They also elect by show of hands a Treasurer of the Paralos and now [or "also one"?] for the Ammon.[f]

62. Of the magistrates chosen by lot there had been formerly one group of those who, together with the nine Archons, were selected from the whole tribes,[a] while another group was selected in the Theseum and divided among the demes;[b] but, since the demes began to sell the offices, they now select those other magistrates also from the whole tribe, with the exception of the Councilmen and the guards,[c] who are still distributed over the demes.

2   The fees received for public services are as follows: the people receive for attendance at the ordinary sessions of the Assembly

e) The Island of Lemnos was settled by Athenian colonists, and an Athenian cavalry corps was stationed there.

f) The two "sacred" ships, which at the time of Aristotle were used for special state services. In former times their names had been Paralos and Salaminia. Whether the papyrus had "now" or a word meaning "separately" seems to be uncertain.

a) Cf. *supra*, Chapter 55, 1.

b) To this group probably belonged the jurors and all those special magistrates who were taken from among the jurors.

c) Probably the ones mentioned *supra*, Chapter 24, **3.**

one drachma and for the "main" meeting[d] nine obols. The jurors have three obols per session, the Council five obols. The Prytanes[e] get an additional obol for their maintenance. Furthermore, the nine Archons receive four obols each for maintenance and have to maintain their herald and a flute-player. The Archon for Salamis[f] receives one drachma a day. The Commissioners of Games[g] are entertained in the Prytaneum during the month of Hecatombaeon, when the Panathenaean festival is celebrated, from the fourth of the month onward. The Amphictyons for Delos[h] get a drachma a day from Delos. The officials sent to Samos, Scyros, Lemnos, and Imbros[i] also get money for their maintenance.

3   The military offices can be held repeatedly, but none of the others can, with the exception of Council members who can belong to the Council twice [in their lifetime].

63. The nine Archons conduct the selection by lot of the jurors for the law courts, tribe by tribe, the Clerk of the Thesmothetae conducting the selection of those from the tenth tribe.[a]   There
2 are ten entrances to the courts, one for each tribe; and twenty allotment machines,[191] two for each tribe; and one hundred chests, ten for each tribe; and other chests into which the tickets of the jurors drawn by lot are thrown. Two urns and a number of staves equal to that of the jurors [to be selected from each tribe] are placed at each entrance. Acorns equal in number to the staves are thrown into the urn. On these acorns are written the letters of the alphabet beginning with the eleventh letter, namely, the "L," using as many [different] letters as there are courts to be filled.

3   All those can serve as jurors who are more than thirty years old, do not owe any money to the public treasury, and have not

d) Cf. *supra,* Chapter 43, 4.
e) Cf. *supra,* Chapters 43 and 44.
f) Cf. *supra,* Chapter 54, 8.
g) Cf. *supra,* Chapter 60.
h) The Commissioners for the funds of the temple at Delos.
i) Military officers sent from Athens to these islands.
a) Cf. *supra,* Chapter 59, 7.

been deprived of their civic rights. If anyone acts as juror who
has no right to do so, information is laid against him, and he is
brought before the law court. If he is found guilty, the jurors
impose on him whatever punishment or fine they think he
deserves. If a fine is imposed, he must be imprisoned until he
has paid both the former debt because of which information had
been laid against him and, in addition, whatever fine the court
has imposed on him.

4   Each juror has one ticket of boxwood, inscribed with his
name, the name of his father, the name of his deme, and one of
the letters of the alphabet up to "K." For the jurors from each
tribe are divided into ten sections, about the same number under
each letter.

5   As soon as the Thesmothet has drawn by lot the letters to be
assigned to the different law courts,[b] the attendant takes them
and affixes to each court the letter which has fallen to it by lot.[192]

64. The ten chests mentioned are set up just outside the
entrance assigned to each tribe. They are marked with the
letters of the alphabet up to K. When the jurors have thrown
their tickets into the chests which are marked with the same
letter as that which is inscribed on their own ticket, the attendant
shakes the chests thoroughly, and then the Thesmothet draws
2   one ticket from each chest. This man[a] is called the ticket-inserter;
he inserts the tickets taken from the chest into the column of slots
which is designated by the same letter as that on the box. This
ticket-inserter is selected by lot so that the same person will not
always act as ticket-inserter and engage in corrupt practices.
3   There are five of these columns of slots in each of the allotment
machines. After he has thrown in the cubes, the Archon draws
the lots for the tribe by allotment machines [that is, first at one,
then at the other allotment machine]. There are white and
black bronze cubes. The number of white cubes thrown in

b) These are, of course, the letters from *L* onward mentioned in paragraph 2.

a) "This man" does not mean the attendant, but the man whose ticket has
been drawn by the Archon. As the following description shows, there are
actually ten such men, one from each of the groups from *A* to *K*.

[that is, into the tube] corresponds to the number of the jurors to be selected in such a way that there is one cube for each five tickets; and the black cubes are handled in the same fashion. As the Archon draws out the cubes, the herald calls those whose lot has been drawn. The ticket-inserter is also one of their 4 number [that is, is one of the jurors selected]. The person who has been called steps forward and draws an acorn from the urn. Then he holds it up with the letter inscribed turned upward and shows it first to the Archon in charge. The Archon inspects it and throws the ticket of the man [selected] into the box inscribed with the same letter as that on the acorn,[b] so that he will go to that court to which he is allotted and not into whatever court he may choose, and so that it may not be possible to bring together 5 in a court the jurors someone may wish [to have in it]. There are lined up at the side of the Archon as many boxes as there are courts to be filled, and each of these boxes is marked by one of the letters which by lot have been assigned to each of the courts.

65. Then he himself [the juror whose lot has been drawn] shows his acorn again to the attendant and then goes inside the grill.[a] The attendant gives him a staff of the same color as the court marked by the same letter which is inscribed on his acorn, so that he is compelled to go into the court to which he has been assigned by lot. For, if he goes into another court, he is shown 2 up by the color of his staff, the courts being distinguished by colors painted on the lintels of their entrances. So he takes the staff and goes to the court which bears the same color as his staff and the same letter as that which is inscribed on his acorn. When he has entered the court, he receives on the part of the state[b] a token from a person selected by lot for this office. Then

b) This shows that the acorns are inscribed with the letters (from L onward) which designate the courts to be filled. Obviously there are as many acorns with the letter, for instance, M, as there are to be jurors from one tribe on the court designated by M.

a) Obviously a swinging gate through which the selected jurors were admitted one by one.

b) The tokens received by the jurors on this occasion had to be surrendered when they received their fees for attendance at the court. They attested their

3 they [take their seats][193] in the court with their staves and acorns after having entered in this fashion. To those who have not been successful in the lottery the ticket-inserters hand back their
4 tickets. The public attendants hand over from each tribe to each one of the law courts the boxes containing the names [of the persons] of the tribe concerned who serve on each of the courts.[c] They hand these boxes over to those persons who have been selected by lot for the task of handing back to the jurors in each law court their tickets, five [?] in number,[194] so that from these tickets they may call out[195] [the names of the jurors] and pay them their fees.

66. When all the courts have been filled, two allotment machines[a] are set up in the first of the courts and also bronze cubes painted with the colors of the courts, and others inscribed with the names of the magistrates. Then two of the Thesmothetae, who have been selected by lot, dump in [into the allotment tubes] the two sets of cubes separately, namely, one of them, the [cubes with the] colors into the one allotment tube, the other, the [cubes with the] names of the magistrates into the other tube. Then the cubes are drawn and the herald announces that the magistrate [whose name was] drawn first will have to work with the law court [whose color was] drawn first, and the second [magistrate] with the second [law court] and [*so forth, so*][b] that no one knows in advance [*which law court he will have to work with*] but [*will be compelled to work with*] the law court which is assigned to
2 him by lot. When the jurors have come [*to the court to which they have been assigned*], the magistrate [*presiding*] in each of the

claim to the payment of these fees from the state treasury. Hence the expression "received on the part of the state."

c) Each of the courts, of course, consists of an equal number of jurors from each of the ten tribes.

a) These allotment machines were obviously different from those described in Appendix, notes 191 and 192. They seem to have consisted merely of two tubes of the same kind as those affixed to the allotment machines of the first type.

b) From here on the papyrus is gravely damaged. Where whole words are missing but can be supplemented with some confidence, we have italicized them and enclosed them in brackets, while suggestions of modern scholars that must remain entirely conjectural have been omitted.

courts [*draws from each*] of the boxes[c] one ticket [*altogether ten*] [tickets representing ten men], one from each tribe, and [*throws these ten tickets*] into another, empty, box. [*Then he draws the lot from*] those; [*of the five*] drawn first [*he assigns one*] to the water-clock,[d] and [*the other*] four he puts in charge of the voting, so that nobody may be able to suborn the man at the water-clock or those in charge of the voting, thus preventing any malpractice
3 in this respect. The remaining five who have not been drawn receive from them[e] the written instruction concerning the order in which and the place where [the jurors from] each of the tribes are to receive, within the court itself, their pay after they have fulfilled their court duties, so that they will stand separated from each other and will receive this pay in small groups and will not crowd together in large numbers in the same place and so be in one another's way.

67. Having done this,[196] they call up the cases. If they handle private lawsuits, they call up the private parties to the suit, taking up four cases, one[a] from each of the types of lawsuits determined by the law.[b] The contestants have to swear that they will speak to the point at issue.[c] If they handle public cases, they call up the public litigants, and they try only one case.
2 There are water-clocks with small outlet tubes; into these [that is, the water-clocks] they pour the water by which the pleadings must be measured.[d] Ten measures are allowed for cases involv-

c) These are the boxes containing the tickets of the jurors assigned to this court from each of the ten tribes. Cf. the end of the preceding chapter.

d) Concerning this water-clock see the following chapter. A photograph of an Athenian water-clock and a detailed analysis of the way in which it worked can be found in *Hesperia*, Vol. VIII, pp. 274ff.

e) That is, the presiding magistrates.

a) This seems to be the meaning, though it is not certain that the papyrus had the word "one."

b) The four different categories of private lawsuits are distinguished in the immediately following section of the present chapter.

c) Cf. Lysias 3, 3; Demosthenes 57, 7 and 59f.

d) That is, the amount of water poured into the water-clock before the beginning of a speech determines the length of time during which the litigant will be permitted to speak.

ing an amount of more than five thousand drachmae and three measures[e] for the second speech; seven measures for those under five thousand drachmae[f] and two [for the second speech]; five measures for those under one thousand[g] and two [for the second speech]; and six measures in the case of rival claims,[h] in which there is no second speech.

3   The man selected by lot to take charge of the water-clock stops the [*water whenever the clerk is going to*] read a [*decree of the people*], a law, the testimony of witnesses, [*or a contract*].[i] [*If, however, the pleadings*] are assigned to proportionate parts [*of the day*],[197] he does not stop the water in the water-clock, but the same amount of water [*is given*] to the plaintiff and to the defendant. The days of the month Poseideon[j] are used [*as the standard*] of the division of. . . .[k] Division of the day into several proportionate parts takes place in cases in which the penalty may be imprisonment, [*death, exile*],[l] loss of civic rights, or confiscation of property, [*and in which the law does not prescribe*] what the penalty shall be.

68. [Most] courts consist of five hundred [jurors]. . . . But when it is necessary . . . [two courts] come together in the Heliaea[a] . . . before one thousand five hundred jurors; that is,
2   three [*courts combined*]. There are bronze voting pebbles, having stems in the middle. Half of these voting pebbles are perforated,

e) The Greek word for "measure" is χοῦς, a measure of not quite three quarters of a gallon.

f) But above one thousand drachmae.

g) The figure is missing in the papyrus, but cf. Chapter 53, 3.

h) For instance, concerning the custody of minors or heiresses, etc.

i) The Greek words for "decree" and "contract" are missing in the papyrus, but would fill the gaps satisfactorily.

j) The month of the Athenian year which, being in mid-winter, has the shortest days.

k) There follow in the papyrus several sentences which are too badly mutilated to be understandable.

l) The words "death," "exile" are supplemented, there being a lacuna of corresponding length in the papyrus.

a) The largest court, which was used when more than one group of five hundred jurors sat together.

half of them are full [non-perforated].[b] When the pleadings are
concluded, the men who have been selected by lot to take charge
of the voting pebbles hand to each of the jurors two pebbles,
one perforated and one non-perforated, in full view of the litigants so that nobody will receive either two non-perforated or
two perforated ones. [*Then the person*] who has been selected
by lot [for this task] takes away [*the staves of the jurors*].[198] In
return for them each of the jurors [*receives*], when he votes, a
bronze [*token*] with the number three on it. For when he returns
it, he receives three obols. This is done to make sure that all
3 will vote. For nobody gets a token unless he votes. [*Two*] urns
are placed in the court, one of bronze, the other of wood; they
can be taken apart [*for inspection*], so that it will not remain
undetected if someone should have fraudulently inserted voting
pebbles before the jurymen are assembled. It is into these urns
that the jurors put their votes. The bronze urn is destined for
the votes which count, the wooden one for the voting pebbles
which are discarded. The bronze urn has a lid which is perforated
in such a way that it lets through only one voting pebble at a
4 time so that the same man cannot insert two. When the jurors
are ready to vote, the herald first asks whether the litigants wish
to protest against the testimonies given.[199] For it [*is*] not
[*permitted*] to enter such a protest after they have begun to vote.
Then the herald makes another announcement, namely: "The
perforated one will count for the litigant who spoke first, the
non-perforated one for the one who spoke second." The juror
takes the voting-pebbles from the lamp-stand,[200] pressing the
stem of the pebble [with thumb and fore- or middle finger][c]
so as not to show either the perforated or the non-perforated
one to the litigants, and throws the one which he wishes to count
into the bronze urn and the one he does not wish to count into
the wooden urn.

69. When all jurors have voted, the court attendants take the
urn containing the votes which count and pour the voting pebbles

b) The voting pebbles which have been found at Athens show that it was
the stems of the pebbles which were either perforated or non-perforated.
   c) *Cf.* Aristophanes *Wasps* 94–96.

on a reckoning board which has as many holes as there are voting pebbles. This is done in order that the votes which are valid may be openly displayed and easily counted, and that the litigants may have a clear view of the perforated and the non-perforated ones. Then the persons who have been selected by lot to be in charge of the voting pebbles count them on the reckoning board, placing the perforated and the non-perforated ones separately. And the herald proclaims the number of the votes, the perforated ones for the plaintiff, the non-perforated ones for the defendant. Whoever receives the greater number of votes wins. But, if the number is equal, the defendant wins. Then again, if it is neces-

2 sary to "estimate" [namely, penalties, damages], they do so by following the same voting procedure, returning the tokens[a] and getting back their staves. For [the speeches concerning] the "estimation," half a measure of water[b] is allowed to each party. Then, when the session of the court has come to an end in accordance with the law, the jurors receive their fees in that part of the court room assigned to them by lot.[c]

a) Obviously the tokens with the figure 3 which they had received in order to make sure that nobody would receive his pay without having voted (Chapter 68, 2 at the end). These tokens must have been returned to the jurors after they voted the second time.

b) See *supra*, Chapter 67.

c) See *supra*, Chapter 66 and Appendix, note 194.

APPENDIX

CHAPTER I.

1) As mentioned in the Introduction (p. 3), the beginning of the treatise is lost. The text preserved in the papyrus begins in the middle of a sentence and toward the end of a chapter. This chapter had obviously dealt with the sacrilege committed by the archon Megacles of the noble family of the Alcmeonidae and with its consequences. A young nobleman by the name of Cylon had tried to set himself up as a tyrant. When his attempt failed, he fled the country and his adherents took refuge in the sanctuary of Athena on the Acropolis. Having left the asylum under a safe-conduct, they were, nevertheless, slain on the order of Megacles and the other Archons near or at the altar of the Erinyes. If, as Aristotle implies, at the time of the trial all those personally responsible were dead, the sacrilege must have been committed many years, or rather decades, before the trial. This assumption in itself does not create any particular difficulty, since it was not uncommon in antiquity that, when, for instance, an epidemic broke out, the cause was found in a sacrilege committed a long time before; and that then, in order to remove the "pollution," a trial was held and a religious purification rite performed. But there are other difficulties.

According to the Olympian list, a Cylon was victor in the Olympian games of 640 B.C. If this Cylon is identified with the main figure of the present story, he must have made his attempt in 632 or 628, since he is supposed to have made it in an Olympian year and since he must have been a very young man when he won the victory in the foot race. If, furthermore, the trial and the "purification" took place before Solon's archonship, as Aristotle implies and Plutarch (*Solon* 13) expressly states, they must be dated in the very early sixth century, though it is strange that by that time all the guilty should have been dead.

Much stranger still, however, if considered in connection with Aristotle's story, are the following facts: In ca. 590 B.C., Alcmeon is said to have led the Athenian contingent in the war against Cirrha (Plutarch, *Solon* 11). At the same time we find Athenian coins with the emblem of the Alcmeonidae.

Finally, according to Aristotle's own account (Ch. 13), the head of the Alcmeonid family was one of the outstanding political leaders in the period preceding Pisistratus' first accession to

149

power. This last statement is especially noteworthy because on this occasion Aristotle makes no mention whatever of the curse. If one accepts Aristotle's story of the Cylonian affair, one would, then, have to assume that, in a very few years after the trial in which the Alcmeonidae were cursed and exiled for all time, they could not only return but could resume their political leadership without difficulty; though nearly a century later, at the end of the sixth century, the curse did acquire political importance (cf. Chapter 20, 2), and though it was still used as a weapon in the political struggle at the beginning of the Peloponnesian War (cf. Thucyd. I, 126/27).

In this connection it may be observed that Isocrates (16, 25f.) tells a story according to which "the tyrants," that is, the sons of Pisistratus, removed the bodies of the Alcmeonidae from their tombs. Since this could hardly have been done without a religious justification or pretense, Isocrates' report seems to indicate that there existed a version according to which the purification of Athens from the guilt of the Alcmeonidae took place, not in the beginning, but in the last decades of the sixth century. If the Cleisthenes, who, according to an inscription published and discussed by B. Meritt in *Hesperia*, VIII, pp. 59ff., was Archon in 525/24, was identical with the Cleisthenes who was responsible for the new constitution introduced in 508/07, as seems very likely, it follows that Cleisthenes was exiled between 523 and 514, for he was in exile in 513. This, then, would make it all the more likely that the purification of Athens took place in that period, as Isocrates indicates, and was used as a political weapon against Cleisthenes at that time. (Cf. also Introduction, p. 23.)

2) There existed a great many different and partly conflicting stories about Epimenides of Crete and his purification of Athens, which is generally assigned to the beginning of the sixth century, though the ancient traditions concerning the chronology of Epimenides are also conflicting. Aristotle supports the version which connects the purification with the Cylonian sacrilege.

CHAPTER 3.

3) The survey of the early history and development of the archonship given by Aristotle in this chapter begins with a period much earlier than the sacrilege committed by the Alcmeonidae. It presents a great many difficulties and problems. According to an almost universal tradition (but *cf.* Plato, *Symp.* 208d), kingship was abolished at the death of Codrus but was succeeded by a long series of archons who ruled for life. It is not quite clear whether Aristotle followed this tradition or wished to express

the opinion that the kingship was abolished under Codrus' second successor Acastus (see *infra*, note 5), the text being somewhat ambiguous. If he meant to follow the general tradition, it is difficult to see in what way the status of the last king Codrus differed from that of his two successors; for they still ruled for a lifetime, the monarchy had never been absolute, and the pole-marchy had been introduced long before. If, on the other hand, one assumes that Aristotle meant to say that the monarchy was abolished under Acastus, it is strange that he does not express his disagreement with the general tradition more clearly. No word, furthermore, is said concerning the question of whether the Polemarch and the Archon proper in the early period also governed for life, which in the case of the Polemarch, who was the actual supreme commander in war, is most unlikely. It is probable that Aristotle himself did not know the answer to the latter question and that the widespread tradition according to which the last king, Codrus, was followed by a series of thirteen Archons, who ruled for life, is a historical construction that originated at a time when reliable knowledge was no longer available. (Cf. also Introduction, pp. 16f and Preface, p. ixf.)

4) In later times, all of the three magistrates mentioned had the title of Archon, being differentiated as the Archon Eponymus (that is, the Archon after whom the year is named), the Archon King, and the Archon Polemarchus. However, in the earlier period (and this is the terminology followed by Aristotle in the present chapter) they seem to have been called simply Archon, King, and Polemarch. The use of this terminology creates an additional difficulty of interpretation. For not in all cases in which Aristotle speaks of king and kingship is it entirely clear whether he speaks of the king as monarch and of kingship as monarchy or whether he speaks of the Archon King and his office.

5) This is the literal translation of what appears to be the text of the papyrus. The text in this form seems to imply that under Acastus the Codridae gave up the kingship, but from then on for some time held the office of the Archon proper. What, how-ever, if this was so, became of the office of Archon King? Was he also chosen from the Codridae? What was then the sense of the separation of the two offices? On the other hand, it seems historically most unlikely that the royal house should have con-tinued in its political functions while giving up its religious func-tions to a man selected from another family, since it was always in relation to the gods that the ancient traditions were most carefully preserved. Many editors, therefore, change the text of the papyrus so that its meaning would be "it was under the

kingship of Acastus that the Codridae gave up those prerogatives which from then on were given to the Archon proper." This certainly makes much better sense historically. But it is difficult to decide whether this is what Aristotle meant to say. (Cf. also Introduction, p. 16.)

6) The expressions used by Aristotle are somewhat vague, and the modern translations of the passage consequently differ widely from one another. The historical evidence shows that the Archon King was entrusted with the ancestral religious functions, while the Archon proper acted as moderator at most of those religious rites which were introduced at a later period. Yet it was not these religious functions that "made the archonship great" but its political functions. Part of these political functions must originally have been performed by the King. (Cf. also the preceding note.)

7) Again the expressions used by Aristotle in this passage are exceedingly vague. Most commentators translate, "it administered the greater and most important part of the government," or something to that effect. This is not only historically wrong but cannot have been meant by Aristotle, as the concluding words of this sentence indicate. The passage must be interpreted in the light of Isocrates' *Areopagiticus* 37, where almost the same terms are used. But Isocrates, in this connection, does not say that the Areopagus dealt with the public affairs, but that it supervised the moral life of the community and saw to it that everybody received his due, both in rewards and punishment. (Cf. also Introduction, p. 17.)

CHAPTER 4.

8) The meaning of these words is rather obscure, since in the preceding chapter Aristotle has described a political development which must have extended over a very long period. Some commentators, therefore, assume that the words "not much later" refer to the Cylonian affair discussed in Chapter I. Concerning this question and the whole problem of the constitution of Draco see Introduction, pp. 8ff.

9) The text at this point is slightly corrupt, making it doubtful whether Aristotle wrote "this" or "his" constitution. (See also Introduction, p. 9.)

10) "Prytanes" in later times was the title of the fifty presiding members of the Council (see Chapter 43). For the old times we have, beside this passage, only one other testimony in Herodotus' version of the Cylonian affair (Herod. V, 71), where the "Prytanes of the Naucrari" are mentioned instead of the nine Archons

referred to in Thucydides' more detailed report (Thuc. I, 126, 8). It is still an open question whether it is permissible to identify Herodotus' "Prytanes of the Naucrari" with the nine Archons (assuming an older terminology), or whether those "Prytanes" had an entirely different function as chairmen of the once important office of the Naucrari (see Chapters 8, 3 and 21, 5), as Herodotus' expression seems to indicate.

11) Because of its more than ambiguous syntactical structure, this is one of the most controversial paragraphs in Aristotle's *Constitution of Athens*. Grammatically, there is no objection to Kenyon's translation: "These officers were required to hold to bail the Prytanes, the Strategi, and the Hipparchi of the preceding year until their accounts had been audited, taking four securities of the same class as that to which the Strategi and the Hipparchi belonged," but the Greek text might also be construed to mean that "the Prytanes, the Generals, and the Hipparchi of the preceding year were required to hold to bail these officers until their accounts had been audited." An explanation of the assumed meaning is difficult and precarious in either case. The translation proposed in our text seems to be more satisfactory. If it is correct, the only necessary assumption would be that the securities for the Generals and Hipparchi of the preceding year, in order to remain valid until the completion of their audit, had to be renewed (in the presence of the "Prytanes" of the new year — whatever these Prytanes may have been).

CHAPTER 5.

12) Since, according to the general tradition, which is also followed by Aristotle, serfdom in Attica was brought about exclusively by the contraction of debts, Aristotle can hardly mean that all those, without exception, who did not belong to the upper class were serfs. But it is quite possible that, in consequence of the ever-spreading distress of the small landholders, which was caused by overpopulation and perhaps also by progressive exhaustion of the soil, the great majority of the poorer people had actually been reduced to serfdom by the time of Solon.

It may also be observed that the resentment of these people was probably increased by two factors. On the one hand, there is some evidence to show that in the period of the monarchy the small landowners, who by that time had not yet been reduced to serfdom, had been considered an integral part of the body politic and had enjoyed the right to vote on major political decisions. A memory of this state of affairs probably survived and made their changed status appear all the more unbearable.

On the other hand, the rapid growth of overseas trade, ship-building, and craftsmanship toward the end of the seventh century would have made it possible for the peasants to leave their farms to take up more profitable professions if, by their indebtedness, they had not been reduced to serfdom and therefore become bound to the soil.

The first factor also explains how the serfs could consider themselves as "the people" of Athens, a term which in the Greek language always implies the possession of political rights. The second factor explains how the simple abolition of debts, effected by Solon, could actually solve the economic problem. For if there had been no new outlet for the peasants, they would soon have become indebted again for the same reasons for which they had become indebted in the preceding period; or, if in consequence of the new rule, which made borrowing on the body of the borrower impossible, they could no longer borrow, they would have been in desperate economic distress.

13) The last word of this quotation is not clearly legible in the papyrus and has been read in various ways by the editors. But the reading κλινομένην makes the best sense, although there seems to be no exact equivalent in English.

14) What Aristotle here calls the middle class is not exactly that which is understood by this term at present. It means rather the "moderately wealthy" or, more specifically, that new class of citizens who engaged in overseas trade. This is also indicated by Aristotle's remark that Solon belonged to the middle class by wealth and occupation (τοῖς πράγμασιν); by this he obviously means that Solon was not a big landowner, which was still considered the most noble status of a man, but belonged to the new merchant class, although he claimed descent from the royal house.

CHAPTER 6.

15) It seems hardly possible that all debts without exception were remitted, especially since trade had already developed to a not inconsiderable degree. But the available evidence does not permit us to establish the exact nature of the measure. At any rate, the immediately following story seems to indicate that the safest way to profit from the seisachtheia was to buy land with borrowed money.

16) The Greek word γνώριμοι is often used by Aristotle to designate the "notables." But it can also mean "friends," "acquaintances." Since in the following sentence it is replaced

by φίλοι, which always means "friends," there can be no doubt as to the meaning of this passage.

CHAPTER 7.

17) By this sentence Aristotle distinguishes between Solon's constitution and the Solonian laws. The laws were inscribed on the Kyrbeis. But it is very doubtful, in fact, impossible, that all the political regulations established by Solon were ever so inscribed. (Cf. also Introduction, pp. 14f.)

18) The translation "higher offices" presupposes that the Greek text, which is slightly mutilated, was μεγάλας (cf. *Politics* 1282 a 41). Most editors read μὲν ἄλλας ("the other offices").

19) The sentence is awkwardly formulated and does not make all points quite clear. The last words indicate that not all the three higher classes were admitted to all the offices mentioned. But Aristotle does not say which of these offices were reserved for which class or classes. According to other ancient authorities, the nine Archons and the Treasurers in the time of the Solonian constitution were taken exclusively from the Pentacosiomedimni, and, in regard to the Treasurers, Aristotle mentions this fact in a casual fashion in Chapter 8, 1.

20) This is obviously a misinterpretation of the epigram, although grammatically it is quite possible to construe the genitive "of Diphilus" with the statue that was dedicated. But since Anthemion's own elevation to knighthood was to be celebrated, the dedication of the statue of another man by Anthemion would have made no sense. Any serious concentration upon the contents of the epigram will result in understanding Diphilus as the name of Anthemion's father. The statue, then, represented Anthemion and not Diphilus. It is, however, by no means certain that Aristotle ever went over his treatise very carefully to check possible mistakes or oversights. (Cf. also Introduction, pp. 11f.)

21) The word used to designate this class is the same as that which designates persons serving in the cavalry. Since a man serving in the cavalry had to supply his own horse and an additional horse for his servant, he had to be a man of some wealth. But Aristotle is undoubtedly right when he contends that by the time of Solon the classes were determined by the amount of income.

CHAPTER 8.

22) With this sentence Aristotle seems to correct a statement made in his *Politics* 1273b 40 and 1274a 16; for in these latter

passages he says simply that under the Solonian constitution the officials were elected (by vote). Practically, at least in the case of the Archons, the difference was not very important, since the lot for the nine archonships was cast among only forty pre-elected men. Isocrates (7, 22) affirms in general that casting the lot for offices, not among all the people but among pre-elected men, was a safeguard for getting only the best and fittest men for each office.

23) The actual procedure in Aristotle's day becomes clear only if we combine this testimony with that in Chapter 55, 1. Each of the ten tribes of that later time selected by lot ten men, and then, again by lot, one of the ten. Of the ten men thus elected, nine would become the Archons of the year, and the tenth would be the clerk of the Thesmothetae. At the same time, it was provided that, in the long run, each of the tribes would have its turn in getting each one of these different offices (the nine archonships plus the office of the clerk of the Thesmothetae). This is indeed a strange procedure which can hardly be explained except as a historical survival from a time when there had been a difference between the two steps in the election. (Cf. also Chapter 22, 5 and note 58.)

24) Again it is necessary to compare the pertinent paragraph in the second part of Aristotle's treatise (Chapter 47, 1) in order to know what actually was done in Aristotle's own day.

CHAPTER 10.

25) This statement seems to contain an implicit polemic against Androtion, the local historian of Attica, who had contended that the diminution of the debts was brought about by a change in the currency. By pointing out that the monetary reforms followed the cancellation of debts, Aristotle tries to show that Androtion's theory cannot be correct. There is a good deal of additional evidence to show that in regard to this point Aristotle is right.

26) The numismatic evidence shows that before Solon the Athenians had used coins of the heavy Aeginetan standard which was attributed to Pheidon of Argos, who ruled over Aegina, and that Solon introduced coins of lighter weight following a standard used in Cyrene, in Corinth, and in Southern Italy. One hundred drachmae of this standard were equal in weight to seventy or seventy-three drachmae of the old Attic standard. This evidence is in perfect agreement with a statement made by Androtion and quoted by Plutarch (*Solon* 15). C. T. Seltman (*Athens, Its History and Coinage*, p. 17) tries to reconcile this evi-

dence with Aristotle's description of Solon's measure by the assumption that by "augmentation of the coin" he meant "augmentation in the bulk of the coinage (that is, of the number of coins in circulation) which automatically resulted from a reduction in the weight of its units." But if Aristotle meant this, the expressions which he uses are certainly very ambiguous and misleading.

On the basis of the numismatic evidence, however, there can be hardly any doubt as to the actual motive of Solon's reforms. Their purpose was probably to facilitate the trade with Corinth and the West.

27) The new talent, like the old one, was divided into sixty minae; but these sixty minae were equal in weight to sixty-three of the old minae. Consequently all the subdivisions of the talent and of the mina, as for instance the stater, which was the fiftieth part of a mina, were proportionately increased in weight. Aristotle expresses this fact by saying that the three odd minae (namely, over sixty) were proportionately distributed over the stater and the other weights. The "old talent" and the "old minae" in this connection are, of course, not identical with the old Aeginetan silver weight units, which were much heavier, but are the trade weights which had been used in Athens before Solon and were now adapted to the new coinage.

CHAPTER 12.

28) Just as the words "noble" and "villain" in early English designate a class distinction, but also include a value judgment and later acquire a strong moral implication, so do the words used by Solon here and elsewhere in his poems. It is characteristic of Solon and his period that he still uses these words to designate the two classes, though he not infrequently uses them also in a moral sense.

29) In this case Aristotle does not quote the whole context. This makes it somewhat difficult to understand the lines which he does quote. But there can be no doubt that Solon again wishes to stress two points: (a) If he had not conceived and carried through the plan by which he tried to give both classes their due, the common people could never have attained the blessings which they now enjoy. Hence, the common people should be grateful to him. (b) Another and more ambitious man in his position would not have tried to prevent a civil war by working out a just settlement, but would have stirred up political passions still more, so that in the resulting turmoil he

could have seized tyrannical power. Hence, the nobles should be grateful to him for having prevented a revolution.

Chapter 13.

30) The words used by Aristotle are usually interpreted to mean "after another interval of the same length." But the more natural translation, according to the Greek idiom, is the one given in the text. This translation seems to make good sense, since the next dated event mentioned by Aristotle occurred 32 years after Solon's archonship (see *infra*, Chapter 14). If this translation is accepted, one avoids a series of chronological difficulties which result from the assumption that Damasias was Archon four years after the second anarchy.

31) It seems that, even as early as the period referred to, many "craftsmen" or Demiurgi owned workshops in which a considerable number of slaves were working under the direction of and for an entrepreneur and mastercraftsman. The Archons chosen from this profession, therefore, may well have belonged to the highest income class.

32) From the indications given, it appears that the party of the Shore was the party of the merchants, shipbuilders, etc., that is, Solon's party; the party of the Plain was the party of the wealthy landed aristocracy; the party of the Highlands or *Diakria* (the mountainous Northern and North-Eastern part of Attica), the party of the poor farmers and of all disappointed groups.

Chapter 14.

33) This is the figure given in the papyrus. Many editors have changed it to thirty-four in order to make it agree with the date given for Solon's archonship by Diogenes Laertius I, 62, on the authority of Sosicrates of Rhodes, namely Ol.46,3 = 594 B.C. But other ancient authorities date the archonship of Solon in 592/91 or 590/89. There is no cogent reason for assuming that Aristotle agreed with Sosicrates rather than with those who placed Solon's archonship in 592/1. In fact, the vague way in which Aristotle determines the time relation between the archonship of Damasias and the preceding periods of "anarchy" would indicate that he himself was not quite sure of the exact chronology (see *supra*, note 30).

Chapter 15.

34) Concerning the figures see *infra*, note 36.

35) This part of Aristotle's story is obviously based in part on Herodotus I, 61, who tells that Pisistratus, when leaving Athens,

went first to Eretria. This explains the "again" in Aristotle, who has not mentioned Pisistratus' first stay in Eretria.

CHAPTER 17.

36) The various figures given by Aristotle for Pisistratus' periods of rule and exile do not quite agree with one another. According to the present passage, the interval between Pisistratus' first accession to power and his death was thirty-three years, nineteen of which he was in actual possession of power. This leaves fourteen years for the two periods of exile. Yet, according to the most natural interpretation of Chapter 14, his first exile lasted eleven years; according to Chapter 15, his second exile lasted ten years, making a total of twenty-one years. Furthermore, since, according to Aristotle, his first rule lasted five, his second six years, his first two periods of rule plus his exiles would have lasted thirty-two years, which would leave only one year for the last period of his rule, though Aristotle clearly implies that the last period was the longest. If, on the other hand, one understands the passage in Chapter 14, which says that Megacles opened negotiations for Pisistratus' return "eleven years later," in such a way as to reckon the eleven years from Pisistratus' accession rather than from the beginning of his first exile, the first exile would still have lasted six years, and the two exiles together sixteen years instead of fourteen; Pisistratus' last period of rule would still have lasted only six years; the total duration, finally, of his actual possession of power would be seventeen years instead of nineteen. The figure of seventeen years for Pisistratus' actual rule is indeed given by Aristotle himself in *Politics* 1315b 32.

It is likely that Aristotle followed two or more different authorities, one of whom was undoubtedly Herodotus. The dates for Pisistratus' accession and for his death are probably correct, at least within the limits of a very few years, but the other dates given are probably derived from rather uncertain calculations. Cf. also Preface p. x.

37) Literally: "from the Argive (woman)." Like Herodotus V, 94 Aristotle implies that Timonassa was not Pisistratus' wife in a legal marriage, because, after the middle of the fifth century, an Athenian could not make a foreigner his lawful wife. But there is no evidence to show that such restrictions existed in the middle of the sixth century, and it is most unlikely that a noblewoman like Timonassa should have consented to enter anything but a fully legal marriage with Pisistratus, and that her relatives

should have considered any other kind of union a reason for supporting Pisistratus politically and militarily.

Chapter 18.

38) With the story told in the rest of the chapter, Aristotle obviously intended to correct Thucydides' account of the assassination of Hipparchus (Thuc. VI, 54ff.). This correction is all the more interesting because Thucydides himself says that he wishes to correct the popular version of the story. Most people in his time, Thucydides states, believed that Hipparchus had been the actual ruler because he was killed by the tyrannicides. But, he points out, Hippias as the elder brother was tyrant (this is also stated by Herodotus V, 55), and Hipparchus was killed because he was involved in a private affair with Harmodius and Aristogeitor. Now Aristotle points out that Hipparchus, though the victim, was not personally involved in this private quarrel, but his half-brother Thettalus was, and that it was merely by accident that the former was the one who was killed. Obviously, there was no reliable tradition, even concerning so outstanding an event of the last quarter of the sixth century. It may be added that it is by no means certain that either the Thucydidean or the Aristotelian version is correct. As to the latter, it is certainly very strange that the tyrannicides should have killed Hipparchus if he was neither the tyrant nor the true object of their wrath, especially since the way from the Acropolis to the Leocoreum, which they had to travel in order to substitute Hipparchus for Hippias, is of considerable length. For a deliberately playful version of the story see Pseudo-Plato *Hipparchus* 228b ff.

39) This remark is again an intended correction of the version of Thucydides, who says (VI, 56–58) that the conspirators selected the Panathenaean festival expressly because on that occasion it was possible for them to carry weapons without arousing suspicion. Thucydides adds that Hippias had those arrested who carried daggers, since the customary weapons carried in the procession were a shield and a spear. Aristotle may be quite correct in his observation that, at the time of the tyrants, no weapons were carried in the procession. But this concerns only one detail in Thucydides' story and is certainly not apt to prove that there was no search for hidden weapons; for men carrying hidden daggers would have been suspected of evil intent even with greater justification at a time when the carrying of weapons in the procession was not usual or was prohibited. So it is a little confusing to find Aristotle criticizing Thucydides' whole story in this perfunctory manner. But Aristotle had to make room

somehow for the probably entirely legendary role given to Aristogeiton in the search for the guilty.

CHAPTER 19.

40) The "hospitality" or *xenia*, referred to in this passage was a generally acknowledged institution or custom among the Greeks of that period. It could exist between individuals and between cities or states, but also between individuals and cities. A special and more official form of this relation between a citizen and a foreign state was the so-called "proxeny." The *proxenos* of a foreign country was expected to entertain outstanding visitors and emissaries of that country in his house and, in general, to take care of its interests as far as this was reconcilable with the interests of his own country. As a representative of foreign interests, the *proxenos* can be compared with a modern consul. There is, however, the important difference that the *proxenos* in this sense was not a citizen of the country whose interests he represented, but a citizen and ordinarily a resident of the state in which he represented the interests of the state whose *proxenos* he was; that is, the *proxenos* of Sparta in Athens, for instance, was not a citizen of Sparta, but a citizen and permanent resident of Athens.

Naturally the *proxenos* of a country was treated with special honors when visiting the country whose *proxenos* he was, and also on any other occasion during which he came in contact with official representatives of that state, even in war. It could also happen that a man connected by ties of proxeny with a foreign state came, for some reason or other, to live permanently in that state. This probably is the origin of the later custom to give the honors and privileges of "proxeny" to especially honored foreigners who took, or had taken, their permanent residence in Athens. These *proxenoi*, however, had not the function of a modern consul, a point that has frequently been missed by modern commentators on Aristotle's treatise (cf. *infra*, Chapters 54, 3 and 58, 2).

41) Cf. *supra*, note 36.

CHAPTER 20.

42) The story of the struggle between Isagoras and Cleisthenes, as told by Aristotle in this chapter, seems, on the whole, derived from Herodotus (V, 66ff.). But Herodotus does not say that Isagoras was a friend of the tyrants. In fact, Isagoras' attempt to set up, with the help of Cleomenes, a council of Three Hundred as a supreme power in the state would rather characterize him as a dyed-in-the-wool reactionary and advocate of a purely aristocratic regime. However this may be, it is a very remarkable

fact that Pisistratus came to power as champion of the poorest classes and that, after his first exile, he was brought back by his alliance with the Alcmeonidae, while his son Hippias, on the contrary, was overthrown by the Alcmeonidae and, according to all reports, seems to have been on less unfriendly terms, to say the least, with the leader of the aristocratic party than with those who wished to give more rights to the people. (Cf. also B. Meritt in *Hesperia* VIII, 62.)

43) These "clubs," or *hetairiai*, were always more or less secret political associations. Both in the period of the tyranny and in the period of Athenian democracy, they were considered the hotbeds of reactionary and oligarchic intrigues against the established government; consequently, both the tyrants and the democracy tried to suppress them. But the internal struggles between different factions within the aristocracy and the oligarchic party seem also largely to have been fought out within these "clubs."

44) See *supra*, note 1.

45) This confirms again that the Council of the Solonian constitution had continued to exist all through the period of the tyranny. Since the "Council" had also existed before Solon (see *supra*, Chapter 4, and p. 3, footnote c), the measure envisaged by Isagoras and Cleomenes would have made the government even more "oligarchic," at least politically, than it had been before Solon.

CHAPTER 21.

46) The fourth year after the overthrow of the tyrants is 508/7, and to this date the archonship of Isagoras is also assigned by other ancient authors. That Cleisthenes began to carry out his reforms in that year is possible on the assumption that the year was named after Isagoras because it began while he was Archon, but that Isagoras was expelled from Athens in his year and was probably succeeded in the archonship by Cleisthenes for the rest of the year.

On the basis of the description of the events by Herodotus (V, 66 ff.), it had been generally assumed that the reforms of Cleisthenes preceded the attempt made by Cleomenes and Isagoras. But Aristotle's story and the reconstruction of the events given above are not irreconcilable with a careful interpretation of Herodotus' version. (Cf. also Chapter 22 and note 55.)

47) The main object of Cleisthenes' reform was undoubtedly to break the influence of the big old families which was exercised through the old tribes. Concerning the question of the new

citizens, we learn from Chapter 13, 5 that immediately after the overthrow of the tyranny there was a revision of the citizen-roll on the ground that many persons participated in the franchise who had no right to it. Since Cleisthenes tried to prevent this rigid investigation, it is clear that it was initiated under Isagoras. Half a century before, those who were afraid of being dropped from the citizen-roll had supported Pisistratus against the other two parties, one of which had been led by the Alcmeonid Megacles. It is characteristic of the position of Cleisthenes that it was he who took up the policy of Pisistratus in regard to the right of citizenship (see also *supra*, note 42). He was supported by those whose citizenship was doubtful, and he did everything to make it secure. This is very plausible. It is also likely that during the tyranny a good many people had acquired citizenship in a not quite regular way and that these also were relieved of their anxieties by Cleisthenes. But apart from a not very clearly formulated passage in Aristotle's *Politics* 1275b 37, which may be based on exaggerated attacks of Cleisthenes' enemies, there is no evidence to prove that he "enrolled many slaves and foreigners in the new tribes," except inasmuch as some of those who had already acquired citizenship may have been suspected of having slaves among their ancestors. In fact, such a policy would have been at variance with the character of his constitutional reforms and might have obstructed his political aims, for to admit slaves to citizenship was always considered a most radical measure and excusable only in the greatest emergencies. (Cf. also *infra*, Chapter 40, 2.)

48) The Greek term $\varphi v \lambda o \varkappa \rho \iota v \epsilon \tilde{\iota} v$ is later used in the sense of "making senseless investigations into the origin of a person or a thing." This later and extended usage is quite understandable if one considers what $\varphi v \lambda o \varkappa \rho \iota v \epsilon \tilde{\iota} v$ in the proper sense must have implied after the Cleisthenian reforms. Obviously the only way of finding out with certainty, whether persons whose ancestors had acted as citizens half a century before could claim citizenship according to the strictest interpretation of the laws, was through the old tribal organizations; and such an investigation became unfeasible after the old organization had been destroyed by the new order.

49) It is clear that, if there had been twelve tribes and these tribes had been identical with the previously existing twelve trittyes, there would have been no rearrangement in the population at all. On the other hand, there is no absolutely compelling reason why the citizens could not have been redistributed over twelve tribes in exactly the same fashion as they were redistributed

over ten tribes, except for the fact that the temptation to carry over some of the bigger units of the old system into the new one would have been greater if this had been made arithmetically possible. In general, one should not forget that in Aristotle's time there existed no reliable tradition that would have explained the details of Cleisthenes' reform. Cleisthenes' preference for the decimal rather than for the duodecimal number system was just as interesting and just as difficult a problem for Aristotle as it is for us, though Aristotle's guesses came probably closer to the historical reality than Herodotus' far-fetched or very vague speculations (V, 66–69).

50) The demes or village communities already existed before Cleisthenes. But it was he who used them as the smallest units in his redistribution of the citizenry in trittyes and tribes, who extended the division into demes to the city, probably making use of the already existing city quarters, and who made it a principle that every citizen must belong to a deme. Since the size of the demes as village communities naturally varied a great deal, the trittyes did not all consist of the same number of demes. As far as can be made out, the number of demes belonging to one trittys varied from one to seven.

51) The Greeks used to call one another by their names plus the names of their fathers. As Aristotle indicates, this would have made it easy to distinguish a newly enrolled Athenian from a native; for, according to Greek custom, the name of the community from which the non-Athenian father originated would have been added to the father's proper name. As Attic literature shows, the people of "good family" continued to call one another by their fathers' names even after Cleisthenes, but, in all official and public affairs, they now were called by their first name and the name of their deme. Gradually, however, it became customary to call people officially by their fathers' names *and* their demes' names, and this is found to be the established practice in the inscriptions of the fourth century. The sentence upon which we are commenting has been pointed out by Kaibel (*Stil und Text*, p. 27) as perhaps the most awkward in the whole book. Aristotle was, of course, quite correct in tracing back to Cleisthenes' reforms two facts of life in the Athens of his own time: (1) that Athenians belonging to the same deme were legally and emotionally attached to one another, and (2) that officially an Athenian was called by his name plus the name of his deme. But one might indeed wish that he had been a little more careful to distinguish between what Cleisthenes actually did, what his

intention was, and what followed as a consequence of a natural development.

52) See *supra*, Chapter 8, 3 and note 10.

53) It is not quite clear whether "all of them" in this sentence means the demes or the founders. Since the demes were certainly localized, it seems that it must refer to the founders. The last sentence in the present chapter shows that there must have been considerably more than one hundred *archegetai*, or founding heroes. Theoretically, therefore, it should have been possible to give every deme a name derived from its founder. But, Aristotle seems to say, not all the founders were still connected with a specific locality which they had founded. Therefore, the names of the demes were sometimes taken from the character of the locality (as is actually the case, for instance: the River, the Hollow, etc.).

54) See the preceding note.

CHAPTER 22.

55) Counting from the archonship of Isagoras, in which year Cleisthenes, according to Aristotle, introduced his reforms, this would be 504/3. But since, a little further down, Aristotle places the same events in the twelfth year before the battle of Marathon (490/89 B.C.), the archonship of Hermocreon must fall instead in the year 501/0. That this is the correct date is also confirmed by the fact that Dionysius of Halicarnassus (*Ant. Rom.* V, 37) gives a different name (Acestorides) as that of the archon of 504/3. The difficulty can probably be solved by the assumption that the reforms of Cleisthenes were not completed in the year of Isagoras (cf. also *supra*, note 46), but extended over three more years, which is very plausible considering the magnitude of the reorganization of the state.

56) This must have been changed not later than 487/76, from which year onward, according to paragraph 5 of this chapter, the Archons were no longer elected by vote; for it is scarcely credible that a man who obtained his office by lot should still have been superior in command to the generals who were elected by vote. Herodotus was obviously wrong (VI, 109) when he thought that Callimachus, the Polemarch of the year of the battle of Marathon (490 B.C.), had obtained his office by lot; and one may also doubt whether his description of the military importance of the office at that time is correct. According to Herodotus' story of the battle of Marathon, the Polemarch had a decisive vote in the council of the army leaders only in the case

of a tie between the votes of the ten elected generals; and his leadership would have consisted in the post of honor on the right wing of the battle-line (VI, 111). This is certainly less than what Aristotle's expression, "leader of the whole army," seems to imply. (*Cf.* Berve, *Miltiades*, 1937 (*Hermes*, "Einzelschriften," Heft 2), pp. 75ff.)

57) Some scholars have argued that Aristotle must be wrong either in stating that the law about ostracism was a part of Cleisthenes' constitution or in dating the first application of the law so late, since it was unlikely that so important a political weapon should have remained unused for such a long time. But cf. B. Meritt in *Hesperia*, VIII, pp. 63ff., who shows that Aristotle's account agrees perfectly with what we learn from Herodotus and from the epigraphic evidence concerning the general political situation in that period.

H. Bloch, in *Harvard Studies in Classical Philology*, special volume (1940), pp. 350ff., points out that part of what Aristotle says about the first ostracism recurs in a fragment from the Atthis of Androtion quoted in the lexicon of Harpocration. Since Androtion praises the leniency of the Athenians in contrast to the cruelty of the Spartans, Bloch believes that the words about the "customary leniency" of the Athenian people are directly taken over from Androtion and do not express Aristotle's true opinion, which was much less favorable to Athenian democracy. However, while Aristotle criticizes Athenian democracy severely, he was quite able to see and acknowledge its better aspects. (Cf. *supra*, Introduction, p. 61.)

58) According to the Solonian constitution, each tribe elected ten candidates for the archonship (forty altogether; cf. *supra*, note 22), from among whom the nine Archons were chosen by lot. "Hence the custom still survives with the tribes that each of them first selects ten by lot, and then they choose, again by lot, from these men" (Chapter 8, 1 and note 23). If Aristotle's expression in this sentence is not directly misleading, the final selection of the nine Archons since the time of Solon must always have been made from a number of men to which each tribe contributed ten men; that is, after Cleisthenes' reform, from among one hundred men. But this is not necessarily a contradiction to the presentation of five hundred men mentioned here, since Aristotle says expressly that the five hundred were elected by the *demes* while the selection by lot was done "tribe-wise" ($\varkappa\alpha\tau\grave{\alpha}$ $\phi\upsilon\lambda\acute{\alpha}\varsigma$), that is, by or before the functionaries of the tribes as such. From the sentence quoted above, we know, furthermore, that the *tribes* selected the nine Archons in two steps, a procedure which in Aristotle's time no

longer made sense, since then each tribe had to select each year
only one of the nine Archons plus the clerk of the Thesmothetae
(Chapter 55, 1).   But, in the constitution based on Cleisthenes'
reform, a preliminary selection of ten men by each of the tribes
was still quite natural.   The whole procedure started within the
demes: the *demes* of a single tribe would present altogether fifty
men to their tribe; from these the tribe would select ten; and the
ten groups of ten men consequently presented by the ten tribes
would be thrown together, so that at the final stage the nine
Archons could be selected from among one hundred men (no
matter whether by vote or by lot).   In this way for each of the
demes and each of the tribes equal chances to get one (or more
than one) of their men into office were secured; but the belief in
the justice of either the vote or the lot had not yet been shaken
to such a degree that the introduction of a mechanical turn, at
least for the single tribes, became necessary.   As late as 399 B.C.,
an accuser of the rhetor Andocides could express himself in the
following way: "Suppose he would participate in the casting of
lots for the nine archonships and would obtain the office of the
[Archon] Basileus" (Pseudo-Lysias 6, 4), which makes it likely
that at that time the mechanical rotation of the archonships
among the tribes was not yet known.

59) The mines of Maroneia belonged to the famous mining
district in the southeast of Attica, where mining had been done
since time immemorial, and are usually called the "silver mines
of Laurium."   Laurium appears to have been used as a general
name for the whole district (Herodotus VII, 144; cf. Thucydides
II, 55, 1; VI, 91, 7).   The Greek verb ἐφάνη means "came to
light" or "showed up," but it is better not translated by "were
discovered," for then a modern reader is inclined to object that
"the mention of the revenue of one hundred talents from the
works comes somewhat suddenly after the first announcement
of the discovery of the mines" (Sandys). Actually Chapter IV of
Xenophon's *Ways and Means* proves that in the old times, when
people had more money, "digging in new places" (καινοτομεῖν)
was frequently undertaken, but that it was done at an enormous
risk; if and when "good work" (καλὴ ἐργασία) was found, "one
became rich" — clearly a case of "striking it rich" — but if it
was not found, the whole investment was lost (*op. cit.* IV, 29).
In other words, the main part of profitless work had to be risked
before and not after an eventual "coming to light" of profitable
mines at a certain place.   It may also be observed that at the
beginning of the same chapter (*op. cit.* IV, 4 and 6) Xenophon
uses the expressions "silver ore shows up" (ἀναφαίνεται) or

"comes to light" (φαίνεται), and "money is found" or "made" as interchangeable.

60) The text of the papyrus says they "must take their residence this side," which does not make sense and is contradicted by the historical evidence; for all the persons ostracized after 481 of whose residence we know took their residence *outside* the points indicated. The insertion of a "not" or change of "this side" to "outside" is therefore necessary.

CHAPTER 23.

61) See *supra*, note 7.

62) *Cf.* Isocrates, *Areopagiticus* 51 and 80–82; *Panathenaicus* 151; and *De Pace* 75–77. See also Introduction, p. 59.

63) The Greek word is "hegemony," which literally means "leadership." In reference to the period with which Aristotle deals in the present chapter, the meaning is that the command at sea against the Persians was transferred from the Spartans and their king Pausanias to the Athenians by a free vote of the majority of the cities which had participated (cf. Thuc. I, 95, 1). Later, however, this "hegemony" became a naval supremacy upheld by force.

64) Attention must be drawn to the fact that here the two outstanding statesmen of the time appear both as "leaders of the people," not one as leader of the noble and one as leader of the "people," as, for instance, Thucydides, the son of Melesias, and Pericles in the period preceding the Peloponnesian War (cf. also the list of the party leaders *infra*, Chapter 28). This designation of Aristeides as one of the "leaders of the people" contradicts Plutarch's statement (*Aristeides* 2) that Aristeides followed an "aristocratic" policy, while his opponent Themistocles sided with the common people. (Cf. also *infra*, note 67 and Introduction, p. 59.)

65) For a more detailed story see Plut. *Aristeides* 23 and *Cimon* 7; cf. also Herod. VIII, 3; Thuc. I, 95; Arist. *Politics* 1307a 2f.

CHAPTER 24.

66) The word used by Aristotle is the same word, ἡγεμονία, which he has used in the preceding chapter. But the following sentences depict the transition from the "leadership" in the confederacy to the control of the "empire" into which the confederacy was gradually converted. Aristotle marks this transition also by replacing the word "hegemony," or leadership, by the word ἀρχή (rule, or empire) in the second paragraph of this chapter.

67) There was a widespread ancient tradition which depicted Aristeides as a conservative statesman, advocate of an aristocratic order (see also *supra*, note 64), and personal friend of the leaders of the aristocratic party, or at least as the leader and representative of the peasants and the country folk in contrast to the forward-looking and progressive Themistocles, the leader of the common people in the city. Traces of this tradition can be found as early as the second half of the fifth century, and it is dominant in later times, as shown in Plutarch's life of Aristeides.

In contradiction to this tradition, Aristotle emphasizes that the most revolutionary changes in the political and economic structure of the Athenian state originated with Aristeides, and that, likewise, the conversion of the Athenian sea-confederacy into an empire was largely his work. That in this respect Aristotle is likely to be right is confirmed by the fact that even Plutarch (*op. cit.* 21 and 25) has to report that some democratic innovations in the constitution were enacted on the initiative of Aristeides and that the latter had a share in the creation of the empire, though he is anxious to explain that in these cases Aristeides acted merely under the pressure of circumstances.

It must, however, also be pointed out that in the present chapter Aristotle describes a development which reached its completion only several decades after the death of Aristeides.

68) See *supra*, note 63.

69) The Greek text reads: "From the tributes ($\varphi\acute{o}\rho o\iota$), the internal levies, and the allies." Since the $\varphi\acute{o}\rho o\iota$ came exclusively from the allies, this reading can hardly be correct, though it is true that the allies made some indirect contributions to the Athenian treasury, in addition to the direct tributes, for instance, by market-dues, court-fees, etc. It is, therefore, likely that the words "and the allies" are a gloss which has penetrated into the text.

70) The judges did not receive any pay before the time of Pericles. But this is quite in agreement with the fact that Aristotle in this chapter describes the results of a policy originated by Aristeides, though many of the consequences became apparent only at a much later date (cf. *supra*, note 67).

71) It seems likely that the figure 700 in this place is due to a mistake of a copyist who inadvertently repeated the preceding figure. Had the two figures actually been the same, Aristotle would have expressed this differently.

72) The Greek text reads: "other ships carrying the tributes ($\varphi\acute{o}\rho o\iota$), that is, 2000 men." Since this does not make sense, the word $\varphi\acute{o}\rho o\upsilon s$ is probably to be changed to $\varphi\rho o\upsilon\rho o\acute{u}s$, meaning

the guardsmen who are mentioned *infra*, Chapter 62, 1, as selected by lot.

CHAPTER 25.

73) That is, all those powers and functions which it had after the Persian Wars, except those which it had from the very beginning. It was believed that originally the Areopagus had the jurisdiction in cases of homicide, though Aristotle in the first extant chapters of the present treatise credits the Areopagus with criminal jurisdiction in general. A large part of this, however, had since been taken over by other courts and to some extent by the Assembly of the People. The additional privileges of which the Areopagus was now deprived included, above all, the guardianship of the laws and the superintendence of public morals.

74) The whole story of Themistocles' participation in Ephialtes' successful attempt to deprive the Areopagus of its power, as told in this chapter, is very strange, to say the least. Since it presupposes that Themistocles was still in Athens in 462 B.C., it is also at variance with Thucydides (I, 137), who dates Themistocles' flight to Persia in the time of the siege of Naxos, earlier than the battle at the Eurymedon, which is dated in 466 B.C. No other ancient author, including Plutarch (*Them.* 23), who quotes Aristotle's treatise for the assassination of Ephialtes, makes any reference to the story. Some scholars have concluded, therefore, that this part of the chapter is an interpolation and was not written by Aristotle. But the style is the same as that of the rest of the treatise.

CHAPTER 26.

75) The expression used by Aristotle is sometimes also used to designate the "higher classes." But, a little farther on in this chapter, he uses the same term to designate the "better men" both of the wealthy and of the poorer classes. The context shows that he means, essentially, people who are moderately conservative and interested in the preservation of the existing social and political order. He seems to imply that, in the period following the Persian Wars, such "conservative" citizens could be found in all classes, not only among the so-called better classes.

76) The Greek text says "rather young." But this is at variance with the fact that Cimon had fought in the battle of Salamis (480 B.C.) and had been in command in the battle of the Eurymedon (466 B.C.). By addition of one letter, however, one can replace the word νεώτερος, "rather young," by the word

ἐνεώτερος, which sometimes means "shy," "inhibited," and which in Pseudo-Plato's *Alcibiades minor* 140c is used specifically to designate a man who is not a good speaker. This is more in agreement with what we hear about Cimon from other sources.

77) Literally, "the majority had perished in the war." Most commentators understand this to mean that the "masses" or "the multitude" had suffered greatly in the wars. But though it is true that *hoi polloi* can also mean "the masses," it would be strange to say that the masses had perished in the war, and it would also be inconsistent with the statement, made at the end of this chapter, that the number of citizens had greatly increased. Above all, however, the statement made a little further down, that "the better men" both of the wealthy and of the common people were decimated by the war, proves beyond doubt that also in the present sentence Aristotle refers to these "better men" and not to the masses. The implication is, of course, that these "better men" would form a larger proportionate part of the army and the expeditionary forces than of the citizenry as a whole, and, therefore, suffered proportionately greater losses.

78) The papyrus, instead of "except in so far as," has a strong "but," which does not make sense. Our translation follows a suggestion originally proposed (but later abandoned) by Blass. If one inserts one letter, the word ἀλλ' (ἀλλά) = "but" is replaced by the expression ἀλλ' ἤ, which means "except in so far as."

Chapter 27.

79) It is noteworthy that in order to understand "after this" correctly, one must not fix one's attention on the last sentence of the preceding chapter. The formulae of transition from one main section of this treatise to the next one generally refer to the principal contents of the preceding section, and not to details that may have been mentioned at its end. Sometimes this tends to obscure the continuity of the narration (cf. the beginnings of Chapters 21 and 34); in other cases Aristotle showed more consideration for his reader, as, for instance, at the beginnings of Chapters 28, 29, and 41.

80) For the connection between the development of sea-power and the increasing political influence of the common people in Athens cf. Pseudo-Xenophon, *Government of Athens* 1, 2 and Aristotle's *Politics* 1274a 12–15.

81) There was a great variety of such regular public services or "liturgies," which were obligatory for the wealthy citizens of Athens: for instance, the arrangement of public festivals, the fitting out of warships, the superintendence of athletic training

schools, etc. In the prosperous times of the fifth century, many wealthy Athenians vied with one another in performing these public services as brilliantly as possible and at great expense, some of them even ruining themselves financially.

82) This is Sandys' translation of the pointed expression. Demosthenes (*Third Olynthiac* 31) applied it to the same practice as it was still used by the politicians of his time: "and what tops everything, you [namely, the people] have to be grateful to them [namely, those politicians] for what is your very own." More explicit, but not less pungent, is what Aristophanes in his *Wasps* (performed 422 B.C.) makes Bdelycleon say (v. 684f.): "If somebody lets you have the three obols [that is, the pay for the dicasts], you are grateful, [forgetting that these are] three obols which you yourself have acquired by toiling and suffering all the hardships at sea and in the land-battles and sieges."

CHAPTER 28.

83) This shows that Aristotle was not an enthusiastic admirer of Pericles. (Cf. also Introduction, p. 59.)

84) Cf. *supra*, note 67.

85) The nature of the "distribution of two obols" (διωβελία) is still controversial. One possible explanation is that it was a daily allowance of two obols to the needy, introduced as a war emergency measure. It may also have been — and this is perhaps more in accordance with Athenian traditions — simply a (limited) restoration of fees, indemnities, or salaries for any kind of civil service; for we know that in the first "good" time after the overthrow of the Four Hundred the principle was upheld that nobody should receive payment for any kind of civil office (Chapter 33, 1; Thuc. VIII, 97, 1). In any case, the *diobelia* was introduced soon after the overthrow of the Four Hundred; according to contemporary inscriptions (*Inscr. Grae.* I², 304), it was already practised in 410/9 B.C. and in the following years, and it was still in existence after the battle at the Arginusae (406 B.C.), as we see from Xenophon's *Hellenica* (I, 7, 2) and Aristophanes' *Frogs* (140ff.). During the short regime of the "Thirty" it was probably abolished like other specifically democratic features of the Athenian political order. After that it must have been restored, for it seems chronologically impossible that Callicrates' promise and the following development, hinted at in the present passage of Aristotle's *Constitution of Athens*, could have taken place before the restoration of the democracy in 403 B.C. Aristotle mentions the *diobelia* also in his *Politics* (1267b 1ff.), on the occasion of an argument concerning the equalization of

property: "furthermore, human baseness is insatiable; first, the comparatively small pay of two obols (διωβελία μόνον) is enough; but when this has become customary [πάτριον, that is, 'ancestral'; cf. Aristophanes' *Frogs* 142!], men always want more, until there is no limit any longer; for it is the nature of desire to be limitless, and the many live only for the gratification of desire." According to the passage in the *Constitution of Athens*, Callicrates' promise of a third obol made an end to the not yet very extravagant distribution of *two* obols; and, from the passage of the *Politics* quoted above, we learn that the first steps in the wrong direction will eventually lead to something far worse, namely, unlimited wasting of public funds. This can scarcely have been anything but the fourth-century institution of the so-called "Theoric Fund" and the development that culminated in the notorious law which reserved all surplus of public revenues for public entertainment of the masses. But at the same time it must be emphasized that there is no evidence for the assumption that Cleophon's introduction of a *diobelia* in 410 B.C. meant nothing but free admission to the theatre for the needy, although it is true that the price of a seat in the theatre was two obols and that (perhaps since the time of Pericles) this sum was supplied by the state for citizens who applied for it.

86) This cliché was applied by Xenophon to the accusers of the generals in command at the Arginusae, especially to a certain Callixenus (*Hellenica I, 7, 35*). Aristotle seems to have been confused by the fact that Xenophon, in this connection, happens to mention Cleophon's death. But it was certainly not the "people" who were responsible for Cleophon's death (Lysias 13, 7ff.; 30, 10ff.). Of Callicrates' death we know nothing.

CHAPTER 29.

87) This emergency committee (or committee of the Probuli), which has not been mentioned by Aristotle before, consisted, according to Thucydides (VIII, 1), of ten elder statesmen, who were elected immediately after the news of the disaster in Sicily had arrived in Athens (in the late fall of 413 B.C.). According to the passage quoted, they were elected to prepare measures to meet the present emergency. In VIII, 67, Thucydides says that, in the spring of the year 411, ten Syngrapheis (συγγραφεῖς), that is, commissioners appointed to draw up laws, were elected with full powers to make proposals for a new constitution. These ten Syngrapheis Thucydides credits with the first proposal which Aristotle ascribes to the thirty commissioners. Thucydides seems to have relied on a report which did not make clear that the

"ten men" were actually the ten Probuli, and only part of the commission of thirty who were entrusted with the task of drawing up a new constitution.

88) This investigation into the ancient laws seems to have continued after the overthrow of the Four Hundred (see Chapters 31ff.); a committee of Anagrapheis remained in office until the dissolution of the democracy in 405 B.C. (cf. Lysias, *contra Nicom.* 2 and 29).

89) Concerning this question see Introduction, pp. 18 and 61.

90) The technical term is γραφὴ παρανόμων. This kind of indictment could be brought against a person who either had violated the rule of procedure when bringing a proposal before the Assembly of the People, or had proposed a law or a decree which could be construed to be at variance with the fundamental principles of the constitution.

91) Thucydides (VIII, 65,3) says: "not more than five thousand." Apart from this, Thucydides uses almost exactly the same words as Aristotle.

CHAPTER 30.

92) The statement that the five thousand elected one hundred men from their own number seems to be contradicted by the statement made a little further down that the five thousand were only nominally selected (Chapter 32, 3), and by a passage in Thucydides (VIII, 93, 2) which says that, in a later phase of the development, the Four Hundred finally promised to make public who the five thousand were. Thucydides (VIII, 92, 11) says that the Four Hundred were anxious that the five thousand should not exist and yet their non-existence not be apparent. Through the pseudo-Lysian speech, *Pro Polystrato*, which seems to have been written in 410/09 B.C., we become acquainted with a man who was a member of the board of a hundred men which, according to the last sentence of Chapter 29 of Aristotle's treatise, was appointed to select the five thousand and to make a list of them. Of this Polystratus it is affirmed (*op. cit.* 13) that he put nine thousand men on the list instead of five thousand, in order to please as many as possible of his fellow citizens. He was also a member of the Council. On the basis of this evidence, it appears certain that the hundred men mentioned by Aristotle at the beginning of Chapter 30, who drew up the new constitution, were supposed to act in the name of the five thousand and to have been selected by them, but that, nevertheless, it was not clear who belonged to the five thousand, and who did not. It

follows that the "election" of the hundred by the five thousand must have been, at least partly, a fake, and the drafting of the constitution of Chapter 30 by the one hundred probably also, since a document of this kind must have actually been drafted by a much smaller committee. What happened in fact cannot be known in detail. But since Thucydides stresses again and again that the population was utterly confused and intimidated, it cannot have been too difficult to arrange what was supposed to be a vote by the five thousand, even though it was not determined who they were.

93) Officially, these one hundred men, supposed to have been elected by the five thousand for the purpose of drawing up the new constitution, cannot have been the same committee as that of the one hundred men (ten from each tribe), mentioned at the end of Chapter 29, who were elected to make up the list of the five thousand. But since everything was obviously arranged by a group of men who wished to restrict actual participation in the political decisions to as few people as possible, it is quite likely that the men serving on this second board of one hundred men were largely identical with those serving on the first board.

94) If one combines this with what Aristotle says a little further on about the creation of four Councils, it becomes clear that all those of the five thousand who were over thirty years old were supposed to serve on the Council, but not all of them in the same year. They were to be divided into four equal sections, probably, at least partly, by lot; and then the lot was to be cast to decide which section would rule in the first year, which in the second, and so on. From this it follows that these four councils could not have had four hundred members each, as many scholars have assumed, though Aristotle does not make any such statement anywhere (a story told by Thucydides VIII, 93, 2, which may be adduced in favor of the assumption that there were to be four Councils of Four Hundred each, is probably to be explained otherwise; cf. *infra*, note 103), but that their number was to be left open and to be determined by the number of men over thirty years old which would be found among the "five thousand" after the list of the latter had finally been settled. It follows further that under this constitution there would have been no Assembly of the People (or of the five thousand) in addition to the Council of each year, but the latter would have had, at least legally and officially, the final decision in everything; though the provision mentioned later, that each member of the Council could bring with him other men from the same age class (out of

the five thousand, of course), would have made it possible actually to assemble in the Council something like a complete assembly of all the five thousand above the age of thirty.

95) The exact meaning of this rule is not clear at first sight. The number of magistrates enumerated in the preceding sentence is about one hundred. Hence the number of members of the Council, even if this Council was to consist of one fourth of the five thousand over thirty, is only seven to eight times as great, at most. Consequently, it does not seem likely that out of this number, first, a smaller group, at least of two hundred to three hundred, was to be chosen, and then out of these the *circa* one hundred higher magistrates. It seems much more probable that the preliminary selection was to be made for each of the offices or groups of offices separately; that is, first, a preliminary election of candidates for the archonship; then, after the Archon or Archons had been chosen from this group, a preliminary election of candidates for the next office, and so forth. The details of such a procedure may be imagined after the model of Plato's *Laws* 753b-d, where the problem of an election of thirty-seven "Guardians of the Law" by and from 5040 citizens is solved in the following way (in Jowett's translation):

> All who are horse or foot soldiers, or have seen military service at the proper ages when they were severally fitted for it, shall share in the election of magistrates; and the election shall be held in whatever temple the state deems most venerable, and everyone shall carry his vote to the altar of the God, writing down on a tablet the name of the person for whom he votes, and his father's name, and his tribe, and ward; and at the side he shall write his own name, in like manner. Anyone who pleases may take away any tablet which he does not think properly filled up, and exhibit it in the Agora for a period of not less than thirty days. The tablets which are judged to be first, to the number of three hundred, shall be shown by the magistrates to the whole city, and the citizens shall in like manner select from these the candidates whom they prefer; and this second selection, to the number of one hundred, shall be again exhibited to the citizens; in the third, let anyone who pleases select whom he pleases out of the one hundred, walking through the parts of victims, and let them choose for magistrates and proclaim the seven-and-thirty who have the greatest number of votes.

96) This seems to imply that not all of the Hellenotamiae were actually concerned with the handling of the money at the same time. Probably there was a rotation of duties.

97) In the Greek text, the word here translated by "term" is λῆξις, which, after the preceding words τὸ λαχὸν μέρος ("that section which would obtain it by lot"), can mean only "apportionment by lot," "allotment" (cf., *e.g.*, Plato, *Laws*, 740a). The wording of the document which Aristotle follows was obviously not very clear, but the idea must have been that, according to the decision of the lot, each of the four sections was to serve as Council for one of four years (cf. also note 99). One may imagine that the lot drawn first would mean service as Council for the first year, the lot drawn second, for the second year, and so forth. As we learn later (paragraph 5), this casting of lots was to be administered by the nine Archons. At its first occurrence, in the present sentence, λῆξις cannot possibly be understood as "section of a body, determined by lot" (Liddell-Scott, New Edition), since the use of lots by the "hundred men" for the purpose of forming the four sections of citizens, which indeed is prescribed in the following sentence, has not yet been mentioned. Accordingly, the reference in the last sentence of Chapter 31 to the "four λήξεις" must mean the four "terms" rather than the four "sections."

98) Since the allegedly one hundred authors of this document can hardly have appointed themselves to this function, the simplest explanation would be that the authors of the new constitution were thinking of the hundred men (ten of each tribe) mentioned by Aristotle at the end of Chapter 29; but cf. *supra*, note 93.

99) Various attempts have been made to give meaning to the words "and for one year" at this place, by adding one or more words either before or after the word βουλεύειν, with which in the text of the papyrus the next sentence begins, and by including this word in the sentence by which it is preceded rather than in the sentence by which it is followed. But none of these attempted restorations is satisfactory, since, on the one hand, the word βουλεύειν (in the sense "to resolve to do," cf. Thucydides VIII, 58, 2) is necessary to the sentence in which it is found, and since, on the other hand, the limitation "for one year" has no direct relation to what the "hundred men" are supposed to do. But the meaning of the preceding passage about the "four Councils," in which βουλεύειν means "to serve as Councilors" would be much clearer if it were expressly stated that the service was "for one

year." A possible explanation for the confusion in the text of the papyrus seems to be that a marginal note: "and the service in the Council was to be for one year," which belonged to this passage, was found in Aristotle's manuscript and that, by a copyist's mistake, the words "and for one year" were inserted where βουλεύειν occurs for a second time.

100) Here we finally learn who was to direct the casting of lots in order to determine which of the "four Councils" would serve in which year. (Cf. note 97.)

CHAPTER 31.

101) These indefinite terms say nothing about the occasion, much less about the date, at which the new constitution described in Chapter 30 is to become valid. This seems to indicate that the managers of the revolution of 411 held out this constitution as a promise for the future, but were determined to retain their power under the provisional arrangement as long as possible, an assumption which is confirmed by the fact that in Chapter 31 provision is made for a government which is to be in office all through the year 410/09. (Cf. also *infra* and Introduction, p. 25.)

102) This probably refers to the existence of a Council of Four Hundred under the Solonian constitution (cf. *supra*, Chapter 8, 4). It must also be observed, however, that by now all parties had become accustomed to the claim that they were restoring or going to restore "the ancestral constitution." (Cf. also *infra*, Chapter 35 and Introduction, pp. 15,18.)

103) Thucydides (VIII, 67, 3) says that the Council of Four Hundred which actually governed in the four months of the oligarchic regime was constituted in the following way: first, five chairmen (πρόεδροι) were elected. Then, these five chairmen selected one hundred men and then each of these one hundred coopted three more members, so constituting a Council of Four Hundred. It is generally assumed that this report of Thucydides describes the exact procedure by which the Council was elected from a larger number previously elected by the tribesmen, as provided for in the constitution described by Aristotle in the present chapter. But it is doubtful whether this explanation is correct. Though the constitution described in the present chapter is in itself a provisional constitution for the immediate future, it contains provisions of a still more preliminary nature, namely the election of ten generals who are to serve until the Council of Four Hundred will actually be established and will be able to elect ten generals with full powers for the coming year. On the other hand, it appears, both from Thu-

cydides and from the dates given by Aristotle in Chapter 32, 1, that a Council of Four Hundred was established almost at once, in which case it can hardly have been actually selected according to the complicated procedure prescribed by the interim constitution. It seems likely, therefore, that the provisional constitution described in this chapter served a double purpose: (a) to give some kind of sanction to a government which had already been established in a rather arbitrary fashion, and (b) to promise a somewhat less arbitrary method of establishing the Council in the near future. This would also explain the passage in Thucydides VIII, 93, 2 (see *supra*, note 94), which says that the present rulers, when getting into trouble, promised actually to appoint the Councils of Four Hundred from the five thousand in the following years. (Cf. also W. S. Ferguson in *CAH* V, pp. 329ff. and the Introduction, p. 26.)

104) *Cf.* Plato, *Politicus* 301a; Aristotle, *Politics* 1292a 4ff.

105) See *supra*, note 94.

106) "They" seem to be the five thousand, since they are differentiated from the Council. But since, according to Chapter 32, 3 and Thucydides VIII, 92, 11 the five thousand were never actually constituted, this also seems merely a sanction of an election which had taken place in an irregular fashion. (Cf. *supra*, note 92.)

107) This obviously refers to that part of the final constitution, which is described in Chapter 30, 2.

108) This second mention of the Councilors and the Generals in the same sentence seems due merely to the perplexing syntax of the Greek text, which, without such repetition, could have been misunderstood to mean that these officials were to be freed, even in regard to other offices, from the restriction forbidding anyone to hold the same office twice.

109) "Ordinary citizens": in Greek simply ἀστοί. This word appears to have been used here to designate the rest of the Five Thousand as distinct from the Four Hundred, because, unlike πολῖται, it does not necessarily imply active participation in the administration of the state.

110) Only in this last sentence has the Greek text preserved the direct discourse of the original document. In other words, Aristotle finally preferred to quote a most intricate sentence literally.

CHAPTER 32.

111) See *supra*, Chapter 30, 1 and note 92.

112) According to Chapter 29 a board of Thirty had proposed

to hand over everything to the five thousand, and according to Chapter 30, 1 this proposal had been ratified by the people. Upon this the five thousand had chosen a board of one hundred, and this board had drafted both the final constitution for the future described in Chapter 30 and the interim constitution of Chapter 31. Accordingly, these drafts should then have been ratified by the five thousand; and it is strange that Aristotle says, instead, that they were ratified by the people. The assumption made by many scholars that Aristotle actually meant to say that the constitution was ratified by the five thousand and expressed himself inaccurately does not solve the problem, since, according to Thucydides (VIII, 67, 3), the establishment of the Council of Four Hundred was accepted by an Assembly of the People on the Colonus, at which the Committee of Thirty presented its proposals and which, both on the basis of the terminology used and from the whole context, cannot have been an assembly of the five thousand, which were not yet determined. All this seems to confirm the assumptions made in notes 92, 101, and 103.

113) Thargelion and Scirophorion are the last two months of the Attic year, the former corresponding roughly to May/June, the latter to June/July. The interval, then, between the dissolution of the democratic Council of the old year and the term on which the Council for the new year should have entered on its office is only one month. It may be observed that, according to Thucydides VIII, 67–69, the democratic Council of Five Hundred continued to sit in the Council house for a few days after the election of the new Council of Four Hundred, until it was ejected by force.

114) See *supra*, Chapter 30 and note 92.

115) See *supra*, Chapter 31, 1, and note 103.

CHAPTER 33.

116) In actual fact, the number of those capable of providing their full military equipment for service in the army was considerably greater than five thousand (cf. note 92). We learn from Thucydides VIII, 97, 1, that from then on all those who fulfilled the military requirement were *ipso facto* considered members of the five thousand so that the figure lost all meaning and became a mere synonym for what otherwise was called the ὅπλα παρεχό-μενοι (those who were able to provide their own heavy equipment for military service). Cf. also the succeeding note.

CHAPTER 34.

117) Most commentators assume that this sentence refers to the five thousand, that is, the government of the Five Thousand

which followed the government of the Four Hundred. It must be observed, however, that in this book the sentences with "then" (in Greek μὲν οὖν) which are found at the beginning of a chapter never continue the narration (as would be the case here if the Five Thousand were referred to) but always give a summary of the main event told in the preceding chapter. This main event is the dissolution of the rule of the Four Hundred, and to it the sentence must refer, not to the government that followed. The latter is mentioned only in the last sentence of the preceding chapter (cf. *supra*, note 79), and mentioned so favorably that, if the first sentence of Chapter 34 actually had been intended to be the statement of *its* short-lived existence, at least a strong adversative conjunction would have been necessary.

In Chapter 41, in which the successive constitutions of Athens are enumerated, the restoration of democracy follows directly upon the overthrow of the Four Hundred. There is no intermediate constitution of the Five Thousand. One must therefore assume that the rule of the Five Thousand which followed the Four Hundred was identical with the restoration of democracy or, gradually and insensibly, led over to the full restoration of democracy. For the change from the rule of the Four Hundred to that of the Five Thousand was sudden and so incisive — it is identified by Thucydides with the overthrow of oligarchy and resulted in the flight of the leading oligarchs from Athens — that Aristotle could not possibly have identified these two constitutions.

That, on the other hand, the transition from the constitution of the Five Thousand as established immediately after the overthrow of the Four Hundred to full democracy was gradual and more or less unnoticeable is confirmed by the fact that neither Thucydides nor Xenophon nor Aristotle nor any other author dealing with the period mentions the date or gives any indication of the time when full democracy was restored. Thucydides (VIII, 97, 2) says that under the new constitution following the overthrow of the Four Hundred, "at first" public affairs were handled well, indicating that there was a gradual change. He speaks of many "Assemblies of the People" which were held immediately after the overthrow of the Four Hundred, which seems to imply that under the new regime the Assembly of the People again had the supreme power in the state. And, indeed, if all those who were capable of providing arms were admitted to the Assembly, with no list to restrict their numbers, the transition to the old form of the Assembly was easy. Likewise, if all the heavy-armed were admitted to the Assembly, there must have also been a Council to deal with current affairs; and the only Council of which we hear after the overthrow of the Council of Four Hundred is the old Council of Five Hundred, which certainly was again in function at the return of Alcibiades in 407.

The assumption, made by K. J. Beloch (*Griechische Geschichte* II, 2², 311ff.), W. S. Ferguson [*Class. Phil.* (1926), pp. 72–75, *CAH*, V, 338ff.], V. Ehrenberg (*Hermes*, LVII, 1922, 613ff.), and U. Wilcken [*Sitz. Ber. d. preuss. Akad., phil. hist. Kl.* (1935) pp. 34ff.], that the constitution following the overthrow of the Four Hundred was identical with the constitution described by Aristotle in Chapter 30 of the present treatise is at variance with the fact that Aristotle does not count this constitution in his enumeration of constitutions in Chapter 41, implying that this constitution was never actually applied, and also with Thucydides' account of the events which followed the overthrow of the Four Hundred. (Cf. also Introduction, p. 25.)

118) This is hardly correct, since only eight of the generals were ever present during the battle. When Xenophon (*Hellenica* I, 7.34) says that the Council decided that "all the generals" should be tried together, he clearly means the eight generals who had participated in the battle (cf. II, 7, 1, where he expressly states that Conon who had been blockaded in Mytilene was not even recalled). But the error can already be found in Plato's *Apology* 32b, from where it may have been taken over by Aristotle.

119) See *supra*, note 102.

120) This corresponds to Aristotle's conviction that the real "ancestral constitution" combined oligarchic and democratic elements in a reasonable mixture. (Cf. also Introduction, pp. 58ff.)

CHAPTER 35.

121) According to Xenophon (*Hellenica* II, 3, 2; 11ff.), the Thirty were chosen to write a new constitution (along the lines of the "ancestral constitution"), and it was by deliberately postponing this part of their duty that they established the oligarchy. In Aristotle's version, on the contrary, the election of the Thirty immediately constituted the oligarchy (end of Chapter 34). But a comparison with Xenophon's text II, 3, 11ff., proves that in Chapters 35 and 36 Aristotle tried to combine what he had said before with Xenophon's narration. In adapting Xenophon to his own version, Aristotle replaced Xenophon's words about the failure of the Thirty to write a new constitution by the rather vague expression, "they paid no attention to the other regulations concerning the constitution." But by using these general terms, Aristotle created a new difficulty. For if the Thirty paid no

attention to anything in their assignment beyond the appointment of five hundred Councilmen and other magistracies (next
sentence), it is hard to see how they could pretend to be aiming
at the ancestral constitution as, according to Aristotle's own
testimony (Chapter 35, 2; cf. also *infra*, note 129), they did during
the first part of their rule.

122) No such body has been mentioned by Aristotle and, what
is more, the number one thousand is too small for the procedure
that is indicated by the text of the papyrus as rendered above.
Hence we must conclude that the text is probably corrupt; but
whether it should be corrected by changing the figure one
thousand, or by any of the other conjectures which have been
proposed, can hardly be decided.

123) This "right" existed only for those who had no legitimate
sons (Dem. 46, 14ff.), and the same limitation must have been
retained in the new law enacted by the Thirty. But Aristotle
need not have mentioned this restriction, since it was a matter
of course and not one of the "troublesome" clauses.

CHAPTER 36.

124) The papyrus reads "two thousand." But since three
thousand are mentioned immediately afterwards, and since the
latter figure is confirmed by other ancient authors, there can
be no doubt that "two thousand" is an error of a copyist.

125) This passage seems to be taken over almost literally from
Xenophon, *Hellenica* II, 3, 19.

126) Aristotle fails to make it clear that, in spite of their
hesitation and the repeated postponements, they finally did
publish the list. (Cf. *infra*, Chapter 37 and note 129.)

CHAPTER 37.

127) This is the usual meaning of the word found in the text.
But since the corresponding noun sometimes is used to designate
the vote, the sentence may mean merely that they ordered the
Council to put the laws to the vote.

128) Or, in other words, that his name did no longer belong
on the list of the three thousand. Xenophon has a more dramatic
version: he does not mention the "second" law; instead, he has
Critias, on the strength of his leadership, "striking Theramenes'
name off the roll" (*Hellenica* II, 3, 51).

129) This shows that by this time it was known who belonged
to the Three Thousand and who did not (cf. *supra*, note 126).
Xenophon, who was present in Athens when the Thirty were in

power, dates the disarming of the people before the arrest of
Theramenes (*Hellenica* II, 3, 20).

CHAPTER 38.

130) The two successive boards of Ten mentioned by Aristotle
in this passage are not distinguished from each other by Xenophon
(*Hellenica* II, 4, 23ff.), by Lysias (*adv. Eratosthenem* 55), and by
Isocrates (*adv. Callimachum* 5ff.). Since all three authors were
contemporaries of the Thirty, some scholars have questioned the
accuracy of Aristotle's account. The latter is confirmed, however,
by a fragment of the work of Andration, a local historian of
Attica of the fourth century. Furthermore, one has to take into
consideration that the name and the task of the board remained
the same, when its members were replaced by others, and that
neither Lysias nor Isocrates had any compelling reason to distinguish between the earlier and the later membership of the
board, though Lysias obviously refers to the board as constituted
in the beginning, while Isocrates mentions one of the members
of the second board. Finally, though Xenophon does not make
a formal distinction, it is clear from his narrative that the board
of Ten was, from the beginning, appointed to open negotiations
with the democrats, but acted contrary to its instructions. (Cf.
also the following note.)

131) The passage in Isocrates' speech against Callimachus
quoted in the preceding note has been understood to indicate
that Rhinon must have been a member of the first board of Ten.
But a careful interpretation of the passage shows that Isocrates'
account is perfectly reconcilable with the assumption that Rhinon
belonged to the second board only, which seems to be implied
by Aristotle.

132) Xenophon (*Hellenica* II, 4, 38) speaks of fifteen.

CHAPTER 39.

133) If these "Ten" are different from the board of Ten which
governed the Piraeus until it was occupied by the democrats, it
must be the first board of Ten which was appointed after the
overthrow of the Thirty. But neither Xenophon (*Hellenica* II,
4, 38) nor Andocides (*de mysteriis* 90) mentions this board among
those excluded from the amnesty, and it is strange that Aristotle
should not have indicated that the first board of Ten is meant.
For the second board was certainly not excluded. It seems
probable, therefore, that the text tradition is faulty and that
Aristotle wrote: "the Thirty, the Ten who governed in the Piraeus,
and the Eleven."

134) By inserting the words "in the city" in this place, where they are missing in the papyrus, Kenyon (preceded to some extent by Gertz) seems to have recovered the simple meaning of this whole sentence.

CHAPTER 40.

135) *Cf.* Xenophon (*Hellenica* II, 4, 43), who tells that this reconciliation took place after a short war against the settlers of Eleusis, in which the latter's generals were killed when trying to negotiate.

CHAPTER 41.

136) Literally translated, Aristotle's words are: "But *then*, the people, having become master of the state, established . . ." This "then" (in Greek τότε, "at *that* time" or, in Kenyon's adequate translation, "at the time of which we are speaking") refers back to the main contents of the preceding chapter, canceling, as it were, for the sake of transition, the remarks at its end. (Cf. *supra*, notes 79 and 117.)

137) 404/03 B.C. According to Chapter 39, the reconciliation of the two parties and the subsequent restoration of the democracy took place in the archonship of Eucleides (403/2), a date which is confirmed by Xenophon (*Hellenica* II, 4, 38) and Plutarch (*de gloria Atheniensium* 349 F.). Since the construction of the sentence as we read it in the Greek text is rather awkward, it is most likely that part of the original sentence is missing in the papyrus.

138) Here the papyrus is difficult to read. But those who have studied it most carefully seem to be agreed that the traces lead to the Greek word μετάστασις ("change"), not to κατάστασις ("establishment"), which, besides, would be difficult to understand in the context.

139) Ion is the mythical ancestor of the Ionian race to which the Athenians belonged. The names of the four Attic tribes occur also in other Ionian cities, and it was believed that these tribes were the descendants of the four sons of Ion and that their names were derived from the names of these sons. But there was also a belief that Attica and its population was older than Ion and the Ionians. This has found expression in the legend referred to by Aristotle that Ion and his followers "came to dwell" in Attica and introduced the division into tribes, though, according to this version, the tribes can no longer be the descendants of the sons of Ion. (Cf. Herodotus I, 143; V, 69; VIII, 44; Thuc. VII, 57.)

140) The number of *eleven* changes of which Aristotle speaks at the beginning of this section comes out only if one begins to count with the political order or constitution of Theseus, not with the settlement of Ion, though Aristotle seems to have designated this as the first change (cf. *supra*, note 138). Aristotle accounts for this by pointing out that the second change was the first which led to something like a constitutional order. But even so, the expressions which he uses are not very clear. For what he actually counts are obviously neither simply changes nor changes of constitutions, but constitutions produced by changes of previously existing conditions.

Concerning the apparent inconsistency which may be found in the fact that Aristotle in his present enumeration seems to omit altogether the constitution or political order which he has described in Chapter 3 and which, according to that chapter, followed the monarchy and preceded the constitution of Draco, see Introduction, pp. 8ff.

141) This little sentence is not so futile as it may seem. For, according to Aristotle's reconstruction of the constitutional history, the origin of both his "sixth" and "seventh" constitution could be traced back to the victory of Salamis (cf. Chapter 23 and *Politics* 1304a 20–24). Aristotle's expression becomes a little involved, because Aristeides' contribution to the development that led to the "seventh" constitution belonged chronologically to the time of the "sixth" constitution.

142) Cf. *supra*, Chapter 24 and note 67.

143) The Greek wording of the last two clauses is even more puzzling than our attempt at a translation. Something must be wrong with the text of the papyrus, but so far all modern conjectures have been unsatisfactory.

144) Heracleides had first been made honorary *proxenos* (cf. *supra*, note 40), and had later been admitted to full Athenian citizenship because of the outstanding services that he had rendered to the Athenians in negotiations with the Persian king.

145) This last step must have been reached before 392, since Aristophanes in his *Ecclesiazusae*, which were performed in that year, refers to the fee of three obols.

CHAPTER 42.

146) There were no birth certificates in ancient Athens, and most people seem not to have known their birthdays (cf. Plato, *Lysis* 207c). The philosopher Epicurus was the first to celebrate his birthday.

147) This means obviously, "that he has not the qualities

entitling him to become a citizen." The Greek word ἐλεύθερος originally designated a person belonging to a family that forms an integral part of the community, which, of course, would not be the case with a foreigner. Later, it is used to designate anyone who is free in the sense of not being a slave. But the original meaning was never completely forgotten.

CHAPTER 43.

148) The lunar year, that is, a year of twelve lunar months, has 354 days, which is equal to $36 \times 4 + 35 \times 6$. In order to keep the lunar year in harmony with the solar year, it was necessary to insert intercalary months. According to the so-called Metonic Cycle, which seems to have been used at the time of Aristotle, eight intercalary months were inserted in the course of nineteen years, that is one intercalary month in every second or third year up to the number of eight in the course of a cycle of nineteen years. For the question of how the days of an intercalary year were distributed over the prytanies, see W. K. Pritchett and O. Neugebauer, *The Calendars of Athens*, 1947, pp. 34ff.

149) The Greek term is εἰσαγγελία which designates an action brought before a political body. The *eisangelia* was supposed to be used in the case of "new and unwritten offenses," that is, offenses not mentioned in the laws, in the case of dangerous and extraordinary offenses against the state (cf. *supra*, Chapter 8, 4), and as an action against public officials for malfeasance in office (cf. *supra*, Chapter 4, 4; *infra*, 45, 2). It is characteristic for the Athenian state that, according to a law quoted by Hypereides, *pro Euxenippo* 7f., *eisangelia* was also used in cases of men who, having accepted bribes, spoke in the Assembly of the People in favor of a measure "which was not in the interest of the people."

150) This is a rather peculiar use of the Greek word ὅσια, which usually means "permitted by divine law." When, as in the present case, contrasted with ἱερά, which means "ordered by divine law," the word ὅσια then often designates those matters that are not sacred and also not in contrast with divine law, that is, secular or profane matters.

CHAPTER 44.

151) The Greek word εὐσημία usually designates a good weather prognostic. But since we know how important omens were considered for the outcome of any military undertaking, it seems clear that here the word is used in a wider sense.

CHAPTER 45.

152) Neither the Lysimachus nor the Eumelides mentioned in this story are known from any other source. But it seems likely that the incident happened in the period after the over-throw of the Thirty. What Aristotle tells in Chapter 40, 2 of Archinus shows that in this period the Council sometimes did inflict the death penalty "without due process of law." On the other hand, it is not very likely that Eumelides would have dared or would have been able to rescue a condemned prisoner just before his execution unless the action of the Council was of doubtful legality. In fact, the Council of the democracy before the establishment of the Thirty had not had the power of inflicting the death penalty without revision by the law courts. It seems likely, therefore, that after the overthrow of the Thirty, under whose regime the oligarchic Council was not bound by such restrictions, the democratic Council for some time usurped such powers, until, on the instigation of Eumelides and on the occasion of the condemnation of Lysimachus, the old rule restricting the juridical powers of the Council was formally restored.

153) The Greek term is ἔφεσις. This term not infrequently means appeal, that is, a request made by the losing party for a revision of a verdict. But in a good many, if not in all, of the cases in which Aristotle speaks, in this chapter, of ἔφεσις, the revision of the decision of the Council by the law courts seems not to have depended on a request by the losing party but to have been obligatory. For the Archons compare *infra*, Chapter 55, 2 and 4, and Demosthenes, *adv. Leptinem* 90. The passage in Aristotle 55, 4 shows also that an Archon was reexamined by the law court, even though he had been passed in the examination by the Council.

154) In these cases, a rejection of the accusation by the Council seems to have been final.

CHAPTER 46.

155) In Aristotle's text it looks as if "they" referred to the shipbuilders. But Demosthenes (*adv. Androt.* 8) mentions a law which said that the Council, if it had performed its duties well, was to receive a wreath as its reward, but that it was unlawful to give this wreath to a Council which had not completed the ships for which the money had been assigned by the Assembly of the People.

156) Here the Greek text is altered by many scholars so that its meaning would be: "and when the *latter* [that is, the Assembly] has passed a verdict of guilty, [the Council] hands him over to

the law court." The preceding chapter, however, seems to indicate that it is usually the Council, and not the Assembly, which passes a preliminary verdict and then hands the case over to the law courts for revision. It seems, therefore, that here, too, the same procedure was followed, except that the offender was also reported (Aristotle here does not use a specifically legal term) to the Assembly of the People.

CHAPTER 47.

157) In other words: the law, though nominally still in force, was no longer observed in fact. A similar case is mentioned at the end of Chapter 7, where Aristotle says that a *thes*, that is, a member of the fourth census class, legally cannot hold any magistracy, but that nobody when the lot is cast will say that he is a *thes*. (Cf. also *supra*, notes 116f.)

158) In the papyrus, this sentence is found after the first part of the following period (see *infra*, note 160), where it interrupts an otherwise good context. Such transpositions are likely to happen occasionally whenever manuscripts are copied from manuscripts. Another explanation would be that the sentence was originally a marginal note in Aristotle's own manuscript, added by him after the whole chapter had been written. In this case the almost unintelligible words "and of the others" might be interpreted as referring to such confiscations as mentioned in paragraph 3.

159) This is a literal translation of the Greek term; the modern technical meaning of "concession" would make good sense in this context; but it is doubtful whether this is what Aristotle meant. Sandys thought of "mines 'let out under special agreement' without the previous payment of purchase money."

160) The words "And . . . the mines which were let out . . . leased for ten years" precede in the papyrus the sentence about "the estates of persons exiled by the Areopagus" etc. (See *supra*, note 158.)

CHAPTER 48.

161) It may appear strange that the magistrates, after having rendered account in a law court and having been either acquitted or convicted, should have been subject to another examination through the procedure described in this chapter, a procedure which might lead to a second trial before a law court after they had been cleared by another law court when rendering account of their administration. It seems, however, that the first rendering of accounts had to do mainly or exclusively with the adminis-

tration of money, while the second examination described in the present chapter and undertaken by the Euthyni extended to all other matters.

CHAPTER 49.

162) In spite of the allowance paid by the state (cf. p. 123, footnote a), a poor man was not able to serve in the cavalry since a cavalryman had not only to take care of his own horse, but also to supply a mounted servant who accompanied him everywhere, his own military outfit, and the mounting of the two horses. He also had to spend much time in military practice.

163) The meaning of this part of the sentence is not certain, and the text may be corrupt. The *peplos* is the richly embroidered robe which was made every year by girls from the old noble families and which was carried in the procession at the Panathenaean festival. If the text of the papyrus is correct, the "models" had nothing to do with the *peplos* and had some specific technical meaning of which we cannot be certain; if we admit a modern conjecture (*"for* the *peplos"* instead of *"and* the *peplos"*), they may have been the designs for the mythological scenes with which the robe used to be embroidered.

164) This sentence (less the words "one may say") is found also at the beginning of Chapter 47, where it served as a transition to the discussion of certain offices with which the Council collaborates closely. Its recurrence here is puzzling, and one would like to remove it as spurious. Yet, as Kaibel remarked (*Stil und Text*, p. 26), neither is it probable that an interpolator should have added it, nor can it be a mere blunder of a copyist. To explain this puzzle, Kaibel suggested that at the end of Chapter 49 the sentence may have remained from a draft (written by Aristotle himself, but rejected subsequently). Wilamowitz (*Aristoteles und Athen*, I, 214f.) believes that Aristotle deliberately repeats, at the end of Chapter 49, the sentence from the beginning of Chapter 47, but uses it now to make it clear that he is not going into any more details. The latter view is to some extent supported by the fact that, on another occasion, too, namely, with regard to the election of military officers, Aristotle uses the same sentence ("They also elect by show of hands all the military officers") twice and in two similarly differing functions, first, in 43, 1 as a brief general statement (cf. Chapter 49, 4), and, then, in Chapter 61, 1, as introducing the single items (cf. Chapter 47, 1).

CHAPTER 53.

165) The expression seems to imply that the Arbitrators handle or prepare all civil lawsuits except the "monthly cases" discussed in the previous chapter, which are placed before the law courts by the Eisagogeis or in a special case by the Apodectae. In Chapter 59, 5f., however, we learn of civil suits which the Thesmothetae and not the Arbitrators have to bring before the law courts and which, nevertheless, have nothing to do with the *endeixeis* mentioned in Chapter 52 as partly belonging to the domain of the Thesmothetae.

166) Since in Attic chronology a year is identified by the name of the ruling Archon of that year, the name of the Archon gives the absolute chronology and therefore can also be used to determine the age of the person. If, for instance, a person had been accepted as *ephebos* (see *supra*, Chapter 42, 1ff. and note 146) in the year of a certain Archon, one had merely to count back to that year and to add seventeen in order to find the present official age of the person. But there was still another method which required no counting. An Athenian had to do military service from the age of eighteen to the age of fifty-eight, or, as the Greeks frequently expressed it, from his nineteenth to his fifty-ninth year. There followed a year in which he was under the obligation of serving as Arbitrator, all in all a cycle of forty-two years. Each year of this cycle, or in other words each of the forty-two age groups which, at any given time, had to keep themselves ready for this kind of public service, was assigned the name of one of the forty-two eponymous heroes selected for this purpose. At the end of each year one age group, namely the age group which had done service on the board of Arbitrators, was relieved of its public duties, and these were taken over by the last of the age groups which in the preceding year had still been subject to military service. The name of the eponymous hero which had been assigned to the outgoing Arbitrators would then become free and would be assigned to the youngest group of *epheboi* just entering military age. Hence Aristotle's statement, a little farther on, that at the head of the list of the newly enrolled *epheboi* one would find the names of the Archon of the year and of the eponymous hero of the outgoing Arbitrators.

CHAPTER 54.

167) This passage is quoted in the *Lexicon Rhetoricum Cantabrigiense*, p. 672, 20 s.v. λογισταί, together with an additional sentence, obviously derived from a different authority. This

additional sentence indicates that, whether or not the auditors found anything wrong during the audit, they had to take the official whom they examined into a court of five hundred and one jurors in any case, and that it was only this court which made the final decision as to whether the official was to be released or whether there was to be a trial.

168) Cf. *supra*, note 40.

169) Kaibel (*Stil und Text*, p. 3) pointed out that the implicit criticism in this section (par. 3–5) is unmistakable. The Clerk of the Prytany, in spite of his responsibilities, is *now* selected by lot, while "this man" is elected by voting! Aristotle does, of course, not object to the procedure in the latter case, for by lot one could hardly pick a man with a good voice; but if, even for this office, election by vote was indicated, the incongruity of selection by lot in the case of a man with the responsibilities of the Clerk of the Prytany appears to be obvious.

170) Whenever a drought, a blight, a pestilence, or the like befell the country, an oracle would be asked what the reason of this misfortune was. The answer was usually that a "pollution" had taken place, or that a god or a hero had been offended, etc., and, among other things, certain expiatory sacrifices were prescribed to remedy this situation. At the beginning of important enterprises, on the other hand, sacrifices were made both in order to propitiate the gods and in order to find out whether they favored the undertaking. For the latter purpose the soothsayers had to be present.

Chapter 55.

171) The expression is not very clear. What Aristotle means seems rather "the various rules according to which and the various methods by which the Archons were selected in the course of time from the beginning until the time when the present method was introduced." For the details, cf. *supra*, Chapters 3, 2–4; 8,1; 22, 5; and 26, 2.

172) See *supra*, note 4.

173) This means that every year each tribe will provide one of the ten highest officials, that is, the nine Archons and their one secretary, and that they will do so in turn, so that, if in a given year a tribe has provided the Archon Eponymus, the Archon Eponymus will not be again taken from this tribe until all the other tribes have had their turn.

174) One might observe that even the Athenian democracy, which has carried to the extreme the principle that everybody is equally fit for the highest positions in the internal adminis-

tration of the state, could not entirely dispense with an examination of the candidates for public office. In fact, while in a modern democracy the examination of the candidate takes place through the public discussion which precedes the election, in Athens it followed the selection for office and was undertaken by two independent public agencies, the Council and the jury court. To be sure, the examination was restricted to questions of citizenship, the performance of certain generally required public services, and of certain basic moral qualifications. There was, at least officially, no examination or even consideration of the intellectual qualities and the administrative ability of the candidate even for the highest civilian office.

175) Literally, "the witnesses foreswear the testimonies." Since the confirmatory oath, that is, the oath by which a witness in a trial or lawsuit confirms the truth of his testimony, was also in use in Athenian law courts, some commentators understand "the witnesses swear *to* their testimony." But the term employed by Aristotle in his sentence seems not to have been used in this sense until many centuries after Aristotle's death. In earlier authors and documents it always means "to forswear, to swear in the negative, to swear to be excused from giving testimony."

176) Cf. also *supra*, Chapter 7, 1, where the promise to set up a golden statue applies, however, to any transgression of the laws, not only to bribery. (Cf. also Plat. *Phaedrus* 235d and Plutarch, *Solon* 25.)

CHAPTER 56.

177) "*Choregos*" originally meant the leader of a chorus, but since the end of the sixth or the beginning of the fifth century, the *choregia* at Athens was one of the liturgies (see *supra*, Chapter 27, 3 and *supra*, note 81) which had to be performed by the wealthy citizens; and a Choregus was a citizen who bore the costs of fitting out and training the chorus for one of the theatrical performances or the choric competitions at the great festivals.

178) This was a rather strange institution. If a citizen was appointed to a *choregia* or another of the more costly liturgies (cf. *supra*, note 81) and was of the opinion that some fellow citizen of his was in a better position to bear this burden, he could challenge this man, either to perform the liturgy in his stead or to exchange properties with him, in which case he would perform the liturgy. This exchange of properties was called "*antidosis*." If the person challenged rejected both proposals, the matter was brought before a law court for decision.

179) There is a lacuna in the papyrus, and the first part of

the figure is not preserved. The restoration of " . . . teen" to "fourteen" is based on a somewhat analogous rule in Plato's *Laws* 833d.

CHAPTER 57.

180) This procedure is called προαγόρευσις. It consists in a public proclamation by which the murderer, whether he is known or not, is warned to stay away from holy water, drink-offerings, mixing bowls, from temples, and from the market place. The custom was very old and had the purpose of preventing the murderer from spreading pollution.

181) A man who has committed involuntary manslaughter has to remain in exile until he can reconcile his prosecutors so that they will agree to let him come back. Since he is an exile, he is not allowed to touch the land. Demosthenes (23, 77) quotes the law referred to by Aristotle as follows: "If a man who has been exiled because of involuntary homicide is accused of another, voluntary, homicide during the time when his prosecutors have not yet been reconciled . . . "

182) The word "Ephetae" is not in the papyrus, which has a lacuna in this place. It is supplied from ancient lexica which probably contain excerpts from the present treatise. The three courts mentioned — the one in the Palladium, the other in the Delphinium, and the third in the precinct of Phreatus — consisted in earlier times of fifty-one members, called Ephetae, who had to be over fifty years of age and were selected according to birth and merit (ἀριστίνδην). Not later than toward the end of the fifth century, these courts must have been replaced by courts consisting of ordinary jurors selected by lot. We know the number of such jurors for two trials held in the Palladium, namely seven hundred (Isocrates 18, 52ff.) and five hundred (Demosthenes 59, 9f.), respectively. The original meaning of the name Ephetae was forgotten in later antiquity and is still controversial. Its insertion into Aristotle's text depends on the assumption that even after the change the ancient name was applied to the jurors in these courts.

CHAPTER 58.

183) The metics were aliens who had their permanent residence at Athens. They were subjected to special regulations and had to pay a special tax. The *isoteleis* were resident aliens enjoying special privileges, especially the privilege of being free from the tax for aliens, and paying the same taxes as the citizens. They also usually served in war within the citizen contingents.

The *proxenoi* mentioned in this sentence are not identical with the representatives of foreign states mentioned in Chapter 19 (cf. *supra*, Ch. 19 and *supra*, note 40), but resident aliens who had a still more privileged and honored position than the *isoteleis* and who often were given the right to acquire landed property in Athens (a right which the ordinary metics did not have), the honor of having a front seat in the theatre, etc.

CHAPTER 59.

184) This would obviously not apply to the cases of homicide discussed in Chapter 57, for which a special court was prescribed by law. But, in all those cases which came before the ordinary law courts, it was the Thesmothetae who determined which of those courts were to handle the actions introduced by the Archon, which courts the actions introduced by the King, etc.

185) See *supra*, Chapter 43, and *supra*, note 149.

186) The word καταχειροτονία is used in two different meanings: (a) a vote against the defendant in case of a *probole* (προβολή); (b) a condemnation by the people, which may consist in the decision to remove a man from office. A probole was an accusation of a person before the Assembly of the People. The vote of the people against a person in sense (a) had no legal effect; it was merely an expression of the opinion of the majority that the person was guilty and that an action against him before a law court was justified. But such a decision would naturally to some extent influence the law court before which the accusation might be brought later. Though as a technical term καταχειροτονία is usually used in sense (a), the context seems to indicate that in the present passage Aristotle used the word in sense (b).

187) "Sycophancy." According to Athenian law, any citizen could prosecute a person who, in his opinion, had transgressed the laws. What is more, the private prosecutor, if successful, received a considerable share (in some cases one third, in some one half, in some even three fourths) of the fines imposed, the property confiscated, etc. In consequence of this, a class of professional informers developed who accused other persons or threatened to accuse them for the sake of blackmail or personal profit. One way of checking these men was the provision that a person who failed to obtain one fifth of the votes of the jurors in a trial, or who withdrew an action which he had started, had to pay a fine of one thousand drachmas. But this provision, since certain actions-at-law were exempt from it, was not always sufficient. Another mode of coping with sycophants was by way of a law which set down the highest penalties, even the death

penalty, for a man who "deceived" the people or a law court. It is probably to actions of this kind that Aristotle refers, though there may have been at his time a special law against sycophancy, the exact nature of which, however, is not known.

188) The actual ratification of these agreements was made by a law court, but it was both introduced and completed by the Thesmothetae. It was the main purpose of these agreements to secure to the citizens of the contracting states the right of suing the other party in a commercial contract. The decision was given in a court of the state to which the defendant belonged, but according to the rules set down in the international agreement.

CHAPTER 61.

189) There is no point of reference for this "also" in Aristotle's text as we have it (and as the grammarians in later antiquity had it). And it has been observed that in our text of Aristotle's work there is also no special chapter concerning those officials who are mentioned by Aristotle in Chapter 43, 1 as being elected by show of hands for *four* years, although at least two of these offices, namely, that of the Treasurer of the military funds and that of the Treasurers of the theatre fund, were extremely important in Aristotle's time. Moreover, in Chapter 43, 1 the mention of these officials is immediately followed by the very sentence with which Chapter 61, 1 begins: "They also elect by show of hands all the military officers." Under these circumstances, different scholars have reached independently (see Wilamowitz, *Ar. und Ath.*, I, 207, note 34) the conclusion that Aristotle, whose last chapter on officials selected by lot dealt with the Commissioners of Games, who served for *four* years, began, or intended to begin, his account of the major officers selected by *show of hands* with the *four-year* terms mentioned in Chapter 43, 1, but that for some reason this section of his work was either not written or was lost early. (Cf. also *supra*, note 164.)

190) Since in the fourth century there was no longer a sufficient number of wealthy citizens who were able to take upon themselves individually the more expensive liturgies, especially the trierarchies (see *supra*, notes 81 and 178), the twelve hundred wealthiest citizens were organized in twenty groups of sixty, called "symmories"; and the "trierarchies," that is, the burden of fitting out and keeping up the warships, were distributed among these *symmories* rather than among individuals.

CHAPTER 63.

191) The Greek word is κληρωτήριον. Until recently it had been generally assumed that this word meant "voting-room,"

and a great many efforts have been made to interpret the text on the basis of this assumption. But a full understanding of the way in which the jurors were selected was not reached. In 1937, however, Professor Sterling Dow was able to show that certain objects which had been found during the excavations at Athens were allotment machines, and that it is these allotment machines which Aristotle designates by the name of κληρωτήρια. Two years later in volume 50 of the *Harvard Studies in Classical Philology* (1939), pp. 1–34, Professor Dow gave a complete description of these allotment machines, together with a drawing of two reconstructed machines, adding an excellent discussion of the way in which, according to the account given by Aristotle, these allotment machines seem to have been used. (Cf. also the succeeding note.)

192) In the preceding sentences of this chapter, Aristotle has described the implements used in the allotment procedure and given an account of the qualifications required for admission to the procedure. In this last sentence he begins his description of the actual allotment procedure which continues to the end of Chapter 64. This description is rather awkward and not quite easy to understand, especially if one does not have the shape of the allotment machines before one's eyes. It may, therefore, perhaps be useful to summarize briefly the different steps of this procedure as they can be reconstructed by a comparison of Aristotle's text with the archeological evidence.

First, the Thesmothet draws letters, one by one, from a box which contains as many letters from L onward as there are law courts to be filled. In the order in which they are drawn from the box, they are affixed to the doors of the various courts.

Then the selection of jurors begins. The men who wish to participate in the allotment for jury duty meanwhile have assembled, the men from each one of the tribes before that one of the ten entrances which is assigned to his tribe. The men from each tribe are divided into ten subgroups designated by the letters of the alphabet from A to K. Each potential juror has with him a ticket inscribed with his name, his father's name, his deme's name, and the letter designating the group to which he belongs. All potential jurors throw their tickets into one of the ten boxes set up outside the entrance, the men belonging to the A group into the box marked with A, the B group into box B, and so on. Then the Archon, Thesmothet, or Clerk, assigned to the tribe, draws one ticket at random from each of the boxes. The men whose tickets have been drawn in this way are selected as jurors. But they have also the task of acting as "ticket-inserters" for the rest of the allotment procedure.

The further selection of jurors is done by means of the allotment machines. These machines are constructed in the following way. Each of the two machines has five vertical columns of slots, into which the ticket can be inserted. At the top of these columns the letters are inscribed: in the first machine A for the first column, B for the second, and so on; in the second Z for the first column, H for the second, and so on — K for the last column. In each allotment machine there are, therefore, five slots in each horizontal line.

The ticket-inserter from group A now takes the A box and inserts the tickets from this box, as they happen to come out, into the vertical row designated by A; the ticket-inserter B, the tickets from box B into column B, etc. When this has been done, the actual allotment begins.

At the left hand side of each of the two allotment machines there is a tube, which in its upper part widens into a funnel, while its lower part is so narrow that the bronze cubes used in the procedure, when dumped in at the top, will form a single vertical row. At its lower end the tube is closed by a handle, which, when drawn, will let fall out one cube at a time.

The Archon has a box with white and black bronze cubes, the total number of which is equal to the number of applicants for jurorship in this tribe, divided by five. The number of white cubes is equal to the number of jurors actually to be selected from this tribe, divided by five. These cubes are contained in two boxes so that each of the two boxes contains the same number of black and white cubes.

After the tickets have been inserted into the allotment machines, the presiding Archon shakes the boxes with cubes and dumps the cubes of the first box into the tube of the first machine, and those of the second box into the tube of the second machine. Then he takes out the cubes, one by one, at the lower end of the tube. If the first cube coming out at this end is white, all the five men whose tickets are inserted in the first horizontal row of the machine are selected as jurors. A herald calls out their names and they are later admitted through the swinging grill of the entrance. If the first cube is black, they are not selected. Their tickets are handed back to them and they can go home. This procedure is continued until all the cubes have been taken out, first from the first, then from the second allotment machine.

The persons who have been selected as jurors must again draw lots in order to determine on which of the various courts they will have to serve.   Only then are they allowed to pass through the gate.   This second lottery is described by Aristotle with sufficient clarity so that a further explanation seems unnecessary.

CHAPTER 65.

193) The words "take their seats" are not in the papyrus. But the sentence as read in the papyrus is incomplete; and something of this kind must therefore be supplemented from the context.   It is also possible that Aristotle stated: "then, in the court, they return (or: lay down) their acorns and staves . . . " (Kaibel, Thalheim).

194) The number "five" is not in the papyrus.   But some figure must be supplemented with the words "by the number," if they are to be understood; and this figure can be supplied from the following chapter, in which we learn that five jurors were selected by lot to divide the jurors into groups for the payment of their fees, at which latter occasion their personal tickets were returned to them.

195) This word is not quite clearly legible in the papyrus, but the essential meaning seems clear.

CHAPTER 67.

196) This is another case which shows clearly that, with the initial words of a transition to something new, Aristotle refers back to the whole preceding section, not to its last part.   What he means is "having completed the preparations described in the preceding section" (Chapters 65 and 66).

197) That is, if the whole day is divided into several parts and these parts are assigned to the several parts of the trial: for instance, one for the prosecution, one for the defense, and one for the finding of the penalty (Aeschines, *adv. Ctesiph.* 197, or, as we find it in Xenophon, *Hellenica* I, 7, 23), one part for the gathering of the judges *and* for their voting, another for the prosecution, the third one for the defense.   However, a division into more than three was also possible.

CHAPTER 68.

198) Instead of "staves" some scholars supplement "tokens," referring to the tokens mentioned in Chapter 65, 2.   Because of the lacuna in the papyrus here and of its somehow defective text in Chapter 65, 3 (see note 193), it is difficult to decide whether the brass token with the figure 3, which the juror receives now, is exchanged against the staff (cf. Chapter 69, 2), or against that token which he had received when entering the court.   In any

case, it seems impossible that the token with the figure 3 was identical with the token mentioned on that earlier occasion.

199) Such a protest seems to have been equivalent to a demand that the witness or witnesses who had given the testimony against which the litigant protested be prosecuted for perjury. (Cf. Plato *Laws* 937b; Isaeus 5, 17; Dinarchus 1, 52.)

200) There seems to be only one way to combine this statement with paragraph 2, namely, to assume that the men whose task it was to hand out the voting pebbles to each of the jurors openly, so that the parties could see that they were one of each kind, put them, for each single juror before he voted, on a "lamp-stand" which belonged to the equipment of the court room, and that then the juror took them off this stand. An ordinary lamp-stand was a simple piece of furniture, of convenient height, widening at the top into a small tray, upon which the lamp was placed. With a little imagination one may find that such a lamp-stand, or something of comparable shape, was just what was needed for a control of the transfer of the two voting pebbles.

Aristotle

THE EPITOME OF HERACLEIDES

FRAGMENTS OF THE CONSTITUTION OF ATHENS

PROTREPTICUS

POLITICUS

ON KINGSHIP

ALEXANDER *or* ON COLONIZATION

Plato

SEVENTH EPISTLE

THE EPITOME OF HERACLEIDES

Introduction

The so-called "Epitome of Heracleides" has come down to us, in a number of manuscripts, under the title "From Heracleides' work On Constitutions."[1] Actually this epitome contains nothing but very badly mutilated remnants of excerpts from the Aristotelian collection of "Constitutions." The work of Heracleides mentioned in the title, therefore, was obviously simply an epitome of Aristotle's work. The text in the manuscripts consists of brief excerpts from this epitome, which probably suffered further abridgement and mutilation by later copyists.

The person and even the period of the Heracleides who was the author of the original epitome had long remained uncertain, and various conjectures as to his identity had been made, until, in 1915, a papyrus[2] was published which contained part of an epitome of Hermippus' work *On Lawgivers*, made by Heracleides Lembus, a statesman and amateur scholar who lived toward the middle of the second century B.C. The method followed in this epitome is so similar to what, as far as one can see from the fragments preserved in our manuscripts, seems to have been the method of the Heracleides who epitomized Aristotle's collection of "Constitutions" that there can be hardly any doubt that this latter Heracleides is identical with Heracleides Lembus.

That part of the "Epitome" which corresponds to the extant sections of Aristotle's *Constitution of Athens* shows clearly that the Epitome is based entirely on Aristotle's work and does not contain

---

[1] Concerning the relation of the manuscripts of the "Epitome" to one another, the question of the authorship of the original epitome, the character of this epitome, and the extent of the damage done to it by later copyists, see the excellent article by Herbert Bloch, "Heracleides Lembus and His Epitome of Aristotle's Politeiai," in *Transactions of the American Philological Association*, Vol. 71 (1940), pp. 27ff.

[2] Oxyrhynchus Papyri, XI, 1367.

anything that cannot be found there.   In fact, wherever possible,
the wording of the excerpts is taken from Aristotle's text.   Nevertheless, since, as a result of the series of abridgements that the
original text appears to have undergone, the connecting links
between the different sections have often disappeared, the text
of the Epitome would be very misleading if we did not have the
original Aristotelian text itself or, where this text is lost, at least
some additional information from other ancient sources.   Thus
the first sentence of Section 7, "he introduced the law on ostracism," follows upon a sentence in which Hippias is the subject.
But we know from Aristotle's treatise and from other sources
that "he" must mean Cleisthenes and not Hippias.   In Section
9 it is misleading to speak of "the successors of Cleon" where the
"Thirty Tyrants " are meant.   In Section 8 the name of Ephialtes
appears instead of that of Cimon.   Section 10 is entirely out of
the chronological order.   What follows (Section 11) is a chance
fragment of equally mutilated excerpts from the second part of
Aristotle's *Constitution of Athens*.

These facts must be kept in mind in any attempt to use the
first three sections of the Epitome for a reconstruction of the lost
beginnings of Aristotle's treatise; especially since, in regard to
the subject matter dealt with in these sections, reliable information from sources other than Aristotle is almost completely
lacking.   Some additional material, however, is found in quotations from this part of Aristotle's work by other ancient authors. [3]

It may also be observed that those sections of the Epitome
that correspond to the lost beginning of the *Constitution of Athens*
amount to nearly one third of the excerpts taken from the whole
work.   If it could be assumed that the Epitome covers the
different parts of the original proportionately, one would have
to conclude that Aristotle wrote rather extensively on the early
monarchic period.   It seems, however, that the excerpts become
more and more fragmentary toward the end, so that no conclusion
of this sort can be drawn.

[3] See *infra*, pp. 208–209.

TEXT

1. In the beginning, the Athenians had a monarchy. When Ion settled with them,[4] then they were for the first time called Ionians. Pandion, however, who was king after Erechtheus, divided the rule among his sons.

2. These quarreled continually with one another. Theseus, however, made a pronouncement by the herald and brought them together on equal terms.[5] But, after having gone to Scyros, he found his death there. For he was hurled down from a cliff by Lycomedes, who was afraid that he would make the island his own. The Athenians, however, at a later time, after the Persian Wars, brought his remains home [to Athens].

3. Beginning with the Codridae, kings were no longer elected, because they appeared to become effeminate and weak. However, Hippomenes, one of the Codridae, wishing to dispel this prejudice, killed the paramour of his daughter Leimone, after having caught him in the act, by tying him to his chariot, and shut her in with a horse until she was dead.

4. The followers of Megacles killed the followers of Cylon because of his aspiration to tyranny when the latter had fled to

[4] The legend of the settlement of Ion and his sons in Athens obviously reflects the historical fact, confirmed by both archaeological and linguistic evidence, that the Athenian people resulted from a mixture of Ionian colonists and a pre-Ionian population. These Ionians, however, did not, like the Spartans in the Peloponnesus, set themselves up as conquerors and rulers, but seem to have lived on equal terms with the pre-Ionian population.

[5] The story of the division of Attica among the sons of Pandion and of its unification by Theseus (cf. *infra*, p. 208, fragment 2) seems also to correspond to certain facts of early history. Archeological evidence and the existence of the festival of the *Synoikia* in later times were used by as early an author as Thucydides (II, 15) to prove that, in an early period, Attica consisted of independent or semi-independent communities under local rule and rulers, and that only later were they united under one central government. Though most modern scholars are inclined to consider this unification as a long and gradual development rather than a single historical event, this development must have been brought to conclusion by a decisive act, which included a thorough reorganization of the whole body politic.

the altar of the goddess; and they [the Athenians] drove those who had participated in the killing into exile as people who lay under a curse [*Constitution of Athens*, Chapter 1].

5. When Solon gave laws to the Athenians, he effected also a cancellation of debts, the so-called "throwing off of the burden." When some people plagued him [with questions and criticisms] in regard to his laws, he went abroad to Egypt [11, 1].

6. Pisistratus, after having been tyrant for thirty-three years, died in old age [17,1]. Hipparchus, the son of Pisistratus, was fond of amusement, had many love affairs, and liked music and poetry; Thettalus was younger and violent [18, 1.2]. Since they could not kill this man [Hippias] who was tyrant, they killed instead his brother Hipparchus [18, 3]. Hippias, however, ruled as tyrant in a harsh fashion [19, 1].

7. He [Cleisthenes] introduced also the law concerning ostracism, which was enacted because of men aiming at tyranny; and, among others, Xanthippus and Aristeides were ostracized [22, 1.3.5.6.].

8. Ephialtes [Cimon!][6] allowed anyone who wished to take fruits from his private estate, and he entertained many people from its produce [27, 3].

9. Cleon, taking over, corrupted the state [28, 3], and those who succeeded him did so even more [28, 4]; they [the Thirty Tyrants!] filled everything with lawlessness and killed no less than 1500 [35.4]. When these had been overthrown, Thrasybulus and Rhinon, who was a man of noble character, were leaders of the people [37, 1. and 38, 4].

10. Themistocles and Aristeides [23, 2]. And the Council of the Areopagus was very powerful [23, 1].[7]

11. They [the City Commissioners] also take care of the streets and see to it that nobody obstructs them by buildings or by bal-

---

[6] Aristotle deals with Ephialtes in Chapter 25, and tells in Chapter 27 the story of Cimon, to which reference is made in this paragraph. The somewhat milder confusion at the beginning of Section 7, where he refers to Cleisthenes who has not been mentioned before, shows by what process Ephialtes could become the grammatical subject in Section 8.

[7] Cf. *supra*, Introduction, p. 204.

conies protruding over the street [50.2]. In the same manner [*sc.* by lot], they [the Athenians] appoint the Eleven who are in charge of the prisoners in the state prison [52, 1]. There are also nine Archons, six Thesmothetae [55, 1], who when they have come up for examination have to swear that they will govern justly and that they will not accept gifts or else will set up a golden statue [55, 5]. The King administers the public sacrifices [57, 1] and the department of war.[8]

[8] "τὰ πολέμια." This passage, of course, ultimately goes back to 58, 1, where Aristotle lists the religious functions (mainly related to war), not of the King, but of the Polemarch. It does not help much to bring "the Polemarch" into the text of our excerpts, for this would still not make the statement correct, and while the *original excerpts* may have been merely misleading, not blundering, he, or rather those, who cut down these excerpts to their present state certainly did not or could not check up with Aristotle's text or any other reliable source of historical information.

FRAGMENTS OF THE LOST BEGINNING OF ARISTOTLE'S *CONSTITUTION OF ATHENS*

1. Harpocration *s.v.* 'Απόλλων πατρῷος: "Since the time of Ion the Athenians revere the 'ancestral Apollo' as belonging to all of them. For when Ion came to settle with them in Attica, *the Athenians*, as Aristotle says, *began to be called Ionians and to give Apollo the name 'ancestral Apollo.'*"

Cf. *scholium* on Aristophanes' *Birds* 1527: "The Athenians revere the ancestral Apollo, because Ion, the Polemarch of the Athenians, was the son of Apollo and of Creusa, the wife of Xuthus."

2. Plutarch, *Theseus*, 25: "When Theseus wished to increase the population of the city further, he called in all people on equal terms, and it is said that the herald's call, 'come hither, all people,' was originated by Theseus, when he was summoning the whole people to convene [cf. *supra* "Epitome of Heracleides," Section 2]. . . . And that *he was the first who was favorably inclined to the common people*, as Aristotle says,[1] and gave up his monarchic power, seems also to be attested by Homer in the catalogue of the ships, where he calls only the Athenians a 'people'" (δῆμος, *Iliad* II, 547).

3. A rhetorical lexicon, the so-called *Lexicon Demosthenicum Patmium*, published by Sakkelion (*Bull. de Corr. Hellen.* I, 1877), in an attempt to explain the term γεννῆται, quotes Aristotle (l.c. p. 152): "as Aristotle tells in his Constitution of Athens, saying as follows: *that they were distributed into four tribes, in imitation of the*

---

[1] Cf. *Constitution of Athens* 41, 2: "The second (change of the original state of things) and the first . . . which implied something of a constitutional order was the one which happened under Theseus. This was a slight deviation from the pure monarchy." This statement is, of course, a summary of Aristotle's narration in the beginning of his treatise. It is from the same lost section of this treatise that Plutarch took his quotation.

four seasons of the year, and that each of the tribes was divided into three parts so that there would be altogether twelve parts like the months in the year, and that they were called trittyes or phratriae: and that thirty clans (γένη) *were grouped to form each phratria, as the days are to form the month, and that the clan consisted of thirty men."*

The same explanation of the term γεννῆται, but in an abbreviated and inaccurate form, is found in other lexicographical sources, but only the *Lexicon Patmium* keeps Aristotle's share in the explanation separate from additions taken from different authors, so that we are able to see clearly: (1) that Aristotle was not concerned with the γεννῆται, but with the alleged analogy of the numbers of tribes, trittyes, and clans with the numbers of seasons, months, and days respectively, which is omitted by the other sources, and (2) that he did not necessarily take the responsibility for this strange piece of pseudohistorical fiction, but was probably quoting other people, as the wording in the *Lexicon Patmium* seems to indicate.   But even so, the fact remains that Aristotle found it worth mentioning, and we must not forget that in Athens, especially after Cleisthenes' reform, which introduced the awkward parallelism of a "prytany calendar" and a "civil calendar," speculations of this kind were, to a certain extent, justified; cf. *Constitution of Athens* 21, 3 and 41, 2; Appendix, notes 49, 50, 148; and also Plato *Laws* 745c ff., 771a ff., especially 771b.

4. Schol. Vatic. ad Euripid. *Hippol.* 11 (edited by Schwartz):
"Aristotle tells *that Theseus, when he came to Scyros for a visit, quite naturally because of Aegeus'[2] family relations, was killed by being hurled down from the cliffs because Lycomedes, who was king there at the time, was afraid.[3]* After the Persian Wars, the Athenians in accordance with an oracle collected his remains and buried them."

[2] The father of Theseus.

[3] According to the "Epitome of Heracleides" (*supra*, pp. 205), the object of Lycomedes' fear, as stated by Aristotle, was "that he (*i.e.*, Theseus) would take possession of the island."

FROM ARISTOTLE'S *PROTREPTICUS*

Introduction

Like all the other early works of Aristotle, the *Protrepticus* (that is, "Exhortation" to the study of philosophy), which he wrote when he was still a member of Plato's Academy, has not been preserved. Considerable traces of it, however, can be found in the *Protrepticus* of the Neoplatonist Iamblichus, who died *c.* 330 A.D.

A large part of this latter work (notably Chapters 5 and 13–19) consists mainly of excerpts from extant dialogues of Plato, which are arranged in such a way that the dialogue is replaced by a continued argument and that the missing links, both between the pieces which are taken from one and the same work and those which are culled from different dialogues, are supplied by Iamblichus himself. It was observed long ago that the intervening Chapters 6–12 have no equivalent in the works of Plato, but contain a number of passages that are identical with quotations from Aristotle's *Protrepticus* found in other ancient authors. A close analysis of these passages and of their relation to the context in which they appear in Iamblichus' *Protrepticus*, which was first undertaken by I. Bywater and further elaborated by W. Jaeger,[1] led to the conclusion that the whole sequence of Chapters 6–12 was essentially derived from Aristotle's *Protrepticus*. This, of course, does not mean that these chapters are one literal quotation from Aristotle. On the contrary, it is quite obvious that Iamblichus in this case has followed exactly the same method that he used in his Platonic chapters. Since Iamblichus was anything but a clear thinker or a good stylist, the formulation of the ideas is often obscure and awkward. These inadequacies of expression must not be attributed to Aristotle, who, if we may trust the judgment of Cicero and the testimony of the literal

[1] In his famous book *Aristoteles* (Berlin, Weidmannsche Buchhandlung, 1923), pp. 60ff.

quotations found in other ancient authors, expressed himself in his published works with admirable clarity and great elegance of style. The ideas expressed in those chapters, however, are most striking, in spite of their often awkward formulation, and far beyond what, from his other writings, is known as the range of Iamblichus' intelligence.

Of Chapters 6–12 in Iamblichus' *Protrepticus*, it is only the tenth that deals with the problem of politics and discusses the importance of philosophy for the lawgiver and the true statesman. This chapter, however, is of fundamental importance for an understanding of Aristotle's development as a political thinker and of the relation of his historical studies to his political philosophy. (Cf. Introduction III, *supra*, pp. 32ff.)

IAMBLICHUS, PROTREPTICUS, CHAPTER 10[1]

That theoretical insight is of the greatest usefulness for the practical life of human beings can easily be seen from the arts and professions. Just as the most intelligent doctors and the majority of those who are expert in physical training agree that good doctors and good trainers must have a general knowledge of nature,[2] so, and even to a much higher degree, good lawmakers must have a thorough knowledge of nature. For the former are concerned only with the health and strength of the body, while the latter are concerned with the excellence and the virtues of the soul and claim to teach what concerns the well-being or distemper of a whole state, and therefore are still more in need of philosophy. For just as in the simple crafts the best instruments or tools are directly derived from [literally: "have been found from"] nature, as, for instance, in the building trade, the plummet

---

[1] The translation is based on H. Pistelli's edition of the Greek text Iamblichi *Protrepticus* (Leipzig, Teubner, 1888).

[2] Concerning the concept of "nature" as used in this context, cf. Introduction III, *supra*, pp. 37ff.

[or carpenter's line], the rule, and the compass,[3] by means of which we determine what is sufficiently straight or smooth in the world of the senses, in the same way the statesman must have certain standards taken from nature and truth itself, by which he arrives at a correct judgment as to what is just, what is good, and what is expedient. For just as there [sc. in the simple crafts], these [sc. the plummet, the rule, and the compass] are outstanding among all tools, so here the most perfect law is that which is set down in the greatest possible harmony with nature.

Nobody, however, who is not a philosopher and does not know the truth, is able to do this. Furthermore, in the other arts and crafts the knowledge of the tools and the most accurate calculations are perhaps not derived from first principles but from secondary or tertiary, or still less primary premises. In other words, they base their theory on empirical observations. The philosopher alone of all men copies from that which is exact (ἀπ' αὐτῶν τῶν ἀκριβῶν); for, what he looks at are not copies, but the original.[4] Therefore, just as that man will not be a good

---

[3] Cf. Plato, *Philebus* 56b ff. Following the word "compass," the manuscripts have some further words, the meaning of which seems to be that the "best tools" mentioned are in some way derived from water, light, and the rays of the sun. This might be an attempt to show how the general thesis that the best tools are derived from nature (cf. also Plato, *Cratylus* 386–390) can be applied individually to the several tools mentioned. But the words as found in the manuscripts cannot be construed grammatically, and their exact meaning remains doubtful. In all probability, some words which would have completed the construction and made the meaning clear are missing in our manuscripts. Unless a more complete text is discovered or a parallel passage can be found in ancient literature, it is not even possible to decide whether the words which we have constitute the remnants of an observation by Aristotle himself or of an addition to Aristotle's text by Iamblichus or somebody else.

[4] This paragraph, if anything in this chapter, seems to be expressed in terms of the doctrine of ideas, and this cannot have been contrary to Aristotle's intentions. Yet, while the whole chapter draws on more than half a dozen different passages or sections from several Platonic dialogues, which were not intended by Plato to be combined into such a whole, the most important among these sources is a section in Plato's *Politicus* (293a–301e); and this section furnishes, at least in so far as lawgiving is concerned, a much less idealistic interpretation of the present paragraph than one might

builder who does not use the rule or the other instruments of this kind but takes his measure from other buildings; so he would, perhaps, not be a good lawgiver or serious statesman who gives his laws or administers the affairs of the state with a view to, and in imitation of, either administration as conducted by other men or the constitutions of actual human communities, as for instance those of the Lacedaemonians or the Cretans or others. For a copy of what is not beautiful itself cannot be beautiful, nor [can a copy] of what is not divine and stable in its nature [be] imperishable and stable. But it is clear that of all the artisans and members of the professions the philosopher is the only one whose laws and actions can be truly correct and good. For he alone lives his life looking at the nature of things and the divine; like a good sea captain [who takes his bearings from the stars], he connects the conduct of his life with what is everlasting and unchanging, and in this way acts and lives as a man who is on his own. This kind of insight is theoretical, but it permits us to handle everything in accordance with it. For just as vision does not produce or create anything (for its only task is to distinguish and reveal the visible things) and yet makes it possible for us to act through its guidance and gives us the greatest help in our actions (for, if we were deprived of it, we would be almost immobilized), so it is clear that, though insight is purely theoretical, nevertheless we do innumerable things, and pursue some things and avoid others, in accordance with its guidance, and in fact altogether acquire the greatest benefits through it.

have expected. The "copies" made by the truly wise statesman are the laws which he is forced to write, although they are too general to apply exactly to individual cases and circumstances; and "that which is exact" is the practical application by the truly wise statesman of the standards of justice and of the well-being of the community to any practical question that he is in a position to decide personally. (Cf. Introduction III, *supra*, pp. 34ff.)

FROM ARISTOTLE'S DIALOGUE *POLITICUS*

Fragment 79 (V. Rose — Syrianus, *Commentaria in Aristotelem Graeca*, Vol. VI, Part I, p. 168, lines 33–35): "in the second book of his *Politicus*, he [Aristotle] writes expressly thus: *for the most exact measure of all things is the good.*"

Commenting on Aristotle's *Metaphysics* 1087b 33ff., the Neoplatonist Syrianus (first half of the fifth century A.D.) is very much displeased with the unorthodox way in which Aristotle deals here with the concepts of "the One" and "measure" and, in order to show that Aristotle himself knew better than that, he quotes one sentence from the Aristotelian dialogue *Politicus*. Syrianus has no doubt that, in this sentence, "the good" is the transcendent "One" or God, who, according to Plato (*Laws* 716c), is the "measure of all things." Probably Aristotle had not said anything in his *Politicus* that precluded this interpretation of the sentence. On the other hand, the fact that the quotation is from a dialogue, the title of which was taken from Plato's *Politicus*, and that the emphasis is on the *exactness* of the "measure" makes it practically certain that the sentence had a specific bearing upon the problems discussed in the Platonic dialogue and must be interpreted accordingly. Now it is the very gist of the argument in Plato's *Politicus* 293a–300e that the only criterion by which the political activity of the truly wise statesman can be judged (or "measured," to speak with Aristotle) is the conformity of his actions with the "good,"[1] and *not* their conformity to written laws, which are necessarily too general and too rigid to cover exactly (ἀκριβῶς) the complexity and instability of human

---

[1] He may do *anything*, if it is "for the good" of the community (ἐπ᾽ ἀγαθῷ Plato *Politicus* 293d), just as the doctor may do anything "if only it is for the good of the body" (*ibid.*, 293b).

affairs.[2] Considering this fact, Syrianus' quotation proves that, in his *Politicus*, Aristotle made the same claims for the political art of his ideal statesman and against written laws and constitutions that Plato had made in his dialogue. As to the "good" which is established as the supreme criterion, it is most interesting to see that, even within the context of Plato's *Politicus*, this "good" is simply the well-being of the community; although it is, of course, possible to consider its scientific cognition dependent on the cognition, or at least the recognition, of the "idea of the good." To that extent, then, Aristotle may still have been an adherent of the "doctrine of ideas" when he wrote the lost dialogue. But, at the same time, we see how easy it must have been, on the basis of the relevant section of Plato's *Politicus*, to emancipate Ethics and Politics radically from the doctrine of ideas, as Aristotle certainly did later. (Cf. Introduction III, pp. 52ff., especially note 77.)

[2] Cf. *supra*, Introduction III, p. 39, and note 20.

FROM ARISTOTLE'S TREATISE *ON KINGSHIP*

Themistius[1] *oratio* 8, p. 128 (Dindorf): "Plato, although divine and to be revered in all other respects, yet simply went too far when he ventured to contend that men will not have rest from their evils until either philosophers will rule as kings, or kings will take to philosophy. This assertion has been tested and time has rendered the verdict. Here Aristotle deserves our admiration for having brought the assertion closer to truth, by a slight alteration of Plato's words, when he said that *it was not only not necessary for a king to become a philosopher, but actually a hindrance to his work; that, however, it was necessary* [for a good king] *to listen to the true philosophers and to be agreeable to their advice.* In this way Aristotle made good practice, not theory, the substance of kingship."

The treatise, *On Kingship*, was addressed to the young Alexander, probably on the occasion of his accession to the throne.[2] Themistius does not specify his Aristotelian source, so that the connection of the fragment with the treatise *On Kingship* is not absolutely certain. But if at the time that *On Kingship* was written there was any human greatness and sincerity in Aristotle's relations to his former pupil, which we have no reason to doubt, the attribution[3] is most probable.

[1] Rhetorician and teacher of philosophy in the fourth century A.D.
[2] *Cf.* W. Jaeger, *Aristoteles*, p. 272 note.
[3] V. Rose, *Fragmenta*, 646 and 647.

FROM ARISTOTLE'S
ALEXANDER, OR ON COLONIZATION

Plutarch *de Fortuna Alexandri* I, 6: "He [Alexander] did not follow Aristotle's advice *to deal with the Greeks as a leader, but with the barbarians as a master*, and to take care of the former as of friends and relatives, while treating the latter as one would treat animals or plants, which would have resulted in continued warfare and would have filled the empire with fugitives and smoldering rebellion. Instead of this he . . . "

The *Alexander*, or *On Colonization*, seems to have been a dialogue and cannot have been written before Alexander's decisive victories in Asia Minor. The attribution of the fragment to it is practically certain.[1] Plutarch bitterly criticizes Aristotle's advice and praises Alexander for not following it. As we learn from Strabo (I, 4, 9), the great Alexandrian scholar Eratosthenes (second half of the third c. B.C.) had expressed similar sentiments. Eratosthenes blamed "those who divided the whole mass of mankind into Greeks and Barbarians and who advised Alexander to treat the Greeks as friends but the Barbarians as enemies." He recommended drawing the line rather between such nations (or tribes) as possess virtue (and good government) and such as do not, and stated that "the advisers" were deservedly disregarded by Alexander, who accepted respectable men wherever he found them. In opposition to Eratosthenes, whom he did not like, Strabo himself tries to reconcile Alexander's practical attitude with the regard due to his "advisers" (that is, Aristotle) by pointing out that Alexander, in acting as he did, was faithful to the spirit rather than to the letter of the advice. This makes some sense, because, according to Aristotle's political theory, the claim of the Greeks to be treated as a free people could be based only on their alleged natural superiority. (Cf. *Politics*, Book I, Chapters 5 and 6.)

[1] Cf. Wilamowitz, *Aristoteles und Athen*, Vol. I, p. 338; and W. Jaeger, *Aristoteles*, pp. 23 and 339.

PLATO'S *SEVENTH EPISTLE*

INTRODUCTION

The complete ancient edition of Plato's works, on which our medieval manuscripts depend, contained, as its last unit, thirteen Epistles, letters of various contents and unequal claims to authenticity. Some of them are, undoubtedly, genuine, and these are the only Platonic writings extant in which the author speaks in his own name. By far the most important is the *Seventh Epistle*, addressed to "Dion's friends and relatives." It was written after Dion's death (353 B.C.), when Plato was about seventy-five years old, as an open letter in order to justify, before the general public, Plato's political attitude in Athens and to explain his entanglement in Sicilian politics.[1] The beginning of the *Seventh Epistle* contains a brief account of the political events that determined Plato's life up to his fortieth year of age, and this part —not more than one eighth of the whole letter — is given below in translation. What we read in this section of the letter about Plato's original aims and hopes is so inconsistent with that picture of the "born philosopher" and his attitude toward life which is familiar to us from the best known of Plato's works that, for a long time, many classical scholars were not prepared to acknowledge the authenticity of this most valuable autobiographical statement that we have of any of the Greek classics. It is very doubtful whether we should ever have been relieved of these scruples had not, during the second half of the last century, careful and clever observation of language and style established an unexpected but absolutely reliable relative chronology of three main groups of Plato's works. The results of these inquiries threw new light on

---

[1] For the results of recent studies and for the still remaining controversies concerning the authenticity of the *Seventh Epistle*, its general intention, and its relation to the *Eighth Epistle*, see J. Harward, *The Platonic Epistles*, translated with Introduction and Notes (Cambridge, England, 1932); G. Pasquali, *Le Lettere di Platone* (Florence, Italy, 1938); and W. Jaeger, *Paideia*, Vol. III, Ch. 9.

a great many other problems, also; and although the necessary revision of opinions held by most earlier scholars cannot yet be considered completed, it may safely be stated that all those Platonic dialogues which, because of their philosophic attitude, seemed incompatible with the report of Plato's early experience in the *Seventh Epistle* (*e.g., Phaedo, Republic, Phaedrus, Theaetetus* belong to a later period of his life. Only three of all extant Platonic writings — namely, the *Apology*, the *Crito*, and the *Gorgias* — can be attributed with practical certainty to the time before Plato's fortieth birthday (that is, before 387 B.C.). Since they concentrate upon Socrates' conflict with the Athenian democracy, they were, of course, written after Socrates' death, in 399 B.C. It is a great help for our understanding of the development of Plato's thought to realize that these early writings do not presuppose the philosophical contents of any other Platonic work, but that they do presuppose exactly those political conditions and personal experiences which Plato, looking backwards, found worth mentioning when trying to explain the growth of his political views.

   The Dion, to whose friends and relatives the *Seventh Epistle* is addressed, was a brother-in-law of Dionysius I of Syracuse,[2] who took Dion's sister Aristomache as one of the two wives whom he married after the death of his first wife. Later, Dion became also a son-in-law of Dionysius I, by marrying his own niece Arete, a daughter of Dionysius I and Aristomache. In 353 B.C., not long before the *Seventh Epistle* was written, Dion was assassinated, after he had expelled Dionysius II,[3] eldest son and successor of Dionysius I, and had ruled in Syracuse for some time. Dionysius I had tried to establish a new dynasty by favoring intermarriages of all kinds within his and Dion's family; and, in the unsettled situation which followed Dion's death, there

   [2] Dionysius I had come to absolute power partly through the support given him by Dion's father Hipparinus. He ruled from 405 B.C. until his death in 367 B.C.

   [3] Dionysius II was a son of Dionysius I and of Doris, whom Dionysius I is said to have married on the same day on which he married Dion's sister Aristomache. Dionysius II married his half-sister Sophrosyne, niece of Dion and sister of Dion's wife Arete.

were, according to Plato's *Eighth Epistle*, three male members of
the dynasty with a "legitimate" claim to the rule of the city,
namely, (1) Dionysius II; (2) Hipparinus, the son of Dionysius
I and of Dion's sister Aristomache; and (3) Dion's own son by
his niece Arete, the name of this son being probably also
Hipparinus.

TEXT

Plato to Dion's Relatives and Friends.   Live Well!

Your letter was written to assure me that you are continuing
in Dion's spirit, and you asked me to lend my cooperation in
a [324] word and deed, to the best of my ability. Let me reply, then,
that I am willing to cooperate if your convictions and aims are
the same as were his, but that I shall reconsider again and again
if they are not. I can tell from intimate knowledge, not only
from conjecture, what his thinking and what his aims were. For
when I first came to Syracuse, about forty years old,[4] Dion was
of the same age[5] as Hipparinus[6] is now, and it was then that he
b became convinced that the people of Syracuse ought to be free,
living under the best kind of laws. This was to remain his firm
belief to the very end. And so, indeed, it would not be unprece-
dented if a God should make Hipparinus, too, adopt these same
political convictions so as to adhere to them in the same spirit
as Dion did.

As to the origin of these convictions, it is a story worth listening
to for a young man, and for an older one also, and I shall try to
tell it to you from the beginning. For now is the time to do so.

Long ago, when I was a boy, I was no exception among many

---

[4] *a*. 388 B.C.   Plato was born in 428 B.C.   In 366 B.C., Plato went to Syracuse
for a second time, and in 361 B.C. for a third time.

[5] Probably a little more than twenty years.

[6] It is still controversial whether Hipparinus, the son of Dionysius I and
Doris, is meant, or whether Plato is thinking of a son of Dion and Arete.

other young people: I expected that immediately after having
c become my own master I would go into politics. Then certain
political events which took place in our city happened to come
my way. What happened was this: the kind of government under
which we were living was blamed and abused by many people,
and finally it was overthrown;[7] fifty-one men took the lead in
the revolt as the new rulers. Of these, eleven were set up in the
city and ten in the Piraeus — these two bodies were concerned
with the market and the whole municipal administration — but
[the remaining] thirty took over the government of the whole
d state as absolute rulers. Some of these men happened to be
relatives and friends of mine, and at once they urged me to do
the natural thing for me and take an active part in the new
regime. And, young as I was, no wonder that I felt as I did. I
expected that their administration would lead the city away from
a life of injustice to a just way of life,[8] so I was very much interested in what they would do. Then, seeing how in a short time
these men made the previous regime appear like gold by com-
e parison — among other things they ordered the elder Socrates,[9]
who was my friend and whom I should not hesitate to call the
justest man of his time, to search, together with some others, for
a [325] one of the citizens and to bring him in by force so that he
might be executed, because they wanted to implicate Socrates
in their acts whether he wished it or not; but he did not obey
and risked anything rather than participate in their unholy
crimes — seeing all this and similar conspicuous misdeeds, I was
horrified and withdrew from any contact with the evils that were

[7] 404 B.C.

[8] Cf. Lysias or. 12,5.

[9] The Greek words φίλον ἄνδρα ἐμοὶ πρεσβύτερον Σωκράτη can mean either "a
dear friend of mine of advanced age, Socrates" or, as translated above, "a dear
friend of mine, the elder Socrates," in contradistinction to the "younger"
Socrates, a mathematician, who had been associated with Plato's Academy.
Concerning the possible objection that, if this was the meaning, the word
πρεσβύτερον should be preceded by the definite article, cf. Plato, Euthyphro 15d:
ἄνδρα πρεσβύτην πατέρα "an old man, your father," where there is no definite
article before πατέρα, although this word obtains the same position as πρεσβύτερον Σωκράτη in the Seventh Epistle.

being perpetrated. And before long the power of the Thirty and their whole political system were overthrown.

Again — not quite so impetuously, but still — I was moved
b by the desire to become active in politics. Now even after the change, troubled as affairs were, many things happened which one would abhor; and it was not surprising that during a revolution some people seized the opportunity of dealing rather cruelly with their enemies, though on the whole those who returned to the city conducted themselves with much decency. But again chance would have it that the friend of mine whom I have mentioned, Socrates, became involved. Some powerful men brought him to trial on the utterly blasphemous charge of
c a crime of which Socrates, least of all men, could have been guilty; they brought him to trial on a charge of impiety. And the judges condemned and put to death the same man who, under the previous régime, had refused to take part in the unholy procedure against one of their friends, who at that time was persecuted — that is, at that time when they themselves were outlawed and in distress. When I looked at that and at the personalities of the politicians, and at the laws and at the new customs, the more thoroughly I looked and the more my age advanced, so much the more it seemed difficult to me to bring
d about a sound political practice; for this did not seem to be possible without the help of friends and reliable associates — but such were not easily found in my own circle, for our city had abandoned the traditions and institutions of our fathers, and, on the other hand, it was impossible to acquire with any ease new friends from elsewhere. For both the written laws and the unwritten laws of good conduct were gradually destroyed,[10] and the state of things became worse and worse at an astonishing
e pace, so that I, who at first had been very eager to go into

[10] Cf. Aristotle, *Politics* 1287b 5–8. The expression in the Greek text of Plato's letter is at least as ambiguous as our translation. It can mean (1) that the laws themselves became less good; (2) that they were no longer properly applied; and (3) that they were no longer obeyed. Probably Plato meant to some extent all three things, but, especially in regard to the written laws, more (2) and (3) than (1).

politics, finally felt dizzy when I looked at it and when I saw things carried in all directions in utter confusion. I did still

a [326] not give up watching for a possible improvement of these conditions and of the whole government; but, waiting all the time for an opportunity to do something, I finally had to realize that all the states of our time without exception are badly administered. For, in regard to the laws, the condition in which they are is almost beyond recovery, so that only some quite extraordinary effort, accompanied by exceptionally lucky circumstances, could possibly change it; and I was forced to say, praising the right kind of philosophy, that it is philosophy that enables us to recognize the claims of justice both in public and

b in private life. Therefore, I said, there will be no end of evil for human beings until either those who adhere to the right and true philosophy will occupy the political offices or those who have the power in the states will, by a grace of divinity, engage in the study of genuine philosophy.

With these thoughts in my mind, I left for my first visit[11] to Italy and Sicily. On this visit, it was[12] just the "happy life" rumored to be found there which I did not like at all — a life full of Italian and Sicilian dishes, with eating a big meal twice a day and never sleeping alone by night, and all the entertain-

c ments that go with this kind of life. For with such habits, practising them from early youth, no man under the sky can become wise, not even a man born with the most marvelous disposition toward virtue could overcome that handicap, and as for self-control, one could not even imagine that it would ever be found in him, and the same might be said of all the rest of virtue. Furthermore, there are no laws whatsoever that could give stability to a state as long as its citizens are men who believe that one must spend without limit, and that one should not waste

d his efforts on anything except on banquets and drinking and the strenuous cultivation of lovemaking. Necessarily, such was my conclusion, these cities will undergo a constant change from and

[11] See note 4.

[12] The Greek text adds αὖ ("for a change," "in turn") emphasizing that this came as a second unpleasant experience after what Plato had learned in Athens.

into tyrannies, oligarchies, and democracies; and those in power in such states will stand not even the sound of words like "just and equitable government."

    With this in my mind, in addition to what I had learned
e before,[13] I went to Syracuse; perhaps it was chance, but it looks more as if a demon had then contrived to lay the groundwork for the latest events concerning Dion and the people of Syracuse and, one has reason to fear, for even more to come, unless you accept my advice, which I am now giving for a second time.

    How can I say that my coming to Sicily was the beginning
a [327] of all that followed? When I had met the young Dion, I revealed to him my thoughts about the best kind of life for human beings and advised him to work for their realization. As it seems now, in doing so, I was not aware that inadvertently I was some-how preparing the future overthrow of the tyranny.[14] For Dion showed the same quick understanding of my words that he had
b for everything, and his response was keener and stronger than I have ever found in any other young man of my acquaintance. Setting his heart, once for all, on virtue rather than on pleasure and luxuries, he resolved that for the rest of his life his conduct would be quite different from that of the majority of Italians and Sicilians. And consequently, until the event of Dionysius' death, he lived a kind of life that was apt to offend the courtiers of the tyrant.[15] After this event . . . [16]

---

[13] The reference is, of course, to 326a–b.

[14] This refers to Dionysius' II escape from Syracuse, in 356 B.C.

[15] With these few words, Plato passes over the two decades between 388 B.C. and 367 B.C., during which he had established his school in Athens and during which Dion had been the most loyal and most trusted supporter of Dionysius I. It is noteworthy that Plato does not say a word about his own experiences with Dionysius I. If we can trust later sources, the manner in which he was sent away from Syracuse was extremely undignified.

[16] At this point begins Plato's detailed report and analysis of what happened after 367 B.C., an account which, according to his words at the end of the letter, "seemed necessary because of the strangeness and absurdity of the facts" (διὰ τὴν ἀτοπίαν καὶ ἀλογίαν τῶν γενομένων).

INDEX OF NAMES AND PLACES

GENERAL INDEX

The Hafner Library of Classics

1. ROUSSEAU, JEAN JACQUES:
   THE SOCIAL CONTRACT

Anonymous translation, published 1791, completely revised, edited, with an introduction, by Charles Frankel, Assistant Professor of Philosophy, Columbia University, New York.

   Trade Edition, Cloth Bound, $1.80   Text Edition, $0.80

2. LOCKE, JOHN:
   TWO TREATISES OF GOVERNMENT

With a Supplement: *PATRIARCHA* by Sir Robert Filmer. Edited, with an introduction, by Thomas I. Cook, Professor of Political Science, University of Washington, Seattle. Edition is based on the sixth edition, published 1764, the first to include all the author's posthumous notes and corrections.

   Trade Edition, Cloth Bound, $2.50   Text Edition, $1.25

3. HUME'S MORAL AND POLITICAL PHILOSOPHY

Edited, with an introduction, by Henry D. Aiken, Associate Professor of Philosophy, Harvard University, Cambridge. Part I: *Of Morals* (Book III of the *Treatise of Human Nature*). Part II: *Enquiry Concerning the Principles of Morals.* Part III: 10 essays selected from the *Essays, Moral and Political.*

   Trade Edition, Cloth Bound, $3.50   Text Edition, $1.75

4. ST. AUGUSTINE: *THE CITY OF GOD*

Translation by Marcus Dods (Books IV, XVII, XVIII translated by George Wilson; Books V, VI, VII and VIII by J. J. Smith). Unabridged. *2 volumes*

   Trade Edition, Cloth Bound, $5.00   Text Edition, $3.00

5. HUME, DAVID:
   DIALOGUES CONCERNING NATURAL RELIGION

Edited, with an introduction, by Henry D. Aiken, Associate Professor of Philosophy, Harvard University, Cambridge.

   Trade Edition, Cloth Bound, $1.80   Text Edition, $0.80

6. BENTHAM, JEREMY: *AN INTRODUCTION TO THE*
   PRINCIPLES OF MORALS AND LEGISLATION

With an introduction by Laurence J. Lafleur, Associate Professor of Philosophy, Florida State College, Tallahassee.

   Trade Edition, Cloth Bound, $3.00   Text Edition, $1.50

7. JAMES, WILLIAM: *ESSAYS IN PRAGMATISM*

Edited, with an introduction, by Alburey Castell, Professor of Philosophy, University of Minnesota, Minneapolis. Contains: *The Sentiment of Rationality; The Dilemma of Determinism: The Moral Philosopher and the Moral Life; The Will to Believe; Conclusions on Varieties of Religious Experience; What Pragmatism Means; Pragmatism's Conception of Truth.*

Trade Edition, Cloth Bound, $1.90   Text Edition, $0.90

8. ADAM SMITH'S
MORAL AND POLITICAL PHILOSOPHY

Edited, with an introduction, by Herbert W. Schneider, Professor of Philosophy, Columbia University, New York. Selections from (1) *The Theory of Moral Sentiments;* (2) *The Lectures on Justice, Police, Revenue and Arms;* (3) relevant passages from *The Wealth of Nations.*

Trade Edition, Cloth Bound, $3.50   Text Edition, $1.75

9. MONTESQUIEU, de: *THE SPIRIT OF THE LAWS*

A reprint of the standard translation by Thomas Nugent. With an Introduction by Franz Neumann, Professor of Government, Columbia University.   Unabridged.

Trade Edition, Cloth Bound, $5.00   Text Edition, $3.00

10. JOHANN GOTTFRIED HERDER
GOD — SOME CONVERSATIONS

A translation with a critical introduction and notes by Frederick H. Burkhardt, President of Bennington College. xiv+247 pages.   *Cloth Bound, $2.50   Text Edition, $1.25*

11. SPINOZA, BENEDICT de: *ETHICS*

Preceded by
THE IMPROVEMENT OF THE UNDERSTANDING

Translation by William H. White.   Edited, with an introduction, by James Gutmann, Professor of Philosophy, Columbia University, New York.

Trade Edition, Cloth Bound, $2.50   Text Edition, $1.25

12. ARISTOTLE: *THE CONSTITUTION OF ATHENS and RELATED TEXTS*

Edited, with an introduction, by Kurt von Fritz and Ernst Kapp, Professors of Classics, Columbia University, New York. Contents: *The Constitution of Athens;* excerpts from the *Protrepticus* and some other relevant passages by Aristotle (translated by the editors); excerpts from Plato's *Seventh Letter.*

13. JOHN STUART MILL'S
   PHILOSOPHY OF SCIENTIFIC METHOD

   Edited, with an introduction, by Ernest Nagel, Professor of Philosophy, Columbia University, New York. Selections from (1) *The System of Logic;* (2) *An Examination of Sir W. Hamilton's Philosophy;* (3) (entire) *On the Definition of Political Economy, and on the Method of Investigation Proper to It.*

Other Hafner Books of Interest

BLAU, JOSEPH L. (Ed.): *SOCIAL THEORIES OF JACKSONIAN DEMOCRACY*

Representative Writings of the Period 1825–1850. (The American Heritage, Vol. I.) intro. biographical notes. index. xxx+383pp.

> *Text Edition, Paper, $1.75   Trade Edition, Cloth, $3.75*

BOISSIER, GASTON:
   THE COUNTRY OF HORACE AND VIRGIL

Translated by D. Havelock Fisher. Maps and plans.
> *xii+346pp.   cl. $4.50*

CAPES, W. W.:
   UNIVERSITY LIFE IN ANCIENT ATHENS
> *xiv+134pp.   ½cl. $1.50*

DUCASSE, CURT. J.:
   ART, THE CRITICS AND YOU
> *170pp.   cl. $2.50*

   PHILOSOPHY AS A SCIENCE: ITS MATTER AND ITS METHOD   *xx+242pp.   cl. $3.50*

GUMMERE, FRANCIS B.:
   FOUNDERS OF ENGLAND *xii+506pp.   cl. $4.00*

LYSLE, A. de R.:
   THE LATEST MODERN ITALIAN-ENGLISH AND ENGLISH-ITALIAN DICTIONARY
> *xvi+768pp.   cl. $4.00*

MUNRO, H. A. J.:
CRITICISMS AND ELUCIDATIONS OF CATULLUS
viii+247pp. cl. $2.50

ORESME, (MAISTRE) NICOLE:
LE LIVRE DE ÉTHIQUES D'ARISTOTE
Pub. from MS. 2902, Biblioth. Royale Belgique, ed. by Albert D. Menut. ill. xii+547pp. unbd. $6.00

PLINY THE YOUNGER:
THE LETTERS OF PLINY THE YOUNGER
Selected with a *Companion to Pliny's Letters* by Helen H. Tanzer. ill. xxiv+292pp. cl. $2.50

PRICE, MARUCIE T.
CHRISTIAN MISSIONS AND ORIENTAL CIVILIZATIONS
Study in Culture Contact. xxvi+578pp. cl. $3.00

SETH, ANDREW:
THE DEVELOPMENT FROM KANT TO HEGEL
With Chapters on the Philosophy of Religion.
iv+170pp. cl. $2.50

SIHLER, E. G.:
ANNALES OF CÆSAR
A Critical Biography. index. x+330pp. cl. $2.50

CICERO OF ARPINUM
A Political and Literary Biography. 2d corrected ed. bibliog. index. xiv+487pp. cl. $4.00

TESTIMONIUM ANIMÆ, OR GREEK AND ROMAN BEFORE JESUS CHRIST
A Series of Essays and Sketches. x+453pp. cl. $3.00

WENGER, LEOPOLD:
INSTITUTES OF THE ROMAN LAW OF CIVIL PROCEDURE
Trans. by Otis H. Fisk. Intro. by Roscoe Pound. Rev. ed. index. glossary. xxx+440pp. cl. $6.00

DATE DUE
